Memory Road Trip

A Retrospective Travel Journey

Krista Marson

MEMORY ROAD TRIP A Retrospective Travel Journey
Copyright © 2021 by Memory Road Press

ISBN 978-1-7373284-0-7 (epub)
ISBN 978-1-7373284-1-4 (paperback)

website: https://kmarson.com
email: memoryroadtrips@gmail.com

book cover photo taken by kmarson near Death Valley

CONTENTS :

PREFACE

Allow Me To Introduce Myself

I have a reputation within my family as being the one who likes to travel. I have no children, I have no pets, and I gravitate toward jobs that offer compressed workweeks. It is no family secret that I enjoy bouncing about the globe, yet no one in my family knows where I go or what I do once I reach a particular destination. I'm not on Facebook, I rarely text, and, quite honestly, I am not close enough to my two siblings to warrant a whole lot of communication with them to begin with. I am the youngest sibling that left Wisconsin for California over 25 years ago and never moved back.

Recently, which now seems like forever ago since the advent of COVID-19, my husband Ryan and I traveled back to Wisconsin to attend my niece's wedding. It was only the second time in 25 years that all three of us siblings were under the same roof (the other time being four years prior at our mother's funeral), and my husband and I sat at a table with my sister and her 12-year-old daughter, Morgan. We all did the usual conversations that people tend to do when they only have a short amount of time to catch up on the last x number of years, but those conversations eventually trailed off when none of us had anything much left to say. We were all just kind of sitting in a food and drink-induced kind of daze when, out of the blue, Morgan turned to me and asked me to tell her a travel story.

"Okay!" I exclaimed. "I got locked inside a cathedral in France once and almost got stuck in there overnight. I eventually figured out how to open a door that hadn't been used for at least 500 years and fell on top of a guy taking a pee."

I proceeded to give her the play-by-play version of how that story unfolded, and when I finished telling her that tale, she asked me if I had any more hilarious stories to share.

"Oh, I have many," I said. "There was this one time in Italy when Ryan and I took this little graffiti train through the countryside, and..." I started but was only as far as I got before the wedding toasts began. The wedding party had their own witty stories to share, and then there was food, and then there was cake, and then there was dancing, and then the whole wedding party thing happened. I never did manage to return to my little graffiti train story. My sister and her daughter drove back to Michigan, and Ryan and I flew back to Arizona, and I was left unsure when, if ever, I was going to be able to tell Morgan where that little tagged to the hilt train took us to.

The story I wanted to tell Morgan was going to be about how we got lost in a 9,000-year-old city filled entirely with caves. The city was called Matera, and the map we had was of no use to us because none of the streets were helpfully named. The map was nothing more than a glorified piece of paper with a bunch of shapes on it, and it looked more like a geometry test than anything that would actually assist us. We could see where our hotel supposedly existed on that little slip of paper, but what we couldn't tell was where that same hotel existed in the Swiss-cheesed landscape that sprawled out before us.

We spent a good 30 minutes searching for the hotel together to absolutely no avail, so we got the hair-brained idea to split up and better our odds. Naturally, splitting up proved to be a colossally dumb decision when we realized that we not only had to find the hotel, but we also had to find one another.

I know for a fact that I went around in circles because I was saddled with a godforsaken roller bag that prevented me from wanting to go up the massively long staircases that graced Matera with much picturesque beauty. Had I been telling Morgan this story in person, I would have paused at this stage of the story, and I would have warned her to never bring a roller bag to Italy. In fact, I would have announced to anyone listening in on our conversation at the wedding reception that if they were even so much as thinking about going to Italy with a roller bag that I was personally there to stop them from doing so. Bringing a roller bag there is a colossally dumb idea, unless, of course, one thoroughly enjoyed the sound of clanging wheels on uneven pavement everywhere one went, one absolutely relished the action of picking up of one's suitcase after it constantly tipped over, and one got one's thrills in carrying the unwieldy thing up oodles of staircases. I would have then, naturally, declared that I had absolutely no intention of dissuading anyone from bringing a stupid roller bag to Italy if such things appealed to them. But then again, I wonder if the conversation would have actually gone in that direction if I was trying to tell Morgan the story about how it took us over an hour to find our impossible-to-locate hotel in the landscape of Swiss fromage.

Ryan gets all the credit for eventually finding the hotel because I simply stopped moving at some point and sat around forever for him to find me. When he finally did locate my pathetic roller bag-laden ass, he proudly announced that he found our hotel. Even though I knew that he would, I was still somewhat genuinely surprised that he actually did. I had no idea how anyone found anything in that cave-riddled town.

When we finally arrived at the hotel together, we were told

that we were the property's only guests. The month was November, and we seemed to be the only tourists in town. The kind proprietor upgraded us to the hotel's finest suite, and within minutes of entering our cave room, we were ready to return to Matera before we even left.

"How many days do we have here?" Ryan asked me.

"Two," I said.

"That's not long enough," Ryan lamented. We were both in our hotel for only five minutes, and, already, we wanted to stay there forever. I would have liked to have told Morgan about how fascinating the city of Matera was, but I didn't have enough time to tell her that it was a place where we even went.

Morgan knew that I liked to travel, but she might have asked me *why* I liked to travel so much. That honestly would have been a good question to throw at me, as I've never really given that inquiry much thought myself. So, I will ask myself now what motivates me to travel? Adventure? Sure. But not "Let's run with the bulls in Pamplona" crazy. I know that I am an insanely curious person, but I generally avoid traveling to places where I might get sick or die. I'm kind of a wimp to a certain degree, but I have known myself to throw caution to the wind when the moment seems to suit me. Overall, the best answer to that question is that I simply like to go.

I've never found it difficult to travel by myself. If I can't find someone to travel with, it often doesn't stop me from going somewhere. I can honestly say that travel is one of the most important things in the world to me, and I regret that I just now reread that sentence to myself in the past tense because a global health pandemic has put most kinds of leisure travel on an indefinite hiatus. Travel will undoubtedly be back someday, but it will unlikely come back looking the same way it once did. Vaccine passports might ultimately become an actuality, so gone will be the ability to just waltz into a foreign country without having to prove one's medical status. I suppose that I have no right to complain if such a change comes about, as doing so would hopefully make traveling safer, but what I can complain about is that something horrible happened that made the world a less safe place to explore. Sure, travel will come back, but I'm not one hundred percent sure right now that I'll want to go anywhere exotic when it does. Saying such things does not roll off my tongue easily but rather dribbles out more like drool and makes me feel like someone I don't recognize. I hate feeling this way because it doesn't make me feel like myself, and I fear that I might lose a sense of who I am because I used to travel to find out who I was.

Traveling has helped me grow as a person. I've always loved how travel is full of moments that lead to experiences and revelations. I know what I look for when I travel, and it's usually around a theme such as art, history, or nature. Food is always a good excuse to go someplace, but it's never the number one reason why I choose to go to a particular destination. I'm not a big shopper, save for my inexplicable penchant for buying coffee mugs. I'll sometimes seek out concerts once I've locked down a destination, but I rarely plan trips around live shows. I would never describe myself as a "people-person," for I get along much better with trees, buildings, paintings, and ghosts. I love rivers. I love forests. I enjoy hiking, but I never care to make it to the top of some towering peak. I love photography, and I am constantly on the internet searching for new ruins to discover. Sometimes, though, I find that I am too late to visit a ruin once I find a particularly ruinous one. Bombay Beach, California, was one that I missed. I had been looking at evocative images of the ruined structures near the Salton Sea for years before I finally made it out there. Once I was there, I discovered that all the ruins I had been admiring online were wasted away, poof, gone. At least Salvation Mountain (a super-sized art piece demonstrating one man's devotion to God) was still there, well, at least in 2012 it was, but that too will most likely disappear with the passage of time.

I have learned that if I want to see something, I must not wait to see it. More than anything, travel is one particular thing: time. It takes time to plan, time needs to be set aside to go someplace, it takes time to get somewhere, and one only has a short amount of time to be someplace before one has to return to whatever it is that one left behind. It's kind of discouraging in a way. For travel to be successful, one must accept all the time factors that are an integral part of it, else travel becomes a drag and an inconvenience.

Traveling is not important to some people, I totally respect that, but traveling has always been important to me. Traveling has become a part of my identity, and I really enjoy going places. I simply love to travel, and I devote quite a bit of time to the whole endeavor, or, I should say, I still *hope* to devote quite a bit of time to it. Travel was always what I thought I wanted out of life. I've never wanted kids, I've always been allergic to most pets, and I am not ashamed to say that I've never really wanted anyone to be dependent on me.

When I travel, I often come back with more questions than answers. I've learned to carry a little notebook with me to write things down to look up when I return. I used to not do this, and would instead make "mental notes" of the things I wanted to learn about, which I would promptly forget to do. Very quickly, the notebooks became full-fledged journals of their own and I amassed many of them throughout the years. I can't express how happy I am with myself that I've kept all those journals because I wouldn't have been able to write this here granddaddy travel journal of them all without them.

I wanted to write this book for my niece, but I also wanted to write this book for myself. In my last 25 plus years of traveling, I have seen many things and have conjured up many ideas. It was my desire to synthesize my thoughts on paper and see how they read on the page. Travel is about feeling and experiencing life in its many facets. Life is too short, and the world is just too big to ignore. I am thankful that I am alive and healthy. I know that I have been supremely fortunate to have been able to travel to wherever it was that I have wanted to go because the world post-COVID-19 might look wildly different. I started writing this well before the coronavirus did a one-two punch into the planet's metaphorical gut, and its effect has already modified my traveling future. Even though it feels weird right now to be writing about travel when it's currently in shambles, I think it is important to remember when travel used to be easy because it may not be so simple to travel anymore. I never necessarily took traveling for granted, but I see now that I took for granted that traveling would always be something that I could easily do.

I initially thought that I would be able to squeeze 25 years' worth of travel stories into one single volume, but a word count revealed that I had enough fodder to fill three individual books. I always knew that I liked to write, but it came as a complete surprise that I had so much to say. It took a little while for me to find my voice, but once I found it, I wasn't able to shut myself up. I didn't want to be quiet anymore once I found my stride, and I found the conversations with myself to be rather cathartic. I liked it that I had somewhere to purge all my thoughts into a single contained space where I could merge my ideas into a synthesized whole.

I love living on planet Earth. If ever the opportunity arose to move to Mars, I will never opt to go there because Earth will always be where I want to be. I may not desire children or even pets, but I do desire to be here, right where I am. If this book is about anything, it is an ode to life here on this pretty blue ball where I'll forever desire to call home.

CHAPTER ONE:
California, 1991-1994

Dying Young

I want to start my first story with an apology. I want to apologize to a boy named Paul for inadvertently contributing to his death at the too young age of 19. I know that it was because I convinced my boyfriend to move back to Wisconsin for me that his best friend wound up dying on a crappy motorcycle on a California freeway. Paul was on his way to the San Jose airport to bid his best friend adieu when the accident occurred. The fact that he never arrived led my boyfriend to conclude that Paul was too hungover to pull himself out of bed, so he boarded the airplane thinking that his best friend was being lazy. My boyfriend didn't know to look out the airplane window and see his own mangled motorcycle resting beside his mutilated best friend somewhere on the road directly below him. The California dream was lain splattered beneath his seat, but he didn't know enough to wave goodbye to the grisly scene that distance, clouds, and ignorance protected him from seeing. Dying young is the most unfair thing that can happen to someone. Life is short enough the way it is, but to die before one even gets a chance to really grab life by its horns is by far the most unfortunate fate. It's been 30 years since Paul died, and I will sometimes think of all the things that Paul never got the chance to experience. Paul never got to live on his own, he never got to backpack around Europe, he never got to marry, he never got to have a career, he never got to buy a house, he never got to have kids, he never got to fight with a spouse, he never got to get divorced, he never got to face his demons, and he never got to hit rock bottom only to come out a better person in the end. Considering that he died in 1991, he also never got to live under any president that came after George H.W. Bush, he never got to listen to any music that came after Nirvana, he never got to hear about The Oklahoma City Bombing or The Columbine Massacre, he never got to worry about Y2K, he never got to experience the internet, he never got to be addicted to a cell phone, he never got to see the Twin Towers fall, he never got to see the Star Wars prequels, he never got to hear about the Mars rovers, he never got to witness the climate change, and he never got to quarantine for a pandemic. In short, Paul ended up missing the rest of his life entirely, and there will always be a big gaping hole in the world where Paul was supposed to be. Somewhere out there, someone was supposed to have built their entire life around him, but that someone never got to meet their future that never had a chance to happen.

Paul just learned how to ride that motorcycle the day prior. The motorcycle still technically belonged to my boyfriend, but he gave it to Paul to ride while he'd be away. Paul was by no means ready to take that motorcycle onto the freeway so soon. The bike was old as hell and had extremely quirky gears. The driver in the car behind him took it for granted that he was going the proper speed and unintentionally hit him from behind. I feel incredibly sorry for whoever hit him because it was a fate that person didn't deserve. It was an accident that should never have happened but unfortunately did.

I brought up Paul's death because I wanted to acknowledge the fact that life can end at any moment. Life can be incredibly short, so life must be lived when one has a chance to live it. Once someone dies, that person's chance to live is gone forever. Paul's early death taught me that, and I can't honestly say that I would have figured that out on my own so incredibly soon. I was living a pretty dysfunctional family life before Paul passed away, but it wasn't so dysfunctional that I ever thought about personally dying. I lived with chronically ill parents, so the thought of their eventual deaths did occasionally cross my mind, but I never perceived those thoughts as being anything unnatural. Paul's early demise struck me as being something incredibly wrong. It got me thinking that if it could happen to him, then it could happen to anyone. Thinking such thoughts made me very introspective and caused me to realize that my time on Earth was temporary. Paul's death taught me that life wasn't going to last forever, and it was a wake-up call that I wasn't initially aware I needed. It was only years later when I really started traveling that the meaning of his death sank in. I felt incredibly lucky to be alive and extremely fortunate to be experiencing the world. Traveling proved to be my way of ensuring that I wasn't squandering away my precious time here on this wondrous planet.

Thought Process

My earliest forays didn't necessarily qualify as "trips" in the traditional sense because they never took me very far, but they served as trips to me because they got me outside of my domestic realm. My boyfriend and I felt really bad that Paul was no longer with us and the only thing that Paul's dying did was leave a big gaping hole for us to fall into. We spent the rest of our ten-year relationship in the bottom of that pit, and we lived together inside the shell of Paul's ghost. We did things and made decisions based on the fact that everything we could do, Paul could do no longer. We felt so terribly responsible for his death, and we never allowed ourselves to break up even when our relationship went to shit a hundred times over because we were too afraid of Paul's ghost punishing us. Ours was the best relationship and the worst relationship because we loved and hated each other in equal measures. Our relationship was volatile, and in the end, I am sure that it was something that caused Paul to do barrel rolls in his grave.

It feels strange to be writing any of this because I harbored no intention of divulging too much detail about my past when I first sat down to write this travel book. It was only when I wrote an outline that I realized that I'd have to look my past straight into its eyes if I wanted to write a genuine account about my travels. I initially tried fighting it and wrote three different outlines with my relationships removed, but each one felt like an ingenuine shell of an inauthentic self. In the end, I ultimately decided if I was going to write something, then I was going to write about the genuine me, good, bad, or otherwise. I figured that since I wasn't going to be on this planet forever, the least I could do was leave a little piece of the real me behind.

In the beginning, I scattered all my travel stories onto the metaphorical table and stared at them as if they were a thousand tiny pieces to a puzzle that I didn't know what the picture was. I had 25 years' worth of travel sprawled out before me, but I was unsure how to arrange them into a cohesive image. After much deliberation, I ultimately decided that it would be best to present my tales in (mostly) chronological order, albeit I anticipated that there would be some moments when I would want to blur the time-space continuum. For the most part, I desired to keep the storyline as linear as possible, but I also knew that there would be moments when I wanted to use some stories as launching pads to explore some current perspectives. My current husband, Ryan, will undoubtedly make an appearance, as he has been my faithful travel companion for the last 15 years. Many of my current thoughts have been formulated with him by my side, and I consider myself incredibly fortunate to have someone so wonderful to share my life with. Given a choice, I would have chosen to be with Ryan since I was 16 years old, but as fate would have it, I didn't meet him until I was 33. Instead, I spent the greater part of my young adult years with someone I shouldn't have been with.

I know that I'm going to have to write about my relationship with a man that I hadn't thought about for at least 20 years because he was a big part of my past, and I'm stuck with my history. Most of my early travel forays came about because I was one half of a not-so-great whole, so I was always trying to find new ways to escape myself. My earliest trips were nothing more than glorified excursions that simply took me out of my house and away from my reality. It didn't take me long to realize that I was finally discovering who I was whenever I stepped away from everything that was familiar. I learned that I tended to think rather profound thoughts whenever I was by myself, so I never particularly minded running off all by my lonesome.

Once I discovered a passion for thinking, I became curious to see where my thoughts would take me. Travel became not only a physical pursuit but a cerebral one as well. It is possible that I approached traveling in my unique way solely because no one per se showed me how to do it. Traveling, for me, grew out of an organic process, and it eventually became part of my lifestyle. Yet, what I perceive as "travel" is a very fluid concept. For me, traveling doesn't require distance so much as it requires intent. One has to *want* to go somewhere, and just about anywhere suffices. Oftentimes, the best trips that a person can take are the ones that don't take them very far. In my experience, it's been the cheap and short trips that most easily satisfy my craving for getting the heck away, mainly because those are the kinds of trips most readily within reach.

Sometimes, though, it's not the end destination that matters, but the journey itself that creates the most memories. For my earliest excursions, it was the vehicle itself that I typically remember the most, so I want to begin my travel stories with the vehicles that took me on my earliest journeys.

Modes of Transportation

I really hate to say it, but my boyfriend and I (okay, fine, I'll give him a name. I'll refer to him as "What's His Name." No? Okay, fine, I'll call him "Joe," as in Joe Blow. Still not good? Ugh, fine, I'll call him Kat because that's what I call him in my head.) Allow me to start that sentence over. I really hate to say it, but Kat and I loved motorcycles. I call him Kat to myself because it's short for Katana, which was the model of Suzuki motorcycle we spent a good portion of our time riding on. Everyone, of course, thought that we were idiots for buying a motorcycle when we moved back to California, and no doubt, we probably were. However, we were too broke to afford a car, so we bought a small motorcycle and gradually worked our way up to that amazing crotch rocket. Well, I should say that we both loved riding motorcycles when California was in a seven-year drought because it allowed us to zoom around in perpetual sunshine. We both cursed the day, though, when the drought morphed into an El Niño, and the sky rained morning, noon, and night for days and days and days on end. It was a good thing that we were both young and happy as those were the two factors that masked how uncomfortable we were riding that bike through a gauntlet of miserable weather. I would get absolutely drenched to the core while riding on the back of that thing. I remember my back going completely stiff from bracing against the cold, and after a few months of constantly feeling like a drowned rat, I tossed in the towel. I had reached my limit of being miserable, so I purchased the worst 1978 powdered blue Mustang still left on the road that soon earned itself the nickname, *The Ghost Rider*.

Ghosty was a perfectly fine car to drive around in the daytime, but Ghosty was a pain in the butt to drive around at night. Whenever I turned on the headlights, the battery would start to drain, and it's doing so would cause Ghosty to lose all its momentum. I discovered the art of ghost riding when I learned that the battery would recharge itself whenever I turned the headlights off. A few miles of riding in the dark usually got Ghosty back up to speed, but then the juice would only last so long when the headlights were on. It became a constant process of turning on and off the headlights just to drive the damn car, and it was more than super annoying, it was super dangerous. I essentially drove around flashing people with my lights, and people always thought that I was asking them to move out of my way. It probably made no sense to anyone why I would never pass them and then inexplicably go completely dark behind them. I was the strangest car on the road, and I always felt like apologizing to everyone for my reckless abuse of road courtesy. I eventually got so used to driving without the headlights on that toward the end of owning that car, it was just easier to pretend that Ghosty didn't have them. It was only when Ghosty started pulling similar shenanigans during the daytime, such as downshifting itself to a leisurely 40 mph on the freeway and refusing to go any faster, that I decided it was probably a good idea to let The Ghost Rider go. I sold Ghosty to someone for $500, but that buyer brought the car back to me the next day and demanded a refund. The last thing I wanted was to have that powder blue goblin sitting in my carport ever again, but 24 hours after I thought that I got rid of it, Ghosty boomeranged right back to me. I had no place to park it, though, as a cherry red 1991 Suzuki Samurai that I had yet to learn how to drive because it was a stick shift was already parked in its place. As a final act of defiance, The Ghost Rider wouldn't even start for me, so I couldn't even experience the joy of driving it to the junkyard. I had to pay $50 for a tow truck to carry it away on a chariot like a spoiled princess.

Santa Cruz

Kat and I started to fight when his drinking became more, and my drinking became less. I waited a year for California residency before going back to school, but when I did return to college, the party pretty much ended for me. I wanted more out of life than just partying every night, but that was the exact opposite of what Kat wanted to do. We were growing apart rather than together, yet we still possessed mutual passions. We both loved California, and nothing kept us more together than driving on its sinuous roads.

Where we lived in San Jose was relatively boring when we compared it to either Santa Cruz or San Francisco, so we usually drove to either of those cities whenever we had time off together. Often, though, our days off failed to coincide, so there were many times when I was left to explore California all by myself. I forged a private relationship with that state, and some of my best memories of being in the throes of my young adult life happened by my lonesome in the rare golden light of a sunny California day. Everyone has their own version of the California dream, and mine looks like a hazy memory of a California that no longer exists.

The early '90s were the Bay Area's last years of calm before the massive internet storm hit the landscape and made it too expensive for any average person to eke out a decent existence. I am glad that I lived there when I did because I wouldn't remotely have the same experience living there today, for life in the Bay Area is totally different now. The internet was only in its incubator when I was there, but it has since emerged from its womb and revealed its ferocious appetite. Unfortunately, society can only feed the internet business so much before it starts taking the food off of everyone's plates. In my opinion, there is nothing left in the Bay Area for me to go back to because it's no longer a place where a person can afford to be poor anymore.

We never had much money when we lived in California, but we always had a little something left over after paying rent, which is not something people with waitressing or oil changing jobs can readily say they have much of today. In my opinion, my version of the Bay Area was better than the version that gets served up now because it never used to feel like the weight of the entire world was dependent upon it. In fact, my version of '90s California was a bit rough around the edges because it was still in the process of putting itself back together after a major earthquake had briefly knocked that part of the country off of its feet.

The Loma Prieta earthquake happened in 1989, yet the beachside city of Santa Cruz was still reeling from its effects three years later. Most Santa Cruz businesses circa 1992 were still operating out of temporary dome-like structures, and their doing so gave the city a sense of suspended existence. My first impression of Santa Cruz was that I thought that it looked like a refugee camp. I wasn't entirely sure if I was allowed to walk around wherever I wanted to, and I noticed those who were walking around were doing so without any shoes on. The sound of bongo drums usually played somewhere unseen in the background and provided a soundtrack to the surreal landscape. The smell of pot smoke typically hung in the air and wafted around as an outdoor incense. It seemed to me that the earthquake cracked the planet open and allowed the 1960s to reemerge from its tomb in all its kumbaya glory. Santa Cruz in the early '90s was where anyone who looked hard enough could find the spirits of Janis Joplin and Jimi Hendrix toking together in a secret alcove somewhere on the beach and not find their appearance strange in the least. Santa Cruz was broken, yet there was a surreal comfort in everything being upended.

There seemed to be a collective desire to leave everything

alone and stretch out the city's temporary existence for as long as possible. The longer they dragged their feet on repairs, the longer they would have the excuse not to bother with reality. It was an intoxicating atmosphere that sucked out all motivation. The easiest thing to do in Santa Cruz was nothing. Unless, of course, staring at the sea was considered as doing something. There is nothing finer in life than letting the mind go. It is essential to occasionally shut off all the clamor and remove oneself from the cacophony that encompasses daily life. Santa Cruz always succeeded in filling my ears with the sweet, sweet sound of static noise.

I always enjoyed listening to the sounds of the wild Pacific ocean as it advanced and receded against an impressive coastline of rocks. I used to sit for hours on a perch that overlooked the ocean and simply stare. I would watch the birds, I would watch the tide, and I would watch the sunlight twinkle on the liquid horizon. I would watch the surfers paddle out and sit on their boards, and then I would watch them wait patiently for the perfect wave. I would watch the surfers bob up and down with the rhythm of the water, and I would allow myself to get mesmerized by their trance. Everywhere I looked, there seemed to be a tempo as if everything was in balance, and I always wished that life looked that balanced the moment I turned my head away from the sea. Dry land lacked rhythm and was the ocean's exact opposite. One needs the sea to restore one's soul and to rejuvenate one's mind. The sea is where one goes to purchase the supplies necessary to navigate the art of living, and it was always there where I tried to wrap my head around the art of dying. I knew that there was an art to life, but I questioned if there was an art to death. Such thoughts tended to put me into a stupor, and more often than not, I simply wound up staring at the sea, which was tantamount to staring at nothing. When I'd go to Santa Cruz, my mind always ended up in the same place, which was absolutely nowhere, and that was where I usually found myself.

It's usual for someone in their young 20s not to know where they are in life. It was never hard for me to find myself in the nothingness because that was where I usually preferred to wander. I wasn't sure what I was doing with my life when I moved to California, but I knew that I wanted to go to school. All I knew was that I really loved history, so aside from the requisite math and English classes, I just signed up for classes that appealed to me with the thought that I'd figure out the rest of my life later. Meanwhile, I had all of the Bay Area at my feet and an adorable Suzuki Samurai to explore it with. I bought that fake Jeep solely based on its looks because I thought it was the cutest darn thing ever. If someone had told me ahead of time how dangerously lethargic that car was, I still would have bought that car anyway simply because I wanted it to be mine.

I was always the slowest car on the road when I was in the Samurai because that four-cylinder glorified golf cart lacked any oomph. Other drivers absolutely hated it when they got stuck behind me on the huge mountain road to Santa Cruz because my looks were deceiving. No one ever assumed that I drove even slower than the slowest semi-truck until it was too late for them to go around me. Sometimes, I would even throw caution to the wind, and I would drive the Samurai to San Francisco. I don't know now why I allowed myself to drive the Samurai all over San Francisco because that car should never have been allowed to stop at a red light on one of those freaky hills. That car despised doing hills, but apparently taking it there was something that my 19-year-old idiot self thought was a perfectly sane thing to do. I must have been a better driver back then or just incredibly naive because there is no way in the world that I would ever drive around San Francisco in a Samurai today as I'm pretty sure that I would see most of that city backward as I'd roll the wrong way down a hill.

San Francisco

I sometimes wish that I was born in the baby boom along with most people in this country because I would have then been able to afford to live my adult life in San Francisco. I assume that living in San Francisco must have been cheap in the 1960s because so many hippies could afford to live there. Even in the early '90s, living in San Francisco wasn't cheap, and I know this because we scoured the city for a cheap apartment and never found one. Rents circa 1992 San Francisco were well over $1,200 for a tiny studio apartment, which made our $795 rent for a two-bedroom apartment in San Jose that we split between three people look like a smoking deal.

We shared our apartment in San Jose with someone I didn't get along with, but to mention him now serves little purpose other than to say that we were not each other's favorite person. I can't claim that I was always at my best when I was around that particular someone because we had a knack for getting under each other's skin. It took a lot of time for us to learn how to get along, but I'd be lying if I didn't admit that some of the least finer moments in my life happened within the domains of that apartment. It took me a little while to figure out that I

25

could simply leave on those frequent days when the two of us were stuck in the apartment together, but I soon gained mastery over the art of escaping to San Francisco.

The critical factor to my routine was always the weather because the San Francisco I escaped to was mostly outside. I knew exactly what streets I needed to take to get myself to Golden Gate Park, and I always parked in the exact same spot just beyond the park's entrance. My absolute most favorite thing to do in San Francisco was to walk the entire three-mile length of Golden Gate Park and to do that walk slowly. I always loved following the tucked-away paths that were nestled in the forest because it was easy for me to pretend that I was hiking in a jungle. Golden Gate Park was where I went when I wanted to get lost because it was easy to pretend that I didn't know where I was. No trip to that park was ever the same journey twice, and there have been many beautiful patches of forest that I've failed to find ever again.

The reward at the end of the hike was always a windmill and a beach. I would spend forever combing for sand dollars on the beach but would only rarely find any. If I was feeling rich, I would treat myself to fish and chips at The Cliff House restaurant. There, I would request a window seat and watch the waves crash against the rocks that majestically rose out of the ocean. The restaurant always had a pair of binoculars that would float around the tables, and when I could get my hands on them, I would look for whales through them, but I never managed to see any. It never mattered to me, though, because I just liked being in there and seeing what the world looked like when I viewed it from that restaurant's window. From their perch, all the world was water. It always made me think about how much of the planet was water and how my day-to-day life had such little connection to the sea. Looking out that window made me think that there was a considerable portion of the world that I wasn't seeing. I had no idea what the rest of the world looked like beyond the horizon, and even with binoculars, I couldn't see past the straight line that divided my world from the world that existed further away from me.

The world always fascinated me, but I had never traveled anywhere besides Florida, which probably didn't even count. I always sensed that a bigger world was out there to experience, but I was unsure how to experience it. The thought crossed my mind several times about joining the Peace Corps, but I always knew deep down that I just wasn't the Peace Corps type. I'm generally too cynical, and I never thought that I could save a village when I couldn't even save myself.

Kat and I should have been broken up by the end of our two years in California together, but we did something stupid and got married instead. I formulated most of my San Francisco memories all by lonesome because that was where I ran to when I needed to escape the life that I supposedly carved out for myself. It's not an understatement to say that I have no idea how many hours I spent looking out that restaurant's window. I spent countless hours there wondering how I could undo all the mistakes I made up to that point in my life. I didn't know what I expected out of myself, so it was really tough for me to figure out what I wanted out of life in general. I was happy, but I also wasn't, and I wasn't sure how to fix anything.

Kat and I loved each other, but we no longer knew how to be together. We filed for a divorce, and Kat abandoned the

California dream for a second time and upped and moved himself to Las Vegas. I wound up moving into my own studio apartment in San Jose, which soon proved to be the worst apartment in the entire city that I could have possibly picked, so my San Francisco forays continued because I had a whole new set of reasons to escape my home life. I thought about talking about those reasons now, but I want to save that topic for later because if I start talking about the apartment fire next, it will cause me to stray too far away from San Francisco, and I have a few more things that I want to say about that city.

In the 1990s, there used to be a vintage arcade in the basement of The Cliff House. That place was a real Victorian phantasmagoria chocked full of turn-of-the-century mechanical games. When I think back on the arcade now, I have a hard time discerning if my memory of it was real or if my memory of it was a product of my imagination because the whole place was one deliriously fantastic claustrophobic mess. I don't remember that arcade as ever having a name back then, for it was just somewhere that one happened to stumble upon because the doors always seemed to be open. It was a place where time forgot to tell it that 100 years had gone by, and when one entered that space, one traveled to the age when the blimp was a popular object to dream about. There were no such things as aisles in that arcade, just small patches of space where a person would rub up against another's back. Inside, the place was steaming hot, and everyone dripped with sweat, but the Victorian chimes that filled the air with turn-of-the-century sounds were so intoxicating that no one ever wanted to leave. Time was hiding from the modern world in that little magical corner of the city, but the modern world found it and made it move.

The Musée Mécanique can now be found in a Pier 45 warehouse where there is all the space in the world to spread out and not touch another person. The Victorian charm has vanished, and a draft now wafts through the arcade. Even though more people visit the Musée Mécanique now than people did back when no one knew it existed, the feeling is nowhere near the same. I still go to that arcade every time I visit San Francisco, but I don't care for it very much in its new cavernous location. I liked it much better when it was the very last Victorian holdout in what was once a very Victorian city. I suppose that there are plenty of places in San Francisco that people would no longer say feels the same, but that's probably because San Francisco has a habit of morphing into an entirely different city the instant someone turns their back on it. I don't necessarily believe that all change is bad, but I sometimes see more value in leaving certain things alone. Wouldn't it be nice if every generation conscientiously left one building behind and bequeathed it as a functioning time capsule for all of eternity? Each generation could then be custodians of the past, one building at a time throughout all of forever. I thought that maybe that arcade would make it into the future, but it didn't even manage to stay in the same spot where I left it in the 1990s.

The one thing that doesn't change much, though, is museums, and they only tend to change when they get renovated for the better. I went to the San Francisco Asian Art Museum many times, but I readily admit that I often found it hard to relate to many of the objects housed there. The Asian outlook on life is so very different from the Western worldview, and I normally failed to comprehend the concepts that many of

29

the objects tried to convey. I went there because I liked exposing my brain to different things, but there were many times when I buzzed past objects because my brain was too full to fit any more foreign concepts into it.

Not many objects there spoke to me, but there was one statue that did, and it was called *The Dancing Ganesha*. Ganesha was the one deity in the Hindu pantheon I reasonably understood because I had come across enough depictions of the elephant-headed deity in literature and art books. The 900-year-old *Dancing Ganesha* at the Asian Art Museum caught my attention when I noticed a little piece of paper tucked into one of its recesses. I thought that it was a piece of garbage, so I reached in and removed it. I could tell that the neatly folded-up paper had some writing on it, but I still wasn't thinking that it was anything other than something that needed to be thrown away. I wasn't necessarily curious to see what was written on it, but I opened it anyway. The note read, "Please, Ganesha, bring my father back," and the handwriting was obviously that of a child's. I was instantly struck with regret for having picked up what was obviously not trash, and it was then that statue got real all of a sudden to me.

What I perceived as a mere object of art, there was a child out there that looked at the same statue and saw hope. To that child, that statue was none other than the real Lord Ganesha, God of New Beginnings, the bringer of good fortune, provider of prosperity and success, and most importantly, the remover of obstacles. Out there, somewhere in San Francisco, a young person was missing his or her father terribly and was desperate for his return. Was the man deceased? Was he living separate from his family, presumably somewhere in far-off India? Who brought the youngster there? The mother? A school group? Did the child write that request down impromptu, unbeknownst to anyone? Did that child know that Ganesha was there? Was it a pilgrimage that the child took to arrive before the statue and plead his or her case? How long had that piece of paper been tucked in there? Were there no other Ganesha statues in the city of San Francisco that could have been receptive to such pleas? Was this statue purer to the Hindu religion because it was so old? Moreover, did I ruin this child's chances of seeing his or her father again now that I read the note? Did I need to put the message back? Was anyone watching me? Great, was I going to get kicked out for participating in a religion that I knew nothing about?

I hurriedly stuck the note back on Ganesha and scurried away. Yet, as I walked past all the other statues, I no longer saw them as inanimate objects. All the statues suddenly became real to me. I started to grasp the concept that the objects had meanings, not just meanings to long-dead people, but meanings to those alive today. The original purpose for each object's existence was still relevant today for those that had faith in such things.

I was puzzled over why Westerners didn't revere depictions of the Christian faith in the same way at their respective museums. I have never seen the faithful pray before a painting of Jesus in the Chicago Art Museum. It is as though it's ritual suicide for a Christian object to end up as a museum piece. The raison d'être of a Christian relic tends to die once it crosses the threshold of a museum door. An object that was once the reason for a medieval pilgrimage becomes nothing more than an anonymous item among other anonymous items once that object enters the confines of a museum. No one ever writes a letter to Saint Such-and-Such's tooth once it's enshrined in a museum display.

I recently returned to San Francisco's Asian Art Museum and noticed a new sign hanging beside *The Dancing Ganesha* statue. The sign requested that no one touch the statue or leave a note upon it. Apparently, what I saw that day was not a solo incident. As I looked over the statue, I saw a little piece of paper tucked deep into one of its recesses. I was half-tempted to reach in and read the note, but I knew from experience that it was none of my business to interfere with someone's plea to Ganesha. Religion is a curious thing and is something very sacred to an adherent. I came to understand that I was not only inside a museum but was also inside a temple. I learned to respect that fact despite not knowing what many of the symbols and iconography meant. I love art, but many, if not all, of the objects in that museum transcended art. Everything in there was infused with a spiritual meaning. I often think that I know what art is, but sometimes I think I see the world too much through a pair of Western eyes.

The Circle of Life

The fact that life doesn't last forever means that everyone will die someday. I really don't like to think that I will eventually die, but the thought of it has caused me to live more fully.

Ryan and I recently cleaned out his deceased mother's condo not that long ago after his step-dad passed away, and seeing their personal objects in situ made going through the condo kind of creepy. Neither of them took anything with them into the world beyond, and for some reason, that struck me as strange. His step-dad's car and motorcycle were still parked in the garage, his keys were still sitting on the table, his wallet was laying out in the open, and everything that was valuable to him was exactly where every item was last left. Time was moving on without them, and time didn't seem at all bothered that those two people were no longer around to move with it. It was a dose of reality that everyone's life was but a blip in the grander scheme of things, and I came to understand how insignificant each individual life was. Everyone only gets one life to live. Once someone dies, their time on this planet is over, and someone else that is not them will be born in their place.

I hope that the Hindus are correct and there is such a thing as reincarnation. Perhaps someday, I will leave that note on Ganesha after all and ask that deity to reincarnate Paul's spirit. My only hope is that whoever takes Paul's place gets to live a much longer life than he did.

CHAPTER TWO:
Lost Vegas, 1994

The Beginning of the End of the Beginning

Kat wanted to move to Las Vegas. He heard rumors that construction was booming over there, so I honestly couldn't blame him when he called up a Vegas construction company one day on a whim when he couldn't stand to sit in Bay Area traffic anymore. He accidentally landed himself a job over the phone as a marble tile setter at Caesar's Palace Forum Shops and told the interviewer that he could start right away. He asked me if I wanted to go with him, and I answered with an emphatic, "No." I had never been to Vegas before, but I had a sneaking suspicion that Vegas wasn't my cup of tea.

I was suspicious of moving to Vegas because I didn't think that Vegas was the kind of place where ordinary people moved to. I thought only eccentric people moved to Vegas, and even though I knew we weren't exactly normal, I didn't consider us as being Vegas-caliber worthy. I never perceived Vegas as being "real," and I was already driving a fake Jeep as it was, so I didn't want to live in what I thought was a fake city too. Vegas might have been booming, but it was possibly building nothing more than a facade. In a way, my whole world was beginning to look like a house of cards because my real life wasn't remotely matching what was supposedly written on paper anymore. Technically, we were getting a divorce, but in reality, we were still acting like a couple.

Ultimately, we agreed to disagree. Kat upped and moved himself to Vegas, and I stayed behind to finish school. We decided to take a break from each other for the eight months that I had left, after which time we agreed to reevaluate our situation and declare whether or not we still wanted to be together. If the answer ended up being yes, then the plan was that I'd move to Las Vegas. If the answer ended up being no, then the plan was that I'd stay in expensive San Jose all by myself. Deep down, I already knew what the answer was going to be. I basically had eight months to avoid the inevitable, and I waited out those eight months in the worst apartment that I could have possibly picked.

The Worst Apartment Ever

The first two floors of the apartment building caught fire at two o'clock in the morning on the second night of my living there because someone thought it would be funny to pile up all the couches in the recreation room and make a bonfire with them. When someone banged on my door and yelled, "Fire!" I half thought I was dreaming until I heard the same yell over and over again as that person made his way down the long corridor. When I opened the door, I smelled the smoke, and my first thought was that I was going to lose everything, so I grabbed nothing. I hurried out of the building in my pajamas and watched the firefighters do their thing while I stood on the curb with a whole bunch of suddenly awake strangers. When the fire was out, they told us that we could go back in to grab some personal belongings, but then we all had to leave. No one was allowed to live in the building until the complex got rigorously assessed, so I was rendered homeless after living only one and a half nights in my very own apartment.

I was half-tempted to move to Vegas that very night, but

school was my priority, so I made myself stay. I moved in with a friend and waited for what seemed like forever to return to my crappy apartment. When I did finally return, I seriously wished that I hadn't because the complex was thoroughly depressing. Nothing had been done to scrub the soot off the walls, and the smell of smoke caused me to gag. Those that could move out did, but those that couldn't stayed and wrote terrible things in the soot with their fingers. The female university student who lived in the studio unit next to mine was one of the lucky ones who got to move away, which worked out nice for me because I then had the kitchen and bathroom all to myself. The whole complex was set up as semi-communal living, and each studio apartment had to share a kitchen and a bathroom with the neighboring unit. The setup was weird, but it made rents reasonably affordable. I seriously thought that I had a chance of having the whole place to myself, which I imagined would make living there at least bearable. But then, one day, about two months later, I heard strange mumblings coming from the other apartment.

Apparently, the apartment manager got the bright idea to pluck people off the streets and tossed them into apartments as a way to fill the units. The lady that I got stuck next to was the kind of lady that talked to herself on buses, and she was definitely not someone that I would have ever chosen to semi-roommate with. She would hold full-on conversations with herself and often impersonated a male voice as if she had someone else in the room with her. Much to my chagrin, she would frequently offer this imaginary person a sandwich.

"Would you like a peanut butter sandwich?" she would ask in her normal voice.

"Yes, I would like a peanut butter sandwich," she would answer herself in her male voice.

"Do you want strawberry jelly on it?" she would ask in her normal voice.

"Yes, I would like strawberry jelly on it," she would answer in her male voice.

Oh, my God, I so wanted to punch her.

I had to pull all my pots and pans out of the kitchen after I discovered that she liked to leave my pans sitting empty on a lit stove. After I took away all the pans, she found a workaround and got into the habit of frying eggs directly onto the coiled electric burner. I more than once had to resort to peeing in my own apartment's sink because she sat in the bathroom for hours on end, and no amount of banging on the door would coax her to get out. She would let out a witchy "maw-whaha," or whatever that word was when I knocked on the bathroom door, and her voice was such a grating noise that I eventually stopped knocking just so I wouldn't have to hear it. I knew that she was mentally ill, but there was nothing that I could do to help her. It irritated me that her presence was invading my life, and it pissed me off that she was a fire hazard in a building that had suffered one too many fires already. Considering how much time she spent in the bathroom, I secretly wished that she would somehow accidentally flush herself down the toilet.

I managed to make my own life more difficult when I made the mistake of hitting a Mercedes with my Samurai on the freeway one morning on my way to school. I was without my car for four months because the shop that I took it to agreed to charge me less so long as I was willing to wait for the mechanic to peck at it during his free time. I lived too far away from school to rely on a bus, so I depended on a cokehead friend who never slept to drop me off there early every morning. It was a win-win for us in a way because he thought that my life was very entertaining. He really enjoyed picking me up because he liked starting his day with a cup of coffee and listening to my neighbor go on about whatever it was that she was going on about every stinking morning. I swear that lady never slept either. I knew that I wasn't thrilled with the idea of living in Vegas, but at some point, I realized that somewhere, anywhere else had to be better than where I currently was. I bought a calendar and started crossing out the days of the longest countdown of my life.

Las Vegas

I went to Vegas intending to talk Kat out of living there, but that proved to be a futile endeavor once I saw how jubilantly he embraced his Las Vegas lifestyle. I didn't know how the constant ching-ching noise from all the slot machines that followed one's every step didn't annoy him because that constant clatter totally annoyed me. I found the entire city to be every bit as grating as I suspected it was going to be, and I really wished that we were living in Tampa or anywhere in Florida instead because then at least we'd have access to a beach. Not a moment went by that there wasn't some constant reminder that I was living in Las Vegas, be it the bright lights that would shine through our bedroom window or the slot machine sounds that were unavoidable even at gas stations. I adamantly refused to exchange my California license plate for a Nevada one because I didn't want to outwardly legitimize the fact that I was supposedly a Nevada resident.

I got the most normal job that I could fathom in the city of constant sound as a waitress at a chain restaurant, where the only real clatter was the sweet, sweet tune of servers occasionally dropping dishes. It was a good enough job, but I didn't know why I was there. I had already forgotten all about the crappy existence that I left behind in San Jose, but it just didn't feel like Vegas was the next best place for me. I wasn't connecting with my environment in the least bit, and I felt entirely out of place. I wanted out. I wanted out of all of it. I wanted to get away and leave myself behind.

On my days off from work, I avoided The Strip altogether and would drive to whatever blank areas I could find on the map. Actually, I should rephrase that sentence and say that I would *attempt* to drive to what I thought were supposed to be blank areas on the map. More often than not, instead of getting out into the desert as I desperately tried to do, I would find myself inadvertently tootling around brand new track home neighborhoods instead. It seemed as though the more I tried to get away, the more Las Vegas managed to keep me in. There was nowhere in Las Vegas that was empty anymore. Las Vegas was getting built up. If I truly wanted to escape the city, I needed to drive a much further distance.

I pored over a map and found a park about 50 miles north tantalizingly called "The Valley of Fire." Just that name alone made me want to visit it because I started to consider fire to be a recurring theme. Moving to Vegas metaphorically made me feel that I went from the frying pan straight into the fire, so the idea of walking around a fiery landscape genuinely appealed to my sensibilities. Unfortunately, I failed to consider that walking around a fiery landscape also harbored the potential to kill me.

Putting the Lost in Lost Vegas

I now know that I went into that desert wickedly unprepared and that I was stupid for hiking in a Nevada desert in the middle of June without any water. I totally get that. However, I didn't set out with the intention of getting lost out there. I went to the park for the first time the week prior and managed to hike a section of it perfectly fine without any water, so I naturally figured that the second time around was going to be more of the same. The park was insanely pretty, and I desired to get more familiar with it because I thought I had found my new Las Vegas escape hatch. Unfortunately, that park ultimately proved to be more like my new Las Vegas escape pit, and I was soon going to fall to the bottom of it.

The Valley of Fire is a 46,000-acre geologic wonderland of red-colored outcrops, canyons, and cliffs. Much of the park can be driven as a road tour, and I drove all over the park the first time I went there. I pulled over at all the scenic overlooks and admired the plethora of beautiful vistas. The park was massive, and I remember thinking that it looked like an easy place to die in. My desert musing was validated near the visitor center when I came across a memorial to some poor chap who died of thirst out there in 1915. The guy's name was John G. Clark, and he was a civil war veteran, but I didn't remember his name when I tried to conjure him up as my spirit animal a week later when I was nearly dying of thirst myself somewhere under the moonlight.

When I went on what I coined my "reconnaissance mission," I discovered a short hike down a slot canyon that was labeled "The Petroglyph Trail." I hiked the trail but thought it was too short and didn't quite satisfy my craving for hiking. The trail did boast some fine petroglyphs, though, and those rock drawings were the first petroglyphs that I had ever seen. I was truly impressed with the ancient figures, and I vowed to return the following week with my camera. After that hike, I proceeded to do the speed demon tour of the park in my car, and I saw more than enough of the landscape to make me want to return the following week and take loads of fabulous pictures.

Kat and I didn't usually have the same days off. As a waitress, I mostly worked evenings and weekends, and Kat worked days during the week, so we just got used to doing our own thing. I only had to work a couple of lunch shifts during the week, so overall, I had more time on my hands than I knew what to do with. I had only been in Vegas for a little over a month when I left Kat a note that said "went hiking" but failed to elaborate where. I initially contemplated not writing a note to him at all because I was pretty sure that I was going to be home before him, but I wrote the note anyway just in case he got home before I did. He and I were slightly slipping toward being on the skids again, and I didn't even mention my Valley of Fire discovery to him the previous week because we were acting more like glorified roommates at this point. Neither of us knew what we were to each other anymore and my being there only seemed to make things more complicated. We knew that we cared for each other, but that was about where our relationship both began and ended. Had I known that he would be up at midnight that evening reporting me as a missing person, I would have left him with a little more information about where to look for me. Unfortunately, he had absolutely no idea where I was when I didn't come home that night, and at some point in the middle of the afternoon, I honestly didn't know where I was either.

My hike started off innocently enough on that same petroglyph trail that I was already slightly familiar with. I knew in advance that the trail was going to be short, but I already had it in my mind that I was going to scale the big rock wall where the trail came to an end. I didn't necessarily think that there would be more petroglyphs on the rocks beyond where the slot canyon ended, but I also didn't rule out that possibility either. I had brought my camera with me, so I was feeling a little bit artsy. Also, I was simply curious to see what was hiding on the other side of the canyon.

There was not a single sign at the end of the trail that said, "Do not climb the rocks," and I saw the shoe prints of plenty of people who had evidently scaled the rocks before me. I in no way thought that I was about to do anything that was going to put myself in any kind of jeopardy when I started to do my climb. I figured that everyone climbed those rocks, so when I went up and over them, I made not a single mental note of where I emerged because I took it for granted that other people would be up there as well. I had absolutely no idea that I was destined to be up there all by myself for the next 22 hours.

I felt as though I was standing on top of the world. The landscape that opened up beyond the rock wall was vast and full of beauty. Before me was a sea of red, and I wanted to dive into it and swim across the stony canyons. I could feel my eyes getting drunk by the intoxicating scenery. It felt special to be standing there in the middle of a silent stone world that gave me a sense of what forever felt like. Forever was red, quiet, still nothingness.

I had brought Yanni with me, so I sat on a rock and listened to the landscape with him. His music fit my mood perfectly, and together we soaked in the wonder that sprawled out before us. There was nowhere else that I wanted to be for that full hour of my life, and it was absolutely marvelous. I was lost in reverie and thought about everything and nothing all at once.

Eventually, the reverie ended. The sun grew high in the sky, and it started to get hot. I snapped a few final pictures and said goodbye to the landscape that was good for my soul, and started to head back down. I climbed down what I thought was the original rock wall that I climbed up and looked for the petroglyph trail, but was flummoxed when I couldn't find it. I supposed that maybe I was just one rock pile off, so I climbed back up the pile of rocks, readjusted my entry point, and descended once again. No petroglyph trail was waiting there for me either. I went back up, readjusted, and repeated, over and over and over again. I went down the same pile of rocks two or three times, convinced that one of them had to be correct, but none of them ever were. I even forged my own path a couple of times, thinking that I could just walk my way out of there, but I failed to find a successful way out.

Hours went by, and I exhausted myself. By about three in the afternoon, I was hot and desperately thirsty. I didn't bring any water or anything to snack on. The only things that I brought with me were a camera and a Walkman. Yanni was the first to go when I got angry and had to pitch something. I unspooled that cassette and tore it up in a fit of fury, so if anyone happened to find a beat-up Yanni cassette in the middle of nowhere, that was unapologetically my doing. I think that I left torn up Yanni next to a beaten-up cactus that I somewhat destroyed in my frantic search for water. I had thought that cacti stored water. I was under the impression that all I needed to do was break open a cactus, and there would be water inside it, but the cactus that I chose was completely dry. I thought that maybe I didn't choose the right type of cactus, so I broke an appendage off another one and was again met with disappointment. I stopped mutilating cacti after that because it was making me feel bad that I was hurting them for no apparent reason.

It was when I eventually realized that I couldn't go down the same rock piles for a gazillionth time that I felt a sledgehammer slam into my gut. I experienced my first wave of real panic when I felt all the blood race from the top of my head and escape through my toes. I felt like a shell of myself in an instant. I suddenly realized that I had nowhere else to go. That was it. I was done.

I was lost.

That realization was devastating once I genuinely admitted it to myself. However, I instinctively knew that I couldn't dwell on the fact because I had to keep a hold of my wits. I had to swallow the panic and figure a way out. The park was massive, but I knew that it had boundaries. I still had the light on my side, so I figured that as long as I ignored my panic, I still had plenty of time to try to work my way through this blunder. The only plan that I could come up with was to pick a single direction and stick with it. I thought that maybe if I kept going in a straight line, I would reach a boundary of some sort. I picked the direction that appeared to offer the flattest terrain and went for it.

About an hour into my jaunt, I had to admit that my prospects of getting out of there were sadly pretty slim. The red rocks that originally surrounded me had gradually turned white, which gave me the sinking suspicion that I chose to walk in the wrong direction. My hunch was that The Valley of Fire wasn't supposed to be white, so I decided to turn around and go back to where I started. I encountered a whole new dilemma when I couldn't recognize which direction I just came from after I did a 360 intake of the landscape. I disoriented myself, and now I was even more screwed because I didn't know where to go from there. It was at that moment when I thought that I was going to die out there.

I was so incredibly thirsty by this point that I didn't even have enough energy to scream, "Help!" anymore. I had been screaming, "Help!" off and on for hours to no avail that I figured it didn't matter if I just stopped yelling it. It was obvious that no one was going to come to my rescue. I got myself into this predicament, so I had to be the one to get myself out of it. The absolute only thing I could do was keep walking while I still had some light. I had to correct my mistake and get back to my starting point, wherever the hell that was. The only thing that I had to focus on was getting back to square one. To do that, I needed to locate the only landmark that I had a mental note of.

When I first went over the rock face, I remember being greeted with a huge rock monolith over my right shoulder. All I needed to do was find that huge monolith once again, and I would get my bearings back. I surveyed the landscape and looked for anything that rose higher than everything else, and once I spotted my monolithic outcrop, I knew which direction to aim for. Unfortunately, I didn't quite make it all the way back to my starting point before everything around me went completely black. The sun had set, and I was still out there. Wherever I was standing was where I was going to sleep that night, and I was standing in a field of fucking rocks.

In an absurd way, I was glad that it was dark. I finally had the perfect excuse to stop moving. I had been constantly walking for over seven hours straight, and I was utterly spent. My mind was taxed beyond its capacity, and I was no longer thinking coherent thoughts. Moreover, I was desperately thirsty, and my body needed to rest. Unfortunately, I had nothing to drink and nowhere to lay my head. I groped in the dark for someplace to plant my body for the long night ahead. I felt around and found the least bumpy spot and tried to make do.

I somewhat managed to lie myself down, but I couldn't relax because the wheels wouldn't stop turning inside my head. I bombarded myself with so many muddled thoughts all at once that I barely recognized the sound of my own voice yelling at me. More than anything, I heard my voice literally scream at me that I desperately needed something to drink. I had to tell myself to shut up about that because there was nothing that I could do to remedy my thirsty situation. Interspersed with my obsessive thoughts about dousing the entire inside of my body with copious amounts of liquid, I sort of managed to think a little about life in general. Actually, it is more accurate to say that I thought a lot about death and only a little bit about life. I reflected on the fact that I never thought that I was going to live to a ripe old age, but I also didn't foresee myself dying at the young age of 20 either. I was thoroughly confused about when I was supposed to die, and I wasn't sure that I was going to wake up the following morning if and when I finally fell asleep that night. So, for a while, I stayed awake solely because I thought that it would be the last night I was ever going to be alive. I was thirsty, but I was alive, and, for that moment, I really felt it. Alive. Life. What did life really mean, I wondered? I had no immediate answer. Not being dead was all I could conclude. Not being dead to life while one had the chance to live it, I also thought.

I wondered to myself if I was living life correctly. At that particular moment, I knew that I was not living life right, but I desperately wanted a second chance at living life better. I didn't want to be punished eternally for my one single mistake of wandering off alone in the desert. I knew that I messed up, and I was very sorry for it, but I wanted the chance to correct my error. The only reason why I was out there at all was because I wanted to get away. I knew that I was in love with an alcoholic. I was unhappy with my life and was perpetually trying to escape it. I didn't want to run from my life anymore. I needed to find my happy place, and I didn't think that I would find it anywhere in Nevada. Was it the state that I didn't like, or was it my home life that I was unhappy with? I knew that the answer was both. I didn't belong there, but I didn't know where I belonged instead. I was lost on too many levels, and my physically being lost was an appropriate outward appearance for how I was internally feeling. I was lost in my own life, and I needed to find a way out as well as a way in. I needed to get inside myself and figure out who exactly was lurking inside me. I resolved that if I ever got out of that desert alive, I would figure out who I was. I didn't want to be dead to me anymore, and I vowed that I wouldn't be if I made it out of that desert as a living human being. What I also didn't want was to be thirsty anymore. It didn't take very long for any profound thoughts to be replaced with obsessive thoughts about dousing my body with bucketfuls of liquid.

I was getting an intimate understanding of what dying of thirst felt like, and it was feeling like something awful. All my thoughts shut down except for the one single thought of wanting something to drink. I was oddly obsessing over Mountain Dew, of all things. I don't even like soda, but my mind was hung up on wanting that sugary drink. I was fantasizing about guzzling down liters upon liters of Mountain Dew, and I couldn't get my mind off of it. I wanted Mountain Dew. I wanted Mountain Dew. I don't think that I even gave a thought about wanting water because I desperately wanted a waterfall of that lime-colored drink.

I believe that I tossed around for an hour with nothing but the thoughts of wanting Mountain Dew before I eventually passed out. Soon, instead of thinking about Mountain Dew, I started dreaming about it. I slept for a bit but was soon woken up by tiny droplets of rain. Little itty bitty droplets of water, too small and infrequent to drink, were dropping on me, and I couldn't tell if I was dreaming or if I was awake. I tried sticking out my tongue, but nothing substantial landed on it, and just enough rain fell to make me curse the sky. The temperature suddenly dropped, and I was instantly chilled. The desert gods evidently hated me, but I couldn't understand why. Being awake caused me to start thinking again, and my thoughts went straight to Mountain Dew. I desperately did not want to think about Mountain Dew anymore because I was tired of thinking about a soda that I hadn't drunk since I was a kid, so I convinced myself to think about something else instead. I started thinking about that memorial guy who died not too far away from where I was now more than officially lost. Up to this point, I prayed to no one. I did not pray to God because I felt forsaken by that deity, but I did wind up pleading my case with the dead ghost of the desert. I begged him to get me out of there come morning. I got on my knees and groveled to his spirit. I mulled over his demise for quite a while and genuinely tried to grasp what he had gone through. I felt akin to his plight, but I desperately did not want to emulate it. I seriously prayed to him. I wanted this to be a matter between him and me like we were some sort of spiritual couple, and I asked him to save me.

"Please get me out of here," I asked him most sincerely. "Please. Please. *Please.*

I must have passed out again after my séance because I slept again until the morning sunlight shone through my eyelids. The sun was shining all happy as if it was the most perfect morning in the whole entire world, and all I could think was, "Goddammit, I'm still out here."

I immediately got up and started the day with a mindless zombie stroll. I saw my landmark monolith rock a short distance away and then mused over what direction to take that morning. I toyed with the idea of going over the rock piles again but discarded the idea as being a waste of time. I chose to stick with the "go with one direction" strategy and went in the complete opposite direction from the one I went in the other day. In a landscape of a million choices, all I could do was hope that I was choosing the correct one.

About a half-hour into my stroll to nowhere, I came across something that I hadn't seen before: another person's shoe prints. "Footprints!" I screamed out loud. It was the first sign of life that I came across. I immediately started to follow them and didn't care where they went. It did, however, strike me as strange that there were even footprints at all, considering that it drizzled a little bit the night before. Either they were fresh from that morning, or the rain the other night was really so pathetic that it didn't even have the stamina to smudge out a trail of footprints. I didn't need an explanation, though, because I was happy to take them wherever they went. The prints led me through a wash, over some rocks, this a way and that a way, and then they stopped.

"Damn it!" I moaned.

In front of me stood yet another looming pile of rocks, so I clambered over them. Once on top of them, I had a fantastic view of even more canyons. Miles and miles of desert canyons were laid at my feet, and I felt completely defeated.

Then, far off in the distance, I saw little figures. People! Actual live human beings! Maybe they were rock climbers.

"Hello!" I yelled and violently waved my arms like an idiot.

"Hello, hello, hello!" Then I thought to shut up and just walk over to them.

As I got nearer to the people, I realized that some vehicles were moving up and down the mountain. They weren't rock climbers after all, but construction workers. They were building something, a lookout tower, or some other contraption. I deduced that if they had trucks, there had to be a road, and, lo, I could probably walk back to my car. I felt a sudden rush of relief. I was going to get out of there alive. All I had to do was wade through another canyon or two, and I was going to be free. I would have whistled while I stepped if I had any saliva left in my mouth to make any sounds with.

As I was making my way over to the small figures, the method of how I discovered them became something of a curiosity to me. There would have been no way that I would have discovered them if I hadn't followed those mysterious footsteps. The prints literally appeared out of nowhere. My rational mind deduced that some hiker who knew the park like the back of his hand roamed through the area that morning, but my irrational mind told me that it was the memorial deity, John G. Clark, who put them there. Whatever the case, I knelt down and said a little thank you to my desert savior, a real heartfelt thank you, to be precise.

Unfortunately, it didn't take long for all the bullshit to begin. I suspected that a road had to be close by, so I intended to quietly slip past the construction workers and high tail it for my vehicle and get the heck away from the park. I didn't want to make small talk with anybody, nor did I want to admit to anyone that I spent a night out in the desert completely lost. I felt stupid that I waved and screamed at the workers way off in the distance, so all I could do was hope that I was far enough away that no one really saw or heard me. Sure, the thought crossed my mind about asking them for some water, but I felt embarrassed that I was lost, and I wasn't in the mood to explain myself. I knew that there was a gas station just down the road, so all I had to do was get into my car and drive to it. I had made it this far without water. I had it in me to push myself to the finish line.

Right as I was about to step onto the paved road to recovery, I was stopped by two construction employees who thought it was worth their time to interrogate me. Someone must have heard my yelling, so I assumed that I got radioed in as a crazy person.

"Who are you, and what were you doing on our set?" they asked me.

I was seriously not in the mood for them.

"I wasn't on your set," I explained. "I was lost all night. I'm just trying to get back to my car."

I could only imagine what I looked like as I was quite sure that I wasn't looking very pretty. I stopped caring about how many thorny bushes I trail blazed through hours ago, so my legs were a scraped-up mess, and I was sure that my hair looked a little beyond bedhead. My mind was complete mush by that point, so they probably saw something a little scary in my eyes. I was only lost for about 22 hours, but it felt like I was lost for at least forever.

"So, you were on our set all night?" they inquired. "What were you doing out there?"

I didn't even answer them the second time around. I had not an ounce of energy available in myself to spend on them, so I walked away while they were in mid-sentence. What I wanted to ask from them was a ride to my car, but I could tell that they were going to be just as useful to me as yet another pile of rocks. I had dealt with enough rocks the last day that I wanted nothing more to do with inanimate objects. Besides, I was becoming quite masterful at walking, so one last thirsty hill meant nothing to me. I was on the homestretch as far as I was concerned, so I just wanted to finish the journey.

I turned around a few times to check if they were following me in their pickup, but they weren't. In fact, not a single car drove by. I walked for I don't know how long, a half-hour or so maybe, and I just about cried when I saw my cute little red Samurai patiently waiting for me. Thankfully I didn't ditch my keys in the desert, and it felt absolutely surreal to put the key into the lock and open that door. I was officially going to get away from there.

The closest pit stop was a 30-minute drive that I managed to do in about 15 minutes. I barreled into the gas station and grabbed the biggest bottle of Mountain Dew and the largest jug of water. I sat in my car and guzzled them both down in record time. I then puked a little for having drunk them so fast before I went back inside and bought some more. Finally, I was able to look around at all the sunlight and agreed that, indeed, this *was* the most perfect morning. I noticed that it was 9 a.m., and I technically had to be at work at 11 a.m., so I hightailed it to make it home.

I walked into our apartment a little after 10 a.m., and I heard Kat's voice say to someone over the phone, "Never mind. She just walked through the door." Kat immediately dropped the phone and gave me a massive hug.

"I feared that you were dead!" he said to me.

"Funny," I said, "I feared that I was dead, too."

I tried to explain in the quickest words possible where the hell I was for the last 24 hours, but it all came out as gibberish. I ultimately managed to convey that I was lost somewhere in the desert and that it took forever to find my way out.

I then took the quickest shower humanly possible and made it to work on time, where I proceeded to act as if nothing out of the ordinary was going on in my life. I was simply happy to have a sense of normalcy again. Not that living in Las Vegas seemed normal to me. Ah, the vicious circle kept turning inside my head. Yet, I was more than happy to be pouring someone a glass of iced tea rather than wandering around aimlessly in a desert, such as how I started my morning that day. Little did people know about the secret life of their waitress. The juxtaposition of my sublime thoughts versus the menial tasks that I was performing was an enduring source of interest for me throughout the day. It baffled me why I was even there, waiting tables. Why didn't I just stay home? Was waiting on tables where I wanted to be? Actually, at that time, yes. I didn't want to have to think of anything heavy for a few hours. I wanted to get my mind off what just happened and kind of take a break from myself. I was way too intimate with my own head for the last 24 hours, so I just wanted to get away from me. Waitressing fit that bill perfectly, and it was probably the only time in my life that I genuinely enjoyed doing that job.

Kat and I had a heart-to-heart that evening, and for the next couple of weeks, we were the best couple in the entire world. By week three, our perfect lives started to unravel, and by week four, I packed whatever I could into my car and drove away. It was obvious that either Vegas had to go or I had to. So, I decided to leave. The thoughts that I had in the desert deeply affected me, so I felt committed to the vow that I made to myself to make my life more like how I wanted it to be. I didn't necessarily know what I wanted my life to look like, but I finally recognized that I didn't want to be unhappy anymore. It wasn't just Vegas that was making me sad, but it was the constant falling out of love that was depressing me. We were not "us" anymore, and I was starting to lose sight of myself.

It was time for me to pick a direction and see where it would lead me.

Again.

CHAPTER THREE:
Finding Where, 1991-1999

The Search

The possibility that my spirit could be anywhere in America made it hard for me to choose which direction to go in. All that I knew was that there was nothing west of Las Vegas for me, so when I got on the road, I headed toward the east. I needed somewhere new to live, and I had no intention of going back to either San Jose or Milwaukee. Mentally, I decided to head for Florida, but physically, I only got as far as Albuquerque. I thought that maybe I was hiding somewhere in the urban sprawl of that semi-arid town, but a few hours of driving on long stretches of monotonous roads ultimately confirmed that I wasn't hiding anywhere there at all. The city was brown and bland and didn't pull on my heartstrings. There was something about Albuquerque that I just wasn't feeling, so I didn't see any point in trying to force myself to fall in love with it. Albuquerque was a bust, so I had to decide yet again which direction to go in. I thought about heading to Texas for a nanosecond and lingered for a while over going to Florida, but a honk of someone's horn behind me caused me to panic. I spontaneously got on the freeway and headed back to Vegas.

I didn't get very far, though, because a moment of clarity caused me to register a motel billboard on the side of the road as being specifically advertised toward me. I got off the highway and checked into that motel in the hope that doing so was going to save me from making any rash decisions. There, I experienced my own dark night of the soul in the middle of the afternoon while I sat on top of a grimy comforter in a generic freeway motel room. It had only been one month since I was physically lost in the desert, but now I was metaphorically lost, which mentally didn't feel all that much different. I honestly didn't know what I was doing there, and I honestly didn't know where I needed to be instead. I felt like I was a human wad of crumpled up paper that got rimmed off the trash can and landed somewhere on the floor next to the garbage. I feared that I would essentially be throwing my life away if I allowed myself to go back to Vegas. I was allegorically identifying with trash, and I recognized that doing so was probably a sign that going back to Kat would be a bad idea. Only eight hours had passed since I left him, and already, I was desperate to return to the crappy familiar because it was the only thing that I knew. Any other choice would have put me into uncharted waters, and I was starting to question my navigational skills. I wanted a change in my life, but I didn't want to be the one to change it, even though I was physically on the road trying to make that change. What I was experiencing was a classic case of cold feet. I made it to the altar, but I couldn't spit out the words "I do" to the future that I so desperately wanted to have.

What I really wanted was for someone else to make my decisions for me. I didn't care what this hypothetical person would decide for me so long as I ended up somewhere decent. I thought that maybe I was being too hard on Albuquerque. I spent a considerable amount of time convincing myself that I wanted to live in Albuquerque because that city was just outside the door. My future could start the very second I left the motel room. I eventually mustered up the courage to walk out of the motel a mere two hours after I entered it because the motel was not where I wanted to be once I decided that I wanted to get on with my life. I wanted to get out there and start my new life in Albuquerque. So, naturally, I was shocked when I watched Albuquerque diminish in size in my rear-view mirror when I allowed myself to drive away from it. My heart took control of the wheel when I entered the car, and it was my heart that wanted to go back to Vegas.

So, the whole time I was heading west, I was still thinking about Florida. I was obviously mentally incapacitated and really shouldn't have been driving. Luckily, I was getting hungry, so I needed to stop and get something to eat. I got off the freeway in Flagstaff, Arizona, and searched for a restaurant but was immediately distracted by how darned adorable the city appeared. In my brain-damaged and malnourished state, I decided within five minutes of tootling around Flagstaff's city streets that I was satisfied with what I saw. I was instantly determined to live in a city that had an old-timey railway station, half a dozen mom-and-pop coffee shops, a gazillion pine trees, and delectable 75-degree weather. My immediate impression was that there was absolutely nothing wrong with Flagstaff, and I genuinely wondered why everyone in the United States wasn't already residing there.

I pulled up to a Denny's restaurant and grabbed one of those apartment rental catalogs that languish outdated in rusty newspaper bins. I quickly got down to business and opened the apartment book before I even thought to glance at the menu. Having the apartment book in front of me was a good excuse to strike up a conversation with my waiter, and I asked him if Flagstaff was a decent place to live.

"Oh, it is if you like driving a snowplow," he quickly replied.

"Whoa, hold on," I thought. How was that the answer when it was so beautiful outside?

"Snowplow?" I asked. "Really? It snows here?"

"It's summer," he explained. "This nice weather only lasts for a few months; then it gets cold for the rest of the year. The elevation here is almost 7,000 feet."

I had never lived in the mountains before, so I didn't quite grasp what high elevation truly meant.

"So, how cold is cold? I asked.

"Really cold," he said.

"Like, Wisconsin cold?" I inquired.

"Maybe not Wisconsin cold," he said, "but pretty darn cold."

"I didn't even know that it got cold in Arizona," I admitted. "I just assumed that the whole state was a desert."

"That's what everyone assumes," he said, "but if you don't like the cold, then you should go down to Phoenix. It's always warm there, and there are tons of jobs. I moved up here from there because I was sick of the heat and tired of all the people."

"Hmmm," I said. "So, you're suggesting that I check out a city that you didn't care for?"

"Phoenix is okay," he said. "Lots of jobs there, and it's cheaper there than here."

It's not that he wasn't selling Phoenix to me; I just wasn't buying it. I was too hung up on how cute Flagstaff was that I convinced myself that it was Flagstaff or bust. It wasn't until I got some food in my stomach that I gradually recovered my brain. I knew deep down that I didn't want to live in a cold city because two mild winters in California positively spoiled me. I spent my entire teenage life shoveling snow, scraping ice, and waiting forever for my rusty car to warm up that I wasn't quite ready to jump right back into that glamorous lifestyle anytime soon. I allowed the idea of living in Flagstaff go by the time I finished my meal. When I walked out of that Denny's door, I found myself one hundred percent homeless once again.

I didn't realize how tired I was until I got into my car and started driving to nowhere in particular. I wisely pulled over on some random side street and promptly fell asleep. I was dead stinking tired, and though I don't remember what I dreamed about that night, I can pretty much guarantee that I didn't dream about how great my life was going to be in Vegas.

I woke up the next morning, grabbed some gas station coffee, and got on the road to Vegas. I was just resigned at that point and didn't even think about any other options. I still had the house keys on my keychain, and I remember looking at them when I put my key in the ignition and thinking how strange the concept of home was. I remember thinking that I wanted to go home, and that was the only thought that possessed my brain as I drove toward the city that I was desperate to leave only 24 hours before.

"Maybe I could convince Kat to move to Florida with me," was what I was seriously thinking when I saw a sign that presented a choice. The road ahead was going to split, and I had to choose between going to either Las Vegas or Phoenix. I had one mile to make a final decision, and I chose without really choosing. Absolutely no thought process was involved at all when I decided to take the road to Phoenix. My entire physical being simply ripped the steering wheel out of my heart's tight grip and took the car in an entirely new direction.

The Discovery

The road to Phoenix was all downhill, and I noticed the scenery change when I looked at the trees. I started my journey at the top of the hill in Ponderosa pines, then descended through curious-looking Joshua trees and other scrubby plants, and bottomed out 5,800 feet later in a land full of saguaros as far as the eyes could see. This is going to sound stupid, but I never thought that the saguaro was real. I honestly thought that those things only existed in cartoons. My inner monologue debated with itself over whether or not those cacti were real or if they were cardboard cutouts. It was an absurdly stupid conversation that I was having with myself, and I couldn't believe it when I saw saguaros standing in traffic islands in the middle of the city. "Who would go to the trouble to stick those silly cardboard cutouts everywhere?" was one of the many stupid thoughts that ran through my head as I progressively made my way to Phoenix's city center. I really didn't know where I was even going, but one of the other thoughts that I had was the thought that I wasn't liking too much how this Phoenix place was appearing. Five miles in, and it was reminding me a little too much of Albuquerque, and that wasn't exactly a good thing.

I happened to enter Phoenix on the longest, most blighted road in town, inappropriately labeled as Grand Avenue. I drove by sorry-looking hotels, large empty lots, I don't know how many humongous industrial-sized buildings, quite a few pawn shops, and enormous strip clubs that were paired with equally enormous signs that advertised their fine establishments with names such as *The Great Alaskan Bush Co* and *Mr. Lucky's*.

"What the heck was I doing here?" I wondered.

I stopped at one of the hotels that openly posted their hourly rates and asked the front desk lady for help. I was feeling pretty desperate, so I didn't care what I sounded like when I asked her where "a nice side of town" was. It wasn't like she didn't know that her hotel wasn't located in an area that most would consider a safe place to leave their car windows rolled down, so without skipping a beat, she suggested that I drive to a suburb called Tempe.

"Lots of young people your age live there," she said to me. "That's where the college is."

I immediately liked the sound of that. She handwrote directions for me on a piece of paper, and I followed them with the hope that her directions were going to lead me to somewhere decent. I got off on the freeway exit as she directed and got dumped onto a street lined with termite exterminating businesses, transmission shops, tire stores, and more empty lots. "Well, this whole town is a dump," I said to myself.

Despite the hideousness that was surrounding me, I kept driving as the hotel lady directed me to do because I hadn't reached the university part yet. As long as there was a pocket of decency, I figured that there existed the slightest possibility of things working out. After driving through five miles of sheer disappointment, I was more than pleasantly surprised when I came upon a city street lined with charming brick buildings. I turned down the attractive avenue and quickly encountered quaint little bookstores, restaurants, bars, a movie theater, and coffee shops. To my eyes, the place looked like a squished-up Flagstaff on a single city street, so I was instantly sold. I was unequivocally going to live in this place called "Tempe."

I turned down the first neighborhood street that I saw and pulled up to the first apartment complex that had a "for rent" sign posted in front of it and landed myself a one-bedroom apartment. I lied to the landlady when I told her that I already had a job lined up at the Chili's Restaurant that I noticed on the corner of the street. I wasn't sure if that Chili's was even hiring, but she didn't call my bluff, so it didn't seem to matter. I did end up getting a waitressing job, though, just it was at a newly opened Applebee's instead. Lucky for me, that Applebee's was so new that it wasn't going to open for another two weeks, so it allowed me some free time to get familiar with my new surroundings.

First off, it was impossible not to notice that it was blazing hot outside. I quickly came to understand why my apartment was vacant when I rolled into town and why the landlady didn't care if I had a job or not, as she was probably just happy that someone was willing to inhabit the unit. The two-story property was built entirely out of cinder block in the 1940s, and it contained a sum total of zero insulation. My apartment was on the second floor, and the air conditioning unit dated from at least the 1970s. Heat definitely rose, and my apartment was so hot inside that no amount of air conditioning could cool the place down. The only saving grace was that my apartment boasted a little outdoor patio that jutted into the neighborhood cat lady's jungly garden. I threw my futon mattress out there and called it my bedroom, as it was more comfortable to sleep outside than in. I thoroughly enjoyed how overgrown the crazy cat lady's backyard was. I adored how her many untrimmed palm trees blew in the breeze at night, and I admired how they took on a thousand different shadows that would sometimes freak me out. It didn't take a leap of imagination to pretend that I was adrift on a little boat somewhere in the middle of the Amazon jungle where I feared any bug could eat me alive.

I soon learned that the drawback of having an Amazon jungle in the backyard was that it increased my chances of having critters crawl into my clothes when I hung them over the balcony to dry. I'm not sure why I didn't think to shake out my clothes before I put them on because I was warned by nearly everyone that I needed to get in the habit of shaking out my shoes every day for scorpions. I even had a desiccated squished up scorpion molded onto my patio's door jamb that I presumed was there to remind me to never let my guard down, but, alas, its disgusting effectiveness wore off on me by day three. Well into my third week of living in Phoenix, I got into the habit of shaking out nothing. I most definitely did not develop the habit of shaking out my work uniform after I washed it in the sink and set it out to dry overnight. The only reason why I washed my uniform in the sink was that I was too cheap to invest in a second uniform. Thus, it was my unabashed willingness to go third-world style that allowed me to tuck in a shirt that had a tarantula lurking inside.

I didn't know what was crawling on me, but I could definitely feel that something was moving across my torso. I untucked my shirt, gave it a shake, and watched in horror as a full-sized tarantula tumbled out. I immediately busted out that creepy spider dance that people do, but my performance was interrupted when I watched the huge arachnid slip under my couch. I couldn't go to work while leaving a tarantula in the apartment, so I had no choice but to capture it somehow. Weren't tarantulas poisonous? Ugh, life before the internet wasn't easy. I had no idea. I thought so. It didn't matter; I had to catch it. I grabbed a coffee mug, moved the couch, and surprisingly secured the mug over the tarantula without incident. Then I was like, "now what?" I had to get it up. I grabbed a piece of stiff junk mail paper, wiggled it under the mug, and walked the whole contraption over to the patio. I intended to toss the tarantula back into a palm tree, but I totally missed and watched the tarantula land on the patio below mine. That was just great. Now I had to tell some guy that I only sort of knew that I just dumped a tarantula onto his patio. I knocked on his door, but he, of course, didn't answer because it was like 10 a.m. on a Wednesday. I left him a note that said, "Sorry, but I accidentally dropped a tarantula onto your patio. I'll be by after work to make sure everything is okay," signed your upstairs neighbor. When I checked on him later that night, he claimed that no such tarantula was there, and he even asked me if I honestly dropped one. "Great," I thought to myself. I was sure that he thought that I was drama. He pretty much accused me of making the story up, and I suspected that he probably thought that he had some lame weirdo living in the unit above him.

I don't know if it was the tarantula in my shirt, the oodles of scorpions that I've nearly stepped on over the years, or the oppressive summer heat that proved to me that Phoenix was a worthy place to call home. This city is crazy cruel, but that's surprisingly part of its appeal. The city might have looked blighted when I first rolled into town, but the tarnish quickly wore off and revealed a polished gem underneath. It didn't take me very long to identify with being a Phoenician. The city had its charms, and I was lucky that Phoenix rescued me when it did because it saved me from going back to Kat at a time when we needed to be apart.

Kat eventually left Vegas and moved to Phoenix, and looking back at it now, I don't know how much of a good thing that proved to be. For the next six years, we were an on-again-off-again couple and continuously moved in and out of each other's apartments. Our relationship was totally absurd in a Stockholm syndrome kind of way, and we should have stopped many times while we were ahead. I don't know if it was animal magnetism, co-dependency, the fact that Paul died, or what, but there had to be a reason why we insisted on making our lives more difficult than they needed to be. The crux of it, I know, was because we were the only family that either of us truly had. Both of us came from broken families, and dysfunction was in both of our blood. It took us both a long while to learn that dysfunction wasn't something that either of us had to accept when we could just choose to be with someone who made us happy instead.

Job Search

Relationships, or lack thereof, aside, I still needed to find myself. I needed to go back to school, but I still didn't know what for. I had always thought that I wanted to be an archaeologist. There was something about putting a spade into the ground and finding remnants of ancient societies that stirred my imagination and made me want to pursue that career. Just the thought that I could possibly become an archaeologist got me really excited, but then the dream deflated once I looked into what it took to become one. Becoming a bona fide archaeologist sounded tedious as hell and way beyond my reach. I possessed zero of the qualifications that were typically necessary to become successful in the field. I was proficient in zero ancient or foreign languages, I had a disdain for reading (and probably for writing) technical publications, and I was way too broke to even think about enrolling in graduate school. My archaeological aspirations were dashed, and I admitted to myself that I would never rise above the status of armchair explorer.

I ultimately decided to become a travel agent because it was the 1990s when I went career shopping, and travel agents were still an actual thing. I enrolled in evening classes at a travel school and graduated with a job at American West Airlines in their package tour department. Unbeknownst to me when I got hired was that their best-selling product was the cheap package tour they sold to Las Freaking Vegas.

Day in and day out, my number one job was to sell Las Vegas to people over the phone. At first, I was abhorred at the thought of having to talk about Las Vegas to people as if I was actually excited about that city, but after a while, I embraced the ridiculousness of my ending up with that job and became what the company called "a million-dollar producer." Hell, I could sell Vegas to anyone, I discovered, and it was easy because that town practically sold itself. My job, though, was to upsell it to people. It was a feat that proved surprisingly easy for me to do once I discovered my knack for painting pretty pictures inside people's heads.

Most callers that I talked to were responding to an ad that they saw in the Sunday paper for a "Super Sale" that promoted an inexpensive Las Vegas weekend getaway. Prices started at $249 for airfare and two nights at the Riviera Hotel. The Riviera Hotel was one of the cheapest hotels a person could stay at on The Strip, and the hotel was just as cheap on paper as it was in real life.

"You don't want to stay at The Riviera," I would say to those who just wanted the $249 deal. "It's worth it to pay a little more and go someplace else. The Mirage hotel is so much better."

I actually liked it when people would press me for more details about why they needed to avoid staying at The Riviera because I perfected my description to elicit the maximum amount of horror. In the 1990s, the worst decorating faux pas anyone could do was deck out a room with 1970s paraphernalia. Unfortunately for The Riviera, the 1970s were boldly soldiering on with its rooms draped in heavy red velvet curtains, floor-to-ceiling mirrors, blue shag carpets, and way too much heavy brown furniture. I assured callers that there was no gaudier hotel than The Riviera and that they should avoid staying there unless they genuinely wanted flashbacks of their disco years. Mostly, no one wanted to be reminded of the '70s, so it was a cinch to convince people to go anywhere else and spend more money. Cha-ching! I was a million-dollar producer in less than eight months, which was a record time for anyone. The company was so impressed with my outstanding achievement that they gave me a little trophy to stand on my desk, and I collected four such trophies over the four years that I was there.

Part of me was genuinely sad when I heard that they tore The Riviera down in 2016. Yet, I did feel a little schadenfreude when the demolition processes got halted because asbestos was found lurking inside one of its old-fashioned buildings. I rather enjoyed knowing that The Riviera proved true to form right until the very end, and I mentally gave the hotel a standing ovation.

In 2017, I visited Las Vegas for the first time in 20 years and made it a point to visit The Neon Graveyard Museum. It was there where I saw it, the one last vestige of my favorite hotel to despise. The old Riviera sign actually looked pretty good sitting there in that motley collection of former Vegas nightlights because it was one of the few signs in that graveyard that still possessed the ability to light up. Demolition workers simply unplugged the massive thing and schlepped it over to the museum, where it will advertise its ghost hotel for as long as forever lasts in Las Vegas. I learned that it cost over $40 million to demolish that beast of a hotel, which implied that the city must have really wanted it gone. Curiously, it's been five years since that hotel got imploded, and still, nothing currently stands in its place. Apparently, nothing was preferable to having something like The Riviera standing there in all its gaudy glory.

Overall, I don't really understand the whole Las Vegas thing, but it's not something that I'll ever need to wrap my head around again. I've been there, done that, and have since moved on. Vegas will always be there for someone else to figure out, and I say let Vegas be someone else's problem. I adore living in the Southwest, and my passion now fully resides in Arizona. It would take me a lifetime to explore every inch of this fabulous state, but just the idea of exploring all of it strikes me as being unrealistic. Arizona is huge, and much of the state is difficult to access. There will always be parts of this state that will be difficult for me to grasp, and for the longest time, Monument Valley was just far enough away that it was out of my reach.

Monument Valley

Monument Valley always looked like it was a good place to escape to, but it was never anywhere I could go to because I only ever owned junky cars that would never make a drive that incredibly far. It wasn't until I was 26 and old enough to rent a car that I was finally able to run away to the place of my dreams that never looked real.

Every photograph that I had ever seen of Monument Valley consistently made the landscape look alien and surreal. I harbored a suspicion that no photograph of Monument Valley could ever substitute for physically being there. The landscape always seemed so quiet, and I imagined that it was where people went to when they wanted to hear their own thoughts. Monument Valley was where one went to hear nothing in one ear and everything in the other. The iconic mitten-like formations appeared to sit on the landscape knowingly, and I believed that all of life's mysteries had been sucked up and deposited inside those formations. Monument Valley looked like a place where one found oneself when one didn't know where else to look.

My approach to Monument Valley occurred in the late evening, just as the sun was threatening to tuck itself into bed for the night. I barely saw the tippy tops of the rock formations looming far off in the distance, and though I put the pedal to the metal, I wasn't able to reach Monument Valley under the auspices of daylight. Just as I got there, all hints of the rock formations filtered away right as the sun descended below the horizon and caused me to think that I just witnessed a mirage. I feared that I quite possibly missed my one and only chance of ever seeing those formations in person, and I was afraid that I'd wake up the next morning and the mittens would be gone. As a precaution, I set my alarm for way earlier than I needed to because I didn't want to risk missing the sun rise over the rock formations that would be in the process of scurrying away.

I did get up insanely early the next day and witnessed one of the world's greatest sights of the sun rising and waking up the slumbering heaps of stone. The sun brought the mittens to life and dressed them in the warmest amber tones that only belonged to them. I was quite certain that the sun always began its morning at Monument Valley, and only after the rocks were awake did the sun begin to wake up the rest of the planet. I truly believed that it was here where time had always begun.

If there were only one word to describe Monument Valley, that word would have to be *shapes*. The whole of Monument Valley was a feast for the eyes, and I couldn't stop looking at the landscape for the mere reason that I didn't want to stop looking at it. I wanted to soak my eyes in the view as if the landscape was a visual bath. Once I turned my head away from Monument Valley, I knew that I would never see anywhere as beautiful again.

I went to Monument Valley feeling lonely. I had just broken up with Kat for the umpteenth time, and I was feeling incredibly low. I felt like I was one-half of an empty whole, so I was feeling incomplete. I wanted to be satisfied with my solitude and enjoy the moment at hand, but my mind wouldn't let me. I kept thinking to myself, "What if I end up alone forever? What if Kat was my only shot at a relationship? Was I foolish to walk away from the only relationship that I will ever have?" It was easy to feel alone in a landscape that had nothing and no one in it. I questioned what it meant to be alone versus what it meant to be lonely. Was I lonely because I was alone? Was I feeling less human for not having another someone in my life? What did it mean to be human? Were we such social creatures that we needed other people to define ourselves? Did we get lost in our own heads if we had no one else to guide us through our own minds? Was I feeling lost in my own life? Did I think that I was going to find myself among the landscape, or was I looking for someone else? Did I need to find another in order to discover my own identity?

"No," I answered to myself. I was there alone because I needed to be me. I needed to realign my heart, head, and soul into a straight line. Yet, what was soul, I wondered? Was the soul merely an idea, or was it an essence? Did one need to believe in a God in order to believe in a soul? Did people believe in God simply because they feared themselves? Were people afraid to be just human? What if that was all we were, humans without souls? Must there always be something beyond ourselves? I questioned if it was right to believe in the invisible only because the only alternative was to believe in nothing. Was it more comforting to take away the singleness of death by replacing it with God and an afterlife? If one took away God, one was left alone. What if there was no God? Where did that leave everyone?

Monument Valley made me think that this life was amazing enough. How could an afterlife be any more beautiful or quiet than the vision that was before me? Why were humans so quick to dismiss the value of our own lives here on this planet? I love it here. I find value in being alive. I am not saying that I don't believe in God, but I sometimes wonder if I do. It's all very cerebral to me. Take prayers, for instance. One might think that they are praying to God, but really, one might simply be talking to oneself. What difference does it make? God is inside the head just as much as God is anywhere else.

I had a hard time deciding when it was time to pull myself away from Monument Valley because life felt too perfect there. Part of me wanted to stay in that landscape forever and do nothing but think and invent new non-religions. I hiked along the provided trails as slowly as I could until there was nowhere left to go but back the same way that I came. I was quite surprised that Monument Valley did not go on forever. I decided that the only way to say farewell was to bow down in honest reverence and thank it for being so beautiful.

I came to Monument Valley alone but left it feeling whole.

CHAPTER FOUR:
Day Trips, 1994-1998

Quick Jaunts

The pay at my travel job was absolute peanuts, but they more than made up for their crappy paychecks by allowing us to fly standby for free on America West Airlines. The only caveat was that standby status was never a guaranteed thing, so there was some level of art in knowing which flights were worth taking a chance on. Usually, the routes serviced with multiple flights a day were the best bets, and those particular flights were typically short jaunts that lasted two hours or less. It became my personal mission to visit every city that I could reasonably fly standby to since it was a benefit granted to me, and it more than made up for the fact that I was earning diddly squat. I barely earned above minimum wage, so I could never afford to stay overnight in a hotel or even so much as think about renting a car, yet, with some clever finagling, I managed to find a way to become the undisputed Queen of Day-Tripping.

I spent a total of four years at America West Vacations, which was plenty enough time for me to rack up quite a collection of day-tripping forays. I typically went somewhere every other week, but sometimes I traveled more often than that. I exhausted all the big cities first before I delved into traveling to the riskier, less-serviced locations. I quickly learned that most airports offered a local bus, so my habit was to fly into an airport and bus to whatever main attractions each particular city possessed. Mostly, I tended to go to museums, but I did rack up quite a collection of capital buildings over time, even though I wasn't always interested in seeing them. I would go to San Francisco a lot because it was still my absolute most favorite city in the world to go to, but I did eventually discover that there was no such thing as going to San Diego too much. Of all the cities that I repeatedly traveled to, I do believe that I popped over to San Diego the most often. I always appreciated how conveniently located their airport was to their city center because it made going anywhere in San Diego super easy. I frequently flew to San Diego just to eat lunch at The Fish Market simply because it was something that I could readily do. I unabashedly lived the life of a jet setter but woefully lacked the income that usually went with it. It didn't matter to me, though, because I had a free pass to most of America, and I took full advantage of that unique privilege. If a museum in some big city had an exhibit that I wanted to see, I simply got on a plane and went to see it. Life at near minimum wage didn't mean that I had to live poorly so long as I basically had a personal aircraft at my disposal. I didn't care that I lived on cereal and toast nearly every day because doing so allowed me to walk around Golden Gate Park on my days off whenever I wanted to. For me, life was good. Real good. I relished the fact that I had no attachments and most of America at my fingertips.

Salt Lake City

As much as I enjoyed repeating familiar and easily accessible destinations, it was the more difficult cities to bag that would always get me the most excited. Some flight routes proved to be too busy to take a chance going standby on, so there were some cities that I was lucky to score only once simply because they were so rarely available. Salt Lake City was one that I remember getting excited about when I got to go there because it was one of the busier cities that rarely offered empty seats. I knew absolutely nothing about the Mormon religion, so I was thrilled when the chance to fly up there finally opened up. As far as I was concerned, the Mormons were a secret sect, so I was very interested in taking a tour of their Mother Ship. I didn't have the remotest clue what to expect because I somehow avoided encountering a single Mormon individual up to that point in my life. However, that fact was due to change after I took a fateful step onto the Salt Lake Temple shuttle bus.

I happened to be the last traveler to board the Temple shuttle bus that was essentially a glorified eight-passenger van. I was the last one in, so I was assigned to ride shotgun with the driver. Sitting where I was meant that I had to talk to the driver, or rather, where I sat meant that the driver thought that he had to make conversation with me. Straight away, he asked me if I was LDS, which quite frankly caught me off guard. I knew nothing of Mormon lingo; I didn't even know that Mormons had their own lingo, so I wondered what I was doing that caused him to ask me that question. Was I drooling? Was I acting weird? Did that man think that he was being funny? Was it because we were riding in a short bus? He didn't realize it, but I thought he was asking me if I was Learning Disabled.

I answered his question with an emphatic, "No, I am not!" Jerk.

I pretty much pouted the whole way to the Temple after that point. I think I remember him asking me some more questions, and I am fairly certain that I gave him curt one-word answers in reply. Thank goodness for the both of us that the ride to the Temple didn't take very long.

I arrived at the Salt Lake Temple and took their hour-long tour. Not too far into it, I learned that LDS meant "Latter-Day Saint," which was the official term for Mormon believers. I thought to myself that they definitely needed to change their acronym. Or, maybe their selecting that acronym was intentional, as I wasn't quite sure. After I took what struck me as a very strange tour, I seriously wondered.

Religions, in general, intrigue me. There are so many of them, and they are all convinced that they are "right." Most religions share a common denominator, yet they all make a convoluted mess out of themselves in their attempt to arrive at their own unique conclusions. I walked away with the impression that the Mormon religion was heavy about initiation. That religion didn't explicitly reveal itself at first glance, and I figured that one needed to be fully immersed in it before one could completely wrap one's head around it. I got the impression that someone could never simply become a weekend Mormoner. Their approach was more like Mormon or bust. MOB could be their new acronym if they were so inclined to change their current one.

As I sat in the Salt Lake airport, I noticed posters enticing travelers to take a quick jaunt over to the Salt Lake Temple. I didn't know if their intention was to encourage religious conversions during connecting flights or not, but I got to thinking that popping over to the Temple must have worked at least once on someone. It was entirely possible that some traveler started his morning in Portland as a Catholic and ended his day in Philadelphia as a newly minted Mormon. It was also entirely possible that such conversions happened often. It got me thinking about the nature of religions and how they are more emotional than anything else. A religion has to speak to someone for that religion to have some kind of value. Religion is only as important as one wants it to be. Some people might find something in the Temple tour that they didn't know they were looking for and decide then and there that they don't want to leave behind whatever it is that they just found. Something similar happened to me once, although it wasn't a religion that I discovered. Instead, it was a person that I found and didn't want to leave behind.

Minneapolis

I met a guy named Ben at a bus stop in front of the Minneapolis airport at six in the morning on some random Tuesday in November. He was in military fatigues and had with him an oversized duffle bag stuffed with, I assumed, everything that he owned. The only reason why he caught my eye was because he was the only other person standing at the airport bus stop at that ungodly hour. We both ended up standing out there for quite a while, during which time we kept exchanging glances. The red-eye flight from Phoenix put me in Minneapolis almost too early in the morning, and even though it might have appeared that I had someplace to be, I actually had four hours to kill before the museum that I wanted to visit was due to open. I honestly didn't know what I was going to do with myself for four long hours and just assumed that I was going to sit in a coffee shop somewhere and read. I was pretty sure that the guy waiting for the bus had somewhere specific to be, yet, he surprised me when he asked me what direction the bus that he had been waiting the last ten minutes for was going.

"Do you know if this bus goes to the Greyhound station?" he asked me.

I genuinely didn't know the answer to that question, but I did know that the bus went to the city center and told him as much. I got a good look at him when we started to engage in conversation and immediately thought that he was attractive in his military kind of way. He had blond hair and broad shoulders. He had a cute way of standing. He looked about my age.

"Where will you be taking a Greyhound to?" I asked him, taking a stab at small talk.

"Duluth," he said. "That's where I'm from. I'm on leave until after the holidays."

I've never been attracted to the whole military thing. I understand the importance of supporting the military and whatnot, but if our country could survive without an army, I think that would be fantastic.

"Where are you heading to?" he, in turn, asked me.

"I'm going to the Art Museum for an Egyptian exhibit, but it doesn't open for another four hours," I said and saw that the bus was quickly approaching. "Do you know where I can get a cup of coffee and hang out for a while?"

"Coffee?" he chimed. "I could use some coffee. I'll go get some coffee too if that's okay with you."

Thus began the fastest one day in my life. The time that I spent with Ben went quicker than a blink of an eye. We did have coffee together, we did shove his enormous bag in a locker that was too small for it at the Greyhound station together, and we did go to the museum together as well. We also talked about life together, we held hands together, and we ended the day with a passionate kiss. Little did I know that I was supposed to be filing nearly every single word that Ben was saying to me as evidence to be recalled upon later when the entire day was going to be called into question. In less than one year, Ben's sister, whom I never met, was going to interrogate me about Ben for reasons that I will soon explain.

Ben joined the navy, I think, straight out of high school. As far as what he told me, he rather identified with being a navy man. He enjoyed seeing the world from the vantage point of a ship, and he didn't find any conflict with being told what to do. Life, he explained, was easier when he didn't have to think for himself. I found his philosophy to be the polar opposite of mine, and the topic made for some seriously good banter. His defense was that the navy provided discipline, which was exactly what he thought was lacking in the civilian world. My argument to that was that the chaos of civilian life was exactly what gave society its lively character, without which life would be terribly dull. We went back and forth with the subject off and on throughout the day as a sort of backdrop conversational piece.

I believed that there was more to Ben than his identification with the navy, although I do think that he had a hard time separating his individual self from his navy persona. I think that he must have felt untethered the day that I met him, and I wonder now if our day together disoriented him even more.

We decided to keep in touch via letter writing. He said that he liked reading letters when he was out to sea. He explained that he was technically based in San Diego, to which I explained that it was super convenient for me to fly out there and visit him sometime. After his leave in Duluth, he said that his ship would depart for Hawaii but that there would be a small window of opportunity to visit him in San Diego before he went out to sea. Nothing was set in stone, but we felt compelled to keep in touch and play things out by ear.

Once home, I wrote to him straight away. I mused about the day that we spent together and how wonderful it was. I got a letter from him the same week. We exchanged a couple of letters before he left Duluth for San Diego. We tried coordinating a rendezvous there, but things just didn't work out for whatever lame reason. The fact that we couldn't squeeze in a bon voyage visit meant that we had to content ourselves with merely being pen pals. He forwarded me the ship's address, and we corresponded while he was out to sea. I got one letter from him after he left San Diego. I, in turn, wrote a total of three letters back. I thought it was strange that I wasn't getting any more replies from him, but then, one day, I got a phone call.

"Hello," an unknown female voice started. "I'm Ben's sister. I'm sorry to have to call you, but I know that you knew Ben because I found a bunch of your letters in his bag."

I wasn't sure what I was supposed to say, so I think I said something along the lines of, "Um, okay."

"Ben's missing," she said. "The navy doesn't know where he is, and I was hoping that maybe you knew something."

The sheer silence on my end, I'm sure, told her the answer that she already knew: that calling me would reveal nothing.

"All I know is that I hadn't got any letters from him for a

while," I managed to say once my brain caught up to my tongue, "so I was kind of wondering what was going on myself."

"Was he...," his sister started to say, "do you know if he was suicidal?"

"Whoa, hold on," I thought to myself. Where was this conversation going?

"Suicidal?" I asked. "No, why? I don't think so."

"How did you know Ben?" she point-blank asked me.

"I met him at the airport the day he flew back home in November," I told her. "We ended up spending the day together."

She basically wanted to know if he said anything to me that day that was akin to dropping hints that he was unhappy with his life. I honestly couldn't say anything negative about him. In fact, I stressed to her how much he seemed to identify with the military lifestyle, and I simply couldn't extrapolate any further.

"He seemed to really like you from what I can tell reading your letters," she kindly said to me.

"Well, I liked him a lot, too," I told her in return. "He seemed like a good guy." It felt weird saying this to someone that probably had spent the last few days picking apart my letters to him, looking for any inferences of turmoil. Meanwhile, my brain was still trying to catch up with the concept of Ben being described as "missing."

"What exactly do you mean by missing?" I asked her.

"He's not on the ship anymore," she flatly stated. "He had night duty and just wasn't there in the morning. They searched the water for him and couldn't find him. He's nowhere on the ship. He's simply gone."

I attempted to compute what she said but couldn't quite manage.

"Do you know if anyone didn't like him?" she wanted to know. "Does he say anything in the letters to you? Would it be too much to ask of you to send me copies of all the letters that he wrote to you?"

I knew that there was nothing incriminating in the letters and told her that he never hinted at anything being amiss. Nevertheless, I willingly agreed to send her copies of the few letters that he wrote to me.

I didn't hesitate in sending the copies of Ben's letters to his sister, albeit it did feel like an odd thing to have to send someone. I didn't really enjoy doing that because it did feel a little invasive, but I did it for her because she already read one side of the story, so I understood why she wanted to read the other half.

After my conversation with her, it wasn't long before I started to receive formal letters from the navy regarding his disappearance.

The letters basically read, "We regret to inform you that Private Ben has been declared a missing person. A search for him has been conducted, and any further information about his whereabouts will be updated as soon as information becomes available," or something to that effect.

The navy replied to each of the three letters that went unanswered by Ben. The first letter they sent me relating to his missing person status was very formal and relatively sensitive to my feelings. The second letter was a bit stern and terse. The third letter basically told me to stop writing to him. I wasn't even writing to him anymore, it's just that the letters were taking so long to get to the ship. My letters were probably getting passed among the chain of command, so it looked like I was ignoring their pleas to halt all communication.

The navy never did figure out what happened to Ben that night, nor did they ever find his body. He remains listed as a missing person to this very day. Did he intentionally jump overboard? Did he accidentally fall off the ship? Did someone push him? No one knows, and no one is saying. My theory is that something accidental occurred. I don't think that Ben meant to fall off the ship, but I suspect that something caused him to tumble into the water. Or maybe he was suicidal; I have no idea. I don't think that he was, but I didn't really know him that well. Probably no one really knew him, or maybe he didn't know himself. What if he did just slip and fall? Such things can happen, right? Or maybe such things don't happen; I don't actually know. Regardless, he somehow ended up in the water in the pitch black of night. How scary was it for him to see the ship slowly slip away from his view? How long did he stay above the water before he succumbed to a watery tomb?

It's sad to think that he wasn't anywhere to witness the sun rise over the horizon the next morning and that life simply went on without him. We are all just little blips in this world, and this was the second time in my life that such a fact was brought to my attention. People eventually die, sometimes sooner rather than later, and I was beginning to wonder what the point was in having attachments to anyone. I started to see the value in being a loner when I could no longer stand the pain of being lonely and depressed. I really started to hate people when I thought that I could no longer trust anyone. I wanted to know if Ben killed himself. If Ben did kill himself, that meant that I meant absolutely nothing to him and my mere existence served zero value in giving him something to live for. I was sure that his disappearance had to have been an accident because I refused to believe that he wanted to kill himself. How did I not know what suicidal tendencies looked like, I wondered? Was there something about Ben that I just didn't see?

People are masters at hiding their emotions. Oftentimes, people show the world only what they think the world wants them to see. People fear to give too much of themselves away, so in protection, people keep too much of themselves inside. No one wants to make themselves vulnerable to whatever it is that they think will penetrate their soul, yet in doing so, many people fail to protect themselves from their own demons. We are more times than not our own worst enemy, and oftentimes we find ourselves storming our own castle. Maybe Ben thought that he had to put out his own fire because if he didn't, he might have thought that the fire would consume him. Of course, that is assuming that he took his own life, but no one knows if he did or if he didn't or if he's still alive somewhere on a remote island that no one other than Ben managed to find.

After the whole Ben thing, I made it a point not to meet anyone when I traveled. Long-distance relationships sucked, and I figured that they would all end in disappointment anyway, which makes it super hard for me to explain why I eventually signed up for some international pen pals. I wanted to travel abroad someday, so I sowed my seeds and made a few friends in England with the idea that I would get more out of my trips if I knew some international people. In actuality, all I did was amass a small collection of blokes that I had to keep pace writing to until it became too much, and I had to whittle my pen pal collection down to just my favorite few. When the time came for my first international trip to Paris, I didn't want to go alone, but I wasn't quite ready yet to meet any of my pen pals, so I broke down and asked Kat if he wanted to go. I don't even remember now if we were on again or if we were off again when I asked him if he wanted to go with me to Paris because whatever we were, we went there together and successfully survived the trip. We must have gotten along pretty well in Paris because we traveled together again a year later to England, and that second trip abroad didn't go nearly as well. I have little memory of the details of the Paris trip, but I do remember all the good and bad parts of the England one because that trip witnessed the inauguration of my journals.

CHAPTER FIVE:
France/England, 1996-1998

Francophile

I have a thing for France. I am an unabashed Francophile despite my complete inability to master the art of speaking the French language. I "took" French in high school, but those lessons proved to be utterly useless. I don't know why the American school system thinks it can teach teenagers a foreign language when their brains are no longer fit to absorb such a thing. I tried "learning" French again as an adult, but I could never get beyond teaching myself how to ask where the bathroom was. Nevertheless, not knowing the French language very well (or barely at all) has not deterred me from loving everything French. I am drawn to French culture, art, design, literature, architecture, history, food, and wine. I just absolutely adore France and would totally marry that country if I could.

My overt love for everything French didn't stem from my undying love for the French language that I never understood. No, my love for France arose because I fell in love with a Disney cartoon. I saw Disney's *The Hunchback of Notre Dame* in a theater in 1996, and there was something curious about how the cartoon was rendered that captured my imagination. I couldn't shake the feeling that there was more to the cartoon than what I was seeing. There was just something *else* about it that was hard to explain. Was it a feeling, a sense, a thought? I couldn't quite tell, but I got the sense that the cartoon was more than just a typical Disney story. I had never considered cartoons to be high art before, but there was something special about that film that made me think otherwise. The film offered a thousand different perspectives, and most of them were from dizzying heights. That film took my mind to places I had never thought about going to before, and it gave me a view of the world that I had never imagined seeing. It took a goddamn cartoon to open my mind to a world that I never knew existed, and I couldn't help but feel a little bit conflicted about that realization. I immediately wanted to know who the cartoonists were that created such a film and discover who their muse was if they were spurred by one.

I got the sense that there was something about the story itself that demanded the artists to look inside themselves and tap deep into their creative cores. I suspected that an unseen driving force pushed the cartoonists to their highest creative limits, so my curiosity was piqued to discover what that force was. I figured that the source of their inspiration was to be found somewhere in the story itself, so I picked up a copy of *The Hunchback of Notre Dame* and started to read it. I had no idea at the time that I just stumbled upon the person who would prove to become my most favorite author.

The author of *The Hunchback of Notre Dame* was a man named Victor Hugo, and he had been dead for 111 years before I learned of his former existence. I didn't bother to read too much about him before I delved straight into reading *The Hunchback of Notre Dame* book, but I did seriously wonder who the writer was by the time I turned the very last page. I wanted to know what kind of person had the emotional capacity to write such an insightful story and give such a deep feeling to an inanimate object as well as to an entire age.

I eventually learned that *The Hunchback of Notre Dame*

was Victor Hugo's plea to save what was left of the Gothic ruins that were crumbling all around him. Victor Hugo opened the Victorian's eyes to see the intrinsic value imbued in ancient stones and got them to rally behind his cause to save the monuments from needless destruction. It's impossible to say how many Gothic monuments would have survived intact today had he never written that one pivotal book, but I personally credit him for being the sole reason why I even know what a flying buttress looks like. Without a doubt, I concluded that it was *his* indomitable spirit that was the unseen creative force behind that Disney cartoon.

Victor Hugo became my personal ambassador to France. He proudly showed me around that country's historical landscape and familiarized me with obscure innuendos. His writings provided me with the French foundation I previously lacked and finally gave me somewhere firm to stand. I was well aware that his historical version of France would prove to be wildly different from the current version of France that I would encounter today; however, I needed to start somewhere, so I felt comfortable starting with him. I will always admire how he was able to see life for exactly what it was. He knew that man was more often ugly than he was attractive, and he knew that most people lived their real lives somewhere below Earth's actual surface. He had a cerebral way with words, and any true meaning of anything that he ever wrote can only be found in the darkest crevices of the collective mind. The essence of humankind runs very deep, and we are all connected by our roots under the soil. He knew well that humans desire to live in beautiful worlds, but he also knew that we make the worlds we live in look terribly ugly.

I never had to worry about finding something decent to read so long as I knew that there was another Victor Hugo book out there waiting for me to devour. I still, and forever will, rue the day I learned that I exhausted everything he ever wrote. I loved mentally traveling to France with Victor Hugo's ghost, and more than anyone, it was he who opened my eyes to a France that I needed to see.

When the time came for me to plan my first international trip, I knew right away where I wanted to go. France had recently possessed all of my thoughts, so I desired to travel to the county that was holding me mentally hostage.

France

Kat and I arrived in Paris late in the evening. I don't remember where we stayed, but I do remember that our hotel was nicely snuggled somewhere deep in the Gothic Quarter. I remember that detail because I never stayed in the Gothic Quarter ever again, even though that was where I always wanted to reside whenever I returned to Paris years later. The Gothic Quarter was and is the area of Paris where everyone desires to be, so I learned to stop looking at hotel prices there ages ago. Either 1997 must have been the last year of affordability for that section of town, or we had just gotten lucky because I recall the hotel where we stayed as not being all that fantastic. Our hotel had dingy rooms, stuffy air, poorly-lit hallways, but also balconies. In truth, that balcony was all we really needed. We were in Paris, and I would have happily slept out there in the rain. Or, maybe I should say that *I* would have happily slept on that balcony as I am not sure that Kat would have appreciated doing so. We were in Paris because that was where I wanted to be. Kat was there because he was along for the ride.

Even though it was late and we were both well beyond jet-lagged, I couldn't allow ourselves to fall asleep without seeing the Notre Dame Cathedral first. I knew that the monument was just down the street, so I convinced Kat that we had enough energy to sleepwalk ourselves down there. I'm not quite sure how we stumbled our way over to the cathedral, but stumble our way, we somehow did. We then both gawked in awe at the beautifully floodlit masterpiece that loomed before us. In front of us was the thing of my dreams, and it looked way better than I even imagined. The cathedral was enormous, and our eyes couldn't take the entire building in with a single glance. The sheer enormity of the edifice made us feel diminutive to the degree that it made us feel like we didn't even exist. We were absolutely nothing compared to that cathedral, and its impact on our psyche was unsettling.

"Crap, that thing is huge," Kat exclaimed.

I just so happened to be looking down right as he said that because something moving had caught the corner of my eye.

"Lookie over here," I said and pointed to something very small scurrying around. "It's the plague welcoming us to Paris!"

We were sitting on brick planters, and running around in the dirt was the most adorable baby rat that had the cutest little feet ever. It was genuinely Disney quality baby rat-ness, but something in me was abhorred by it because its presence was lending a too authentic medieval feel to the scene.

"Do we capture it?" I asked as it puttered around on its adorable little feet.

"I don't think so," Kat said, not because he didn't think that we needed to, but more because he didn't know what we'd do with it if we caught the adorable potentially plague-ridden thing.

"How weird is it that the first thing that we see in Paris happens to be a rat?" I asked, not specifically to Kat, but more to the gods that destroyed the perfect vision of Paris that I had pre-built inside my head.

"This is Europe," Kat said. "There's probably rats eveywhere."

In a sense, what he said ended up being kind of true because we did end up seeing way more rats than we really wanted to whenever we went underground to ride on the metros. Rats constantly ran along the tracks and seemed to know the precise moment they needed to get off of them to avoid getting squished. Watching the rats gave us something to do when we waited for a metro to arrive, so after a while, we just kind of appreciated that they were there because their antics made the waiting time seem incredibly less painful.

While we were in Paris, we did all the usual Paris things, and our trip was so typical that there is almost nothing for me to retell. However, I should really take a moment to mention that I did develop a brand new habit on this first-ever trip to Europe and that this new habit struck Kat as being a particularly annoying one. Much to Kat's and most everyone else that I have since traveled to Europe with's chagrin, I discovered that there was a certain special magic about getting up ridiculously early. I probably would have never gotten the wild hair to start our Paris days before the sun rose had I not seen the photographs made by the nineteenth-century photographer, Eugene Atget. However, I *did* see his images of a quiet Paris before everyone awoke, so all the blame technically rested upon him. Atget's Paris was filled with quiet, contemplative spaces of zen, and it was his visions of a Paris frozen in time that I wanted to discover for myself. I learned that he took most of his photographs right as the sun rose and that it was the quality of the light that made his images of empty streets and people-less parks especially striking. His was the Paris before everyone else, and it was the same sort of Paris that we could have for ourselves so long as we dragged our butts out of bed at an unreasonable hour every morning.

Getting up super early did nothing to endear me to Kat, but we soon discovered that a decent cup of French coffee was all that we needed to wipe the sleep out of our eyes. Coffee in France is always the best, I don't know why it is, but it just is. Parisian coffee became our gasoline, and we needed the stuff coursing through our veins to get us out the door and onto the quiet city streets. The early mornings were ours for the taking, and we took them to the Luxembourg and Tuileries Gardens, the Louvre, and the banks of the Seine. We took empty pictures of all of those contemplative places, and when I say "we," I really just mean me. Kat didn't know who Atget was nor what kind of spell I was mysteriously under. He wasn't seeing the same kind of beauty that I was seeing, and it wasn't a kind of beauty that I could easily explain. He understood the value of not having any random people in my pictures, but he was struggling to understand what I was going on about the light. I had only recently learned about photography myself through the art of Atget's images, so all I could tell him was that I was experimenting with an idea. I wanted to see if I could recreate the same kind of feelings that Atget's images gave me. There was something about the early morning glow that made his images seem both timeless and ephemeral, and I was convinced that the secret to his photos resided with the sun.

Dining was never an elaborate affair because we were way too poor to even think about poking our heads inside any fancy restaurants. We took most of our meals al fresco at the little food carts that stood in front of the major parks. However, when we did splurge, it was either on a doner kebab (a handheld meal similar to a gyro, but served with a pile of fries on top) or at the cheap Chinese restaurant that we discovered across the Notre Dame that served the meanest French wine on that side of the Seine. We got lit on that objectionable wine quite frequently because it was one of the few restaurants that we could afford to dine at, but also because the view from its window was absolutely unparalleled. It was tempting to get drunk there every night, but the hangovers were just as brutal as the wine itself. We reserved going there only when we felt masochistic, which was admittedly more frequent than was healthy for us.

We did take a couple of excursions outside of Paris, but distance-wise, we didn't go very far. We did the requisite Versailles romp and complained that the gardens were too big and the weather was too cold. I only vaguely remember what the palace looked like inside, and when I think back on it now, all I recall is its long hall of mirrors. I particularly remember the hall striking me as feeling rather somber. I'll never forget how the gray October light reflected off the glass and filled the space with a weight that didn't seem to befit the room. I knew that the Treaty of Versailles was signed in that mirrored hallway, and with that gray light, it seemed as though the World War I era was still ensconced in there. Overall, my memories of Versailles are not memories of gaiety and light but more seem to be memories of someone else's history. Versailles was a place that seemed very detached from the current world. The palace didn't seem to know where it was, and I got the sense that Versailles felt that it was left behind when the rest of time moved forward without it.

The other major excursion that I remember us taking was to Chartres Cathedral. I had read about its famous stained glass windows that gave off a hue coined the "Chartres Blue." Allegedly it was a blue that only medieval artists knew how to create, so I was excited about experiencing a color that my eyes had never seen. Just the mere thought that there was a lost color out there in the world greatly intrigued me and got me inventing all sorts of imaginary colors that my eyes would never see.

Chartres Blue was indeed an actual color, but it was also something more than that. It was also an element that we instinctively breathed. Breathing in that stained glass light was invigorating and made me think that there was more to life than what we typically saw. There was something about that blue that I physically felt, and it gave me the sense of a fourth dimension. Life had complexities that I never understood, and I started to wonder if the medieval mind had a mastery over mysteries that we no longer possessed. Modern man likes to belittle his medieval ancestors, but perhaps we need to tap into the power that was once the medieval brain. Medieval man believed in something that was greater than himself, and because he had such faith, he was able to push himself to his greatest creative limits. Chartres Cathedral was proof of what man was capable of when he not only believed in God but also believed in himself. It was a tandem experience that caused Chartres to be born, and the result was a new element that deserved a place on the periodic table. Somewhere between oxygen and hydrogen, there needed to be a place for Chartres Blue.

Lastly, there was one place that I wanted to see on this particular trip but didn't get to experience because it was unfortunately closed. That place was, of course, the Victor Hugo museum. It was there, in front of my beloved author's time capsule of a museum, that I learned a word that I would come to detest as being the most ubiquitous word in all of the French language: fermé. Fermé, I quickly learned, meant closed. The Victor Hugo museum was closed for renovations, and it would remain closed for one reason or another every time I tried to go there for the next six trips that I took to Paris over the following 21 years. I also learned a second detestable French word: la grève. La grève, I learned, meant strike. I soon gained a proficiency in French that I never possessed before when I could completely understand a sentence like, "Le musée est fermé pour cause de grève." French strikes are common and unavoidable, and they have left me out in the rain and stranded in the countryside, yet they still haven't completely ruined my ardent love for France, although they have managed to somewhat tarnish it.

Whenever I travel to France, I have to prepare two itineraries. The first itinerary is always my preferred one based on trains, and the second is my backup one based on buses. I, unfortunately, had to learn the hard way the reason to do this. Being stuck in the French countryside might have sounded romantic to me until the day that I actually did get stuck in the French countryside when a train decided that it was no longer in the mood to pick passengers back up. Had I prepared a backup itinerary, I would have known not to travel to that particular city because I would have been privy to the knowledge that no buses ever ventured there. Alas, that is a story that merits its own retelling, which I will have to touch upon in some other installment. Until then, I will attempt to segue into the topic of England as gracefully as I can.

England

Ah, yes, England and the trip into bad relationship dystopia. Oh, how I so don't cherish the memories that we made there together. It was almost hard to believe how much we changed in a year, but we didn't see the change in ourselves until we were over 5,000 miles away from where we were familiar. Looking back on it now, I don't even know why we went to England together because we didn't even fly over there on the same airplane. That probably wouldn't have been a detail that I would have remembered had I not written it down in the first travel journal that I started to keep. I was essentially traveling to England all by myself, so I was concerned about being lonely. I decided to bring along a journal just in case I needed a way to talk to myself and keep myself company.

The very first journal entry revealed the state of mind that I was currently in when I copied down a quote from Caspar David Friedrich that said, "The painter should not paint just what he sees before him, but also what he sees within him. If, however, he sees nothing within him, let him also give up painting what he sees before him." Caspar David Friedrich was a 19th-century German artist whose paintings of crushed ice floes, denuded trees, and ruined cathedrals were images that I greatly admired. However, I knew when I copied that quote down that I wasn't really thinking about art but was instead thinking about my relationship with Kat. I didn't believe that I saw anything in us anymore. Our relationship had become artless. When I looked at us, I saw nothing worth commemorating on canvas.

On the very next page, I wrote down a quote by Alfred Lord Tennyson that said, "It is better to have loved and lost than to have never loved at all." I think that I knew that this trip was going to be a heartache that probably didn't need to happen, so why we insisted on going to England together likely stemmed out of habit rather than an actual desire to spend some quality time together. We were two people who were essentially already apart, but we refused to admit that reality to ourselves. We weren't even living together anymore, and by all appearances, it looked like we finally started to move on with our separate lives. We were still "dating," but we were definitely not the world's happiest couple. There were lots of fights and reckless evenings that I am not even about to get into because doing so would fill an entire book in and of itself. Deep down, I think that we both suspected this trip was going to be our last farewell, so we presumably wanted to shout our goodbyes to each other in London, in front of everyone, preferably on opposite sides of the Thames. We desired to make a spectacle of ourselves for our last huzzah, and why not? Our relationship deserved that much. We totally earned it.

The first thing I did in London was get lost on the tube. I somehow kept ending back at the Earl's Court platform even when I wasn't trying to. By some grace of God, I eventually figured out how to get to my hotel, and the first thing that I did was throw open the curtains. The view from the window was of the next door's rotting garret that looked extremely Londonesque with its exterior pipes and moldy bricks. The view was decidedly decrepit, so I pulled out my sketchbook and attempted to immortalize its appearance on paper. I had a dead-on view into the neighbor's flat, but whoever lived there was evidently tired of people looking directly into their apartment because their curtains were drawn tightly shut. I was rooting for an exhibitionist to suddenly fling the curtains wide open and give me a free "watch a British person live his life in his apartment" show, but that, unfortunately, didn't happen. My voyeuristic opportunities stymied, I sat down and resignedly sketched the moldy pile of bricks that looked to have stood in that very spot for at least 300 years.

Kat arrived later that evening. We immediately took a stroll around central London together and sucked in loads of car fumes straight into our lungs. It was shocking how incredibly stinky London was, and the pervasive smell of car exhaust gave us both instant headaches. What London could have used was a heavy dose of Chartres Blue pumped into their atmosphere but I figured that the odds were pretty low that France would allow their secret element to travel across the Channel given their historic rivalry. We proceeded to wander around in search of a pub but ultimately failed to find one. We ended up buying some cheap beers from a convenience store and then celebrated our mutual London arrivals in our non-glorious hotel room. Our London adventure was off to the exact sort of start that we both probably expected, and we didn't seem to have a whole lot of cause for celebration. We were just there, together, doing the one thing that usually led to us fighting. The drinking was a constant source of friction between us, but I was desperate for sleep and needed a dose of alcohol to put myself to bed. So, devil be damned, I was going to drink, and so was he.

We went for a stroll along the Thames the next morning and surprisingly managed to do so without arguing. We unexpectedly came across an ancient Egyptian obelisk plopped on a spot that struck us as being nowhere in particular. I am a rabid Egyptian fanatic and always revere an Egyptian obelisk as being a big deal. It takes a whole hell of a lot of effort to carve, transport, and raise one of those monstrosities, and transporting one to England only compounds the amount of effort involved even more. Normally, if an ancient Egyptian obelisk makes a harrowing journey overseas, that obelisk usually gets duly rewarded with a prominent location. This obelisk, however, looked as though it landed on a nondescript location for no particular reason. Thankfully, the story of its harrowing journey to London was described on a nearby plaque. The adventurous tale was a tragic one that saw six crew members die and the obelisk feared lost at sea. By some miraculous stroke of fortune, the obelisk was rescued and completed its journey to London, but the passion for the monument had apparently waned. Initially, the plan was to plant the obelisk in front of the Houses of Parliament, but when the obelisk arrived, it was regulated to stare at the waters from whence it came. In essence, I guess that it didn't really matter where that obelisk was left to stand because its true meaning was lost ages ago when the entire ancient Egyptian culture faded into the pages of history. That obelisk will never again be what it once was, and it wasn't because the object itself changed over time, but more because everything and everyone else around it did.

From the obelisk, we walked over to Big Ben and found it way shorter than we expected. After that, we strolled over to Westminster Abbey and spent what felt like forever and a day inside that cavernous church, cathedral, museum, or whatever that hallowed structure was officially deemed. Finally, we tubed over to the Victoria and Albert Museum and stayed in there until it closed.

At one point in the V&A, I heard someone say, "Hi," to Kat like he actually knew him, and it turned out that he actually did because he sat next to him on the plane from L.A. to London. Mind you, the V&A was not a small museum by any stretch, and when the two guys ran into each other, they were both in the tiniest, most cubbyhole-ist room in the entire place where the only objects on display was a small collection of Albrecht Dürer prints. It was more than a little weird to think that all of London, like, literally, *all* of London, was just outside that building, yet, the stars aligned in such a way to cause those two men to catapult into the city on the exact same trajectory for some bizarro reason. I can never understand how moments such as those actually happen, but everyone takes it for granted that moments such as those just randomly occur. No rhyme, no reason; the world sometimes suddenly feels incredibly small even though the world is insanely massive.

For the next couple of days, we did more of the usual London things. However, to relate what most of that entailed would make for some incredibly boring reading. The only thing probably worth mentioning, though, was the day trip we took over to Wales to see a castle in Cardiff. That castle fascinated us because it was the first time in our lives that we saw an authentic motte and bailey construction, and its appearance was something straight out of a movie. I did, however, get more than a little drenched wandering around that magnificent edifice because my umbrella was of no use to me while it was still sitting somewhere alone on the train. Luckily, it wasn't raining that hard, and I honestly didn't realize how soaking wet I was until I shook myself out like a wet dog the moment we entered the castle.

It was possible that walking around Cardiff in the rain made me cranky, and it was highly probable that I took that gray mood back with me to London. Up to that point in the trip, Kat and I had been relatively cordial to each other, but our patience with each other was eroding fast, and by the time we got back to London, we were incredibly snappy. I felt a potential cold coming on, so I bickered with Kat about not wanting to go out that night and drink. I lost the argument and was dragged all over London, looking for somewhere to go. Our London hotel was inconveniently situated somewhere in the middle of a barren pub desert, so it took an extremely long time to find a place that served alcohol. We managed to get in some heated bickering during that time, so much so that we could see our relationship disintegrate before our very eyes. I was sick, he was thirsty, and it all boiled down to him accusing me of being a dictator. He claimed that I had too much control over him and over what we were doing on this trip. So from there on out, he declared that he was going to do his own thing. He really meant what he said because I can honestly say that I never really saw Kat ever again after that particular evening, at least not the same Kat I used to know. The scales that we once stood on were swept out from under our feet, and whatever equilibrium we once had was instantly removed. Our relationship was left in the air, and it stayed in that space from that moment onward.

Scotland

Relationships are hard, and sometimes they are just downright impossible. Ours was officially in the impossible stage; however, we still had several days left on the trip to go. When I woke up the next morning, I wasn't sure if Kat was even going to bother to travel on the next leg of the trip with me. Yet, he surprised me when he got out the door the same time I did and walked in the same direction I was going. I was admittedly not too thrilled to see him trailing behind me all the way to the train station, and I was even less thrilled to watch him board the same train to Scotland as me. From all that he said the night before, I was under the impression that he wanted to go his separate way, so I was really baffled as to why he decided to take the seat next to mine. I remember looking out that train window and wanting to run out into that landscape, far into the nowhere that existed somewhere between land and sky. The Scottish Highlands beckoned me with its surreal beauty. I couldn't discern if The Highlands felt very high or if the clouds felt very low, for it felt as though we were barreling through a narrow sandwich of space. This landscape was nowhere I had ever been to before, yet the feelings that the landscape aroused in me were very familiar. The Scottish Highlands gave me an outward appearance for how I was truly feeling inside, and it wasn't until I saw that landscape that I recognized my true self. There was a beauty in misery that I just wasn't seeing until I cast my gaze outside that window. I was out there somewhere on that landscape, so I scanned the hills and desperately searched for the outlines of myself.

When we arrived in Edinburgh, I fully expected that we'd go our separate ways, but I guess that old habits die hard because Kat chose to trail me to the Scottish National Gallery. Ten minutes into it, I seriously wished that he hadn't bothered because he was in too fidgety of a mood to be inside a museum. The last thing that he wanted to do was look at paintings, so after a brief period of irritating huffs and grunts, his presence just vanished from my side. I supposed that he would do the museum at his own pace, and I would do it at mine, but not too shortly into it, he found me again and told me that he wanted to leave. I remember nothing of what I saw in that museum solely because I didn't have a chance to see very much of it. For someone who declared that he wanted to do his own thing, I was rather perturbed at how he insisted that it was my turn to be the one to tag along beside him. I suppose that the only reason I left with him was that I was afraid of being alone, but had I known that he was going to abandon me at every turn from there on out, I would have stayed and finished the rest of that museum without him.

Kat seriously could have left me at the Scottish National Gallery, and I would have been alright, but I didn't know that at the time. In the heat of the moment, I genuinely thought that maybe I did need to learn how to be a better follower, so I obediently trailed him like a puppy dog to Edinburgh Castle, where he promptly ditched me at the first display. I am always someone who reads every plaque that gets put in front of my face, so I stopped to read a thing about some cannons or whatever, but Kat wasn't interested and instead pressed on until he disappeared over a cobblestone hill. I knew that I was to interpret his leaving me behind as somehow being my fault, but I made the conscious decision not to take the blame. I was officially sick of us being pissed at each other all the time.

"Fine," I thought to myself. "We'll see Edinburgh Castle by ourselves then. Like I give a shit."

And that was what we did. We both did that castle entirely on our own, and it was stupidly weird. We'd sometimes catch glimpses of each other turning a corner or walking out of a room, and we each pretended that we didn't see the other. For something like three hours, that charade went on until the day grew very late, and I knew that it was time to go. When I went to look for him for real, I, of course, couldn't find him anywhere. After a while, I didn't even know why I was looking for him because I wasn't even sure if we'd be sharing the same hotel that night. I ended up scouring the entire castle about three whole times over until I finally leaned over a ledge and found him milling around outside the castle at the very base of the hill. He wasn't even inside the goddamned castle anymore, and it was so infuriating to find him out there that it made me want to scream.

Edinburgh Castle was nice and all, but I wasn't in the frame of mind to truly appreciate it. The whole time I was there, I was absorbed in the thoughts of a myriad of other things. Naturally, it rained the entire time, and the gloomy atmosphere was the perfect backdrop for all my muddled thoughts. All my ideas were as damp as the air, and I could see my thoughts drip behind my eyeballs as they trickled from my brain in little snippets of images. My synapses were firing, and I was exactly where I wanted to be, and I was with exactly who I wanted to be with. It was at Edinburgh Castle where I discovered that my best travel companion was myself. By the time I walked out of Edinburgh Castle, any fear that I had about traveling alone was completely erased, and I was emboldened to see the world entirely on my own. I didn't want to deal with the bullshit anymore, and I didn't want to constantly justify myself. All I wanted was to be happy, and if that meant having no one else around me, then so be it. I wanted to embrace being on my own.

Entirely on my own, though I yearned for it, I definitely wasn't. The following day saw both of us sitting on the edge of Loch Ness, where we scoured the lake for a sight of Nessie. Watching for the Loch Ness monster definitely tested our patience, but it was kind of fun to mindlessly gaze at the drop-dead gorgeous scenery and allow our minds to go completely numb. We both fell into a zone, and doing "The Loch Ness stare" did have a relaxing effect upon us. Inwardly, we were both simmering with hatred for each other, but outwardly, it was too beautiful of a landscape to get angry in. A nearby plaque described the facts about some 14th-century war for Scottish Independence that occurred near the spot where we were sitting, but I just couldn't fathom people fighting on the gorgeous emerald hills that encompassed the lake. The concept just seemed too incongruous that my mind didn't even attempt to imagine it.

When it was evident that the Loch Ness Monster was not going to grace us with her presence, we scampered all over the excellent ruins of nearby Urquhart Castle, where its position on the lake allowed us to keep a one eye vigil out for Nessie. Any movement on the lake caught our immediate attention, but there wasn't much happening on the water to catch our glances because the surface remained eerily still. Loch Ness remained resolutely quiet, and the lake was just too beautiful to get mad at Nessie for not making an appearance. In the end, we never did see anything that even hinted that a mysterious creature lurked in the depths below, but we did see a minor car accident happen in the parking lot while we waited for the bus to arrive, which was probably way more than what most people get to see when they go in search of the Loch Ness Monster.

We took the bus back to Inverness and proceeded to go to some annual Gaelic Festival that was supposed to be a highlight of our trip, but the "festival" ended up being a total bust. I think we went to the right place, but even when we were there, we had to second guess if what we really did was crash on some older people's 50th high school reunion instead. The "festival" was being held in what looked like the Scottish equivalent of an elementary school cafeteria, and our eyes immediately started to water at the sight of too many pasty white legs. Nothing remotely was going on that even hinted that we walked into Gaelic Festival; we heard no music, and we saw no dancing, so we tried to ask someone if this was where the festival was. I swear that the answer was given to us in Gaelic, though, because neither of us understood a single word the man said in reply. We left the cafeteria room thoroughly confused and decided to cut our time in Inverness short and get a head start on making our slow crawl back down to London.

I just now took a moment to look up what date the search

engine, Google, was invented and learned that its founding date was September 4, 1998, which explains why the next set of events happened the way they did. Life before the internet was colossally stupid sometimes, and people did things while crossing their fingers and hoping for the best outcome to simply happen. Before the internet, it was perfectly normal to just show up somewhere, say, at a train station or a box office, and inquire about availability. Without the internet, there was hardly such a thing as booking ahead. So, when we showed up at the train station in Glasgow and asked for two tickets on the night train to London, we had to contain our anger when we were told that the train was completely sold out. The only train that still had any seats available on it was the one that was going to Edinburgh, so we hopped on that, thinking that we could maybe catch a night train to London from there instead. Unfortunately, our train to Edinburgh was slightly delayed, so by the time we reached Edinburgh, the last train to London was already gone. We were told that there was only one more train going anywhere that night, and that train was heading back to Glasgow. We basically had a choice of being stranded in either Edinburgh or Glasgow for the duration of the night, so we opted to be stranded in Edinburgh since we were already there. We bought our tickets for the 6 a.m. train to London and started racking our brains over what to do with ourselves for the next seven hours. We were way too cheap to get a hotel, so we started to make ourselves comfortable on the train station benches, but we were kicked out by the station master at midnight when he went around locking the doors. Tossed out to the streets, we found ourselves homeless for the night, and right as we realized that, the sky cracked open and started to rain.

Naturally, our next plan of action was to find a pub and take root in it until morning. We dipped into the first pub that we saw and ordered some beers, and I had every intention of nursing mine for the next six long hours. I took my first baby sip and started to read a book, but I only got one page into it before the server told us to chug our drinks because the pub would be closing soon. Not 20 minutes later, we found ourselves back on the streets, searching for somewhere to stay dry. Unfortunately for us, the entire city was shuttered. It was 1 a.m., and we had nowhere to go.

We wandered around and eventually stumbled upon a glass shelter bus stop where we decided to make camp like bona fide homeless people. We had our bags with us, so one of us needed to stay awake while the other tried to sleep on a skinny bus stop bench that was the furthest thing from being comfortable. The benches provided weren't even really benches at all, but rather these small little flippy things that weren't even as wide as an average-sized tush. One needed to sit on it just right to avoid flipping completely off of it, and doing so required an element of gymnastics that involved calculating a proper body weight to shoulder formula. Sitting on that flippy seat took way too much concentration, so both of us "slept" much better standing up. When it was my turn to be on the watch, I noticed way too many 17 to 25 year-olds running around at four in the morning. I was desperate to ask them where they lived so I could crawl into the beds that they obviously weren't using.

Kat and I didn't talk at all the whole time we waited through those long five hours. We had absolutely nothing left to say to each other. We both just wanted to get through this, the midnight marathon. My stupid rolling suitcase broke at one point during the night, and it caused me to trail way behind him when the time came for us to race to the train station. I didn't really care about him, about me, or about anything at that point. That bus stop night was the worst. The only thing that I did care about was getting on a train and speeding as far away as possible from what we were that previous evening. We were literally nothings, human blobs. Never before had I felt so blobby. For five long monotonous hours, I just was. I was blah. We were blah. The whole world was blah.

We continued our non-communication all the way to London and set the new standard for how we dealt with each other: in silence. I used to wonder if we were the only ones whose relationship functioned like crap, but I now know that dysfunction is, unfortunately, normal. People sometimes just don't know how to act around each other, and it's a wonder to me why humans are considered social animals. We need each other, but we act like we don't, so we are our own dichotomies. Our relationship quietly slipped away, and I still, to this day, do not remember how or when we finally said our official goodbye. We said goodbye to each other so many times that when we said it for the last time, neither of us probably heard it.

For nearly every trip after that, I typically traveled alone.

CHAPTER SIX:
Spain/France, 1998-1999

Barcelona

Okay, I admit it. Old habits die hard. I am not proud to say this, but...I went on another European trip with Kat again after I just swore that I would travel by myself. Embarrassingly, Kat and I stayed together as an on-again-and-off-again couple for at least another year beyond the England trip. For whatever lame reason, neither of us put forth any effort toward finding a new someone to start a relationship with, so we sort of stayed together even though we were barely even friends. We mastered the art of tolerating each other, and it never surprised either of us when people sometimes mistook us for siblings because we stopped behaving like lovers long ago. Ours was a relationship solidly built on love and hate to the extent that we personified the concept and became the picture that people saw when they looked up that term in the metaphorical dictionary. The long and the short of it was that we were just there. We were always just there. We never really left, but we also never really stayed. We were just too close to each other, and we didn't know how to be emotionally independent of one another. We never matured past a certain point in our relationship, so we couldn't help but get stuck in the quagmire that we created. We both constantly tried to leave, but the quicksand that surrounded us always managed to grab our ankles and pull us back under. Overall, it seemed as though our lungs actually functioned better whenever we sucked in big gulps of sand, so we made it a habit to take in large breaths of it.

Barcelona was, for me, love at first sight, or rather I should say that it was love at first sound. I had always been a dark wave kind of a girl, so it made a supreme impression on me to hear someone blare The Sisters of Mercy from their car as they cruised around the perimeter of Barcelona's Gothic Quarter. In my opinion, no other band could have better matched in sound what the historic neighborhood looked like in appearance, and it was the perfect pairing of the two that made me say out loud that Barcelona was the best city ever. However, I would find out the very next day that I uttered those words too soon after my backpack with all my money and bus tickets in it would get stolen. Yet, until that moment occurred, I was the ultimate Barcelona groupie who would have followed the city all over the world if it hopped on a bus and went on a tour.

Much of Barcelona was pure eye candy which made my eyes feel like they were devouring an entire birthday cake every time I stared at some whimsical building that looked like it was made with way too much sugar. Most of the city's fantastical architecture was attributed to the man known by the single name of Gaudí, and it took seeing his buildings in person for me to solve a private chicken-or-the-egg conundrum that had been secretly brewing inside of me for a number of years. My mom was fond of using the word "gaudy" to describe anything that she found to be exceedingly tacky, and it was a word that she used liberally throughout the whole of the '70s and '80s. Those were some fugly ugly decades, and my mom used the word gaudy so many times that she personally owned the term as far as I was concerned. I generally thought that I knew what gaudy looked like because I had grown so adjusted to seeing the world from my mother's point of view. I imagined my mom would have rolled her eyes into the back of her head if she got magically plopped in front of a Gaudí creation. Sure, his buildings were weird, wacky, and whimsical, but I personally liked them and couldn't stop admiring all his eccentric structures. I never knew which came first, Gaudí, the architect or gaudy, the term, but after I admired several Gaudí designed residences, I gradually realized that the word gaudy was the linguistic bastard child that Gaudí never knew he had.

There was no doubt in my mind that my mom would have called La Sagrada Familia cathedral as easily being the gaudiest building that she ever laid her eyes on. I tried really hard to look at the cathedral without thinking about my mother's opinion, but the more I looked at it, the more I had to admit that the unfinished monstrosity did look rather tacky, but it at least looked tacky in a good way. Looking tacky suited Gaudí's cathedral in a way that not looking tacky wouldn't have, so it was super easy for me to embrace the cathedral's atrocious tackiness in all its gaudy glory. That, and it also made for a way more fun conversation when we tried to figure out what all the weirdness was when Kat and I climbed to the top of one of the cathedral's silly bell towers.

"Is that an egg sitting on the top of that spire over there?" I asked Kat while I pointed to something weirdly indeterminate.

"No," Kat said and squinted his eyes, "I think that's supposed to be a pine cone."

We both scrutinized the peculiar display for a longish moment.

"Actually," Kat corrected himself, "I think that it's supposed to be a nest."

"Yes," I agreed, "...of *dragon eggs*."

We silently mused over the object for a little bit before Kat changed his mind once again. "Now I'm leaning toward it being a fancy bowl of fruit."

"Whatever it is," I said and pointed at something else equally indeterminate, "it's got nothing on that whole Christmas tree thing over there with all the doves on it."

Kat cast his gaze to the next big thing that I was pointing at and questioned my interpretation of it being doves on a Christmas tree.

"I don't think those are doves," he said and squinted his eyes again. "I think those are paper airplanes taking off in a pillar of smoke."

"Hum, maybe," I said and scrutinized the pillar thing a little bit more, "but now that I'm really looking at it, I think that it's a sculpture of an entire nuclear war."

It was painfully obvious that we had no idea what any of the sculptures were supposed to be. Or maybe we had too many ideas, it was really hard to say. Either way, the cathedral was brilliant because it was so utterly different. It was as if Antoni Gaudí dumped the entire contents of his brain all over that cathedral and implored God to sanction his insanity while leaving the rest of us to question it.

For the last decade of his life, Gaudí devoted himself entirely to the endeavor of building La Sagrada Familia, and I imagined that he grew more pious as the cathedral rose taller. He designed the cathedral in inspirational bursts of creativity which he likely believed were telepathic designs sent directly to him by God himself. To get the cathedral built, he threw in every cent that he was worth, and he tossed in his health and hygiene as well for good measure. When a tram accidentally ran Gaudí over, no one knew who he was because he didn't look like anyone that people needed to care about. He simply looked like any other homeless person who wandered into the street, and because he appeared to be worth nothing, that was the exact amount of medical attention that he unfortunately received. The public found out that Gaudí was run over 24 hours too late, and by the time they realized their mistake, he was already residing with the God that he longed to be with.

If Gaudí had drafted any blueprints to build La Sagrada Familia by, it wouldn't matter if someone finally found them today because it wasn't like the cathedral was shaping to look anything like what he might have jotted down on paper. He was creating an outward expression of the spirit that he felt inside himself, and he knew what that spirit looked like even though no one else did. More than 100 years later, the cathedral that Gaudí started remains partially unfinished. I got the impression that everyone likely assumed that Gaudí was going to live forever or at least until his cathedral was complete. A Japanese firm was continuing to build La Sagrada Familia in 1998 when I saw the cathedral in person. My overall impression was that they must have been consulting an Ouija board because they seemed to be doing a fine job expressing what I was sure they thought was Gaudí's original vision.

We had two full days to spend in Barcelona. I voted to spend most of the second day holed up inside museums, but I got overruled by Kat's burning desire to hang out at the beach. In October. Without swimsuits.

"Why in the hell do you want to go to the beach?" I wanted to know. "That sounds like a really lame idea."

"Because I'd rather go to the beach than go to another museum," Kat barked back. "All we ever do is go to museums, and I'm soooo sick of them. Going to a beach sounds like way more fun, and I'd rather do something that I want to do."

It wasn't that he didn't have a point because I admitted that he totally did, but it was obvious that he didn't do any of the reading that I requested he do before we traveled to Barcelona.

"Did you read that Barcelona guidebook I gave you?" I asked him.

"Yes," he emphatically declared.

"Bullshit," I retorted. "You apparently didn't read the part that advised against going to the beach because people get pickpocketed there all the time."

"Bah, I don't believe that," Kat said as if it was perfectly in his right to pick and choose what guidebook facts were worth believing.

Long story short, I wasn't in the mood to start a fight on day two of our trip, so we went to the stupid beach, and three hours later, I found myself no longer in possession of any cash, credit cards, bus tickets, or hotel key because someone nabbed my backpack. I wanted to scream, "I FUCKING TOLD YOU SO!!" so fucking loud at Kat, but I only mumbled the phrase to him because I felt a tiny bit bad that he was now going to have to brunt the entire cost for the rest of the trip.

"How did you get your backpack stolen?" he asked me.

"How did you *not* get your backpack stolen?" I asked him in return.

"I used it as a pillow," he flatly explained.

Yup, we went to the beach alright, and there we fell asleep. We were still a little jet-lagged, and after a few minutes of staring at the water, we both went into a trance and completely dozed off.

"Well, the bus tickets that we literally just bought were in there," I said to him, "so we'll have to buy those things again."

"Seriously," Kat still wondered, "how did someone get your backpack away from you? Where did you have it?"

"I thought that I was holding on to it," I explained and then shuddered at the thought of someone getting so close to me that they plucked my bag away. "I guess that I'm glad that I didn't wake up because I probably would've gotten punched."

At that thought, we dropped the subject because we both knew that we were equally in the wrong for A) being at the beach and B) for being careless. We were both just glad that at least one of us had money to spend, although neither of us was impressed that we had to rebuy some bus tickets. We marched on over to the bus depot and reluctantly made the exact same purchase that we did just hours earlier. In fact, we were even less excited to be buying bus tickets the second time around because we didn't even want to purchase bus tickets in the first place. What we really wanted to do was take a train from Barcelona to Toulouse, but the trains in France were on grève (strike), much to our dismay. I didn't know it at the time, but French strikes were destined to be something of a fixture in my travel forays to that country. I have since decided that if I ever move to Paris and get a cat, which I will never do because I don't speak French and I am allergic to cats, but if I ever do, I am so naming my cat Grève because I can think of nothing more quintessentially French than a blasted strike.

Carcassonne

Had the trains not been on strike, we could have gotten from Barcelona to Toulouse in roughly three hours, but the same journey by bus was going to take us over six, and our bus driver was only going to drive sober for the first half of it. To get to Toulouse, we were going to be traveling on some seriously twisty roads high up in The Pyrenees Mountains. The last thing that we wanted to see was our bus driver down an entire liter of wine all by himself when we stopped for lunch mid-way through what was already a harrowing enough journey, but that describes exactly what we ended up seeing.

Kat and I could scarcely enjoy our coffee and sandwiches as we watched our bus driver down an entire carafe of wine all by his lonesome. It would have been one thing if we were driving on super flat roads because I didn't doubt any French man's ability to drive a car with a little bit of wine under his belt, but we were in the middle of *The Pyrenees Mountains*, where the distance between a guardrail and an abyss wasn't all that generous. Before we left the restaurant, I wanted to give our driver the benefit of the doubt that he was going to stay behind and we were going to board the bus with a brand new driver. However, a new driver failed to materialize when the time was nigh, and I wasn't able to suppress an audible gasp when we watched the wino get comfortable in the driver's seat.

"He's French," Kat tried to assure me. "He probably had wine for breakfast, too."

"A whole carafe, though?" I asked.

"Ya," Kat lamented, "that was a lot."

When we took our seats, we both scoured the cushions for the seat belts that were nowhere to be found.

"Whelp, this trip just keeps getting better and better," I said really super loud.

"Well, at least the road up here wasn't all *that* terrible," Kat tried to reassure me. "Hopefully, it'll be just like that for the rest of the way."

Well, of course, the road wasn't "just like that" for the rest of the way, not even close. It turned out that we hadn't even gotten to the genuine harrowing part yet, but then again, our driver would have made any road harrowing simply because of the way he drove way too freaking fast. Curves were completed with the aid of only two wheels instead of the usual four, and every person that sat at a window seat got really nice close-up views of all the grass that pleasantly grew directly below the stubby guardrails that I feared would tempt our driver to test its effectiveness at holding back a careening bus. I don't know why I kept looking out the window because it was making me carsick to watch the scenery whiz by a mile a millisecond, but not even nausea and a splitting headache could get me to turn my head away.

"Stop looking out of the window," Kat tried to order me.

"I can't help myself," I stubbornly replied. "If I'm going to die, I want to see what my death is going to look like."

"Well, of course, we're going to die on this thing," Kat flatly stated, "but it doesn't mean that you have to watch it happen. You really just need to look away and read one of your books."

His nonchalant attitude really perturbed me.

"How are you not nervous?" I asked him as the bus listed for the umpteenth time on a hairpin curve.

"Are you kidding?" he asked back. "I'm totally crapping my pants here, but he probably drives this road completely wasted every day."

"Ya, I'm sure he does," I agreed, "but doesn't that concern you?"

"Of course it does," Kat said, "but we all gotta die someday."
I turned around and gave him the stink eye.

"At least we'll die someplace pretty?" Kat asked rather than stated.

My face was still plastered to the window when I saw the pointy turrets and crenulated walls of the medieval village Carcassonne looming over the horizon. I was ready to get off the bus at any moment, so I seized the opportunity to leap off it a good 60 miles away from what was supposed to be our final destination. The whole reason why we were even heading to Toulouse in the first place was so that we could backtrack and spend the day in Carcassonne, so it made sense to get off the bus sooner rather than later. Just the mere sight of that charming walled city caused my heart to flutter, for I had been poring over photographs of that city for many months. I excitedly tapped Kat on the shoulder and told him to grab his bags because we were getting off. We then both jumped off the bus as if we were stuntmen leaping from a burning building. I almost didn't care when I noticed hours later that I accidentally left the Catalan Art book that I didn't even read inside one of the bus's seat pockets. "Hell," I consoled myself, "it wasn't as if I was going to see any Catalan Art anyway since Kat put the kibosh on museums." It was probably better that I left that book on the bus because it likely would have just pissed me off to look at pictures of artwork that I was deprived the opportunity of seeing.

The city of Carcassonne had been inhabited since Neolithic times, but the town really came of age during the medieval era when it rose to prominence as a fortified stronghold. The compact village was enclosed with two rings of walls and punctuated with a total of 53 towers whose silhouettes cut an impressive skyline. Yet, when the medieval era ended, the village of Carcassonne went with it, and the fortified city fell into a romantic state of decay. Lucky for us today, the Victorians had an artistic eye for such things, and they loved running around Europe in search of a new medieval ruin to resurrect in some fashionable way. A certain Victorian by the name of Viollet-le-Duc set his claws on Carcassonne and remodeled the crumbling village into a modern medieval fantasy. His results looked convincing enough to me that it made me want to be locked inside a dungeon by an evil stepmother and wait for a knight in shining armor to rescue me.

Everyone has their fantasy of what a medieval village should look like, and Carcassonne, with its collection of turrets, curtain walls, pointy roofs, and cobblestone streets, fulfilled all my fantasies, and then some. Carcassonne matched my mind's eye so perfectly that it appeared as if my imagination was realized in stone. It also seemed as though someone had turned time inside out, for I had a hard time discerning if I was living in the now or if I was living in the alternate version of what now used to be. Time seemed like such an arbitrary concept, and it didn't take a very long time for me to give in to the irresistible urge to set Kat up for some photographic role-playing.

"Go inside that little window will you?" I kindly directed Kat.

"Oh, okay," he said and dutifully complied.

"Okay, now put your hands in prayer and look up to the sky like the good little medieval monk that you are in your hoodie and blue jeans," I instructed.

"Really?" Kat bemoaned. "You're going to make me do this silliness?"

"Oh, come on!" I exclaimed. "It will be fun!"

Not that I'm ashamed to admit it, but every single picture that we took at Carcassonne was an image of either Kat or I posed in some ridiculous situation. There were a hundred different ways that we could have posed in front of ramparts, windows, bridges, and tombs, and we always tried our best to choose the most archaic pose that we could possibly do despite how un-medieval we looked in our 20th-century clothes. We had so much fun running around Carcassonne and doing stupid little things that I wanted to go back there even before we left. It came as no surprise to me when I found myself there again on my own about seven years later, but the experience was totally different the second time around. Carcassonne wasn't quite the same without someone else around to share the experience with, and I damn near met my demise there when I became the target for a flying patio umbrella, but that's a story that I will have to share in some future chapter.

First Time Solo

Kat and I had long been broken up by the time I returned to Carcassonne in 2005, but I almost didn't think of him when I went there without him because I had traveled to France solo at least three or four times in the interim. I have a slightly addictive personality, so France became my heroin after I stopped using Kat as my illicit drug of choice, and I wasn't the least bit ashamed of my newfound addiction. Working in the travel industry meant that getting over to France was not a matter of cost but simply a matter of time, so I made it a habit to blow all my vacation time in one extravagant trip per year. I was always aware that I had pretty much the entire world available to me on the ridiculously cheap, but France was my addiction, so that was where I invariably chose to go.

For the first handful of years, I flew to Paris from LAX on a carrier known as AOM French Airlines because they only charged travel agents the taxes for a ticket which amounted to something piddly, like $250. Unfortunately, I had to stop using them after they ceased operating in 2001. Until then, though, theirs was one of the best deals out there, so they made it super easy for me to get addicted to France. I really enjoyed using that airline, and I always found it strange that they put in absolutely zero effort toward advertising in the US market. Practically no one in the United States knew who AOM was even when they were at their peak as the second-largest airline in France, and there were a couple of times when the plane showed up at LAX, and I ended up being the only American who got on it. The airline was a big hit with French people, though, and the planes that I boarded in LAX were usually already packed with French nationals who were on their way back home from Tahiti. Los Angeles was simply a pit stop for the plane to fill up on some gas and maybe pick up whatever French people were through with holidaying at Disneyland and maybe on the rare occasion, to pick up some random American like me.

I remember one particular time I boarded that plane, and it was packed full of 20-year-old dudes who all looked identical because every one of them sported the same Polynesian-style shirt. Only about ten of us boarded the aircraft in LAX and it was immediately clear to us newcomers that we totally missed the Tahitian bachelor party when the aroma of stale beer tickled the back of our nostrils. Once the plane got back in the air, the party instantly resumed, and the aisles quickly transformed into prime real estate for hacky sack games. I recall a Frisbee flying over my head and being perturbed about it, but not really. Adam Sandler's movie *Big Daddy* aired on the overhead screen, and his voice was dubbed over in French, which made him look really silly, but it was a perfect visual for how the flight felt. In short, it was hands down my favorite flight ever because it was like Mardi Gras in the air. The only thing missing was beads to toss out the windows and seeing the flight attendants walk around topless.

Always, my solo trips to Paris began at the cheap Chinese restaurant where I made it a tradition to sip on the worst wine in all of France while gazing upon the best Parisian view. I just now took a moment to look on Google maps to see what that restaurant's name was, but I virtually went up and down the street and failed to find it. I'm not entirely assuming that the restaurant is gone because I remember it being just a postcard size of a place, but I do fear that it has since been transformed into a Subway shop, as that's what's there where I thought it used to be. It looks like there are still some seats plopped behind the windows, but unless they serve repugnant wine, I can't imagine the experience dining there being anywhere near the same. Still, theirs was always my favorite seat in all of Paris, and I never wanted to start a journey in France on any other perch.

In the journal that I took with me in 1999, I tried my hand at drawing the Notre Dame Cathedral while I downed the abomination that the restaurant passed off as being wine, and the result of my efforts was not something that I would ever consider framing. I don't know why I thought that drawing the Notre Dame Cathedral was a doable endeavor because just one glance at it should have been enough for me to see that sketching it was way beyond my artistic ability. For every line that I put down on paper, I failed to put down a hundred lines more, and for every window that I drew, I failed to draw the three other windows beside it. I tried drawing the flying buttresses, but I drew them so completely out of perspective that I left them hanging in mid-air. Having gasohol surging through my veins only caused me to draw progressively worse, so by the end of my second glass of engine fluid, I covered up what I drew with a whole bunch of trees. I titled my picture *Notre Dame* probably because I needed a reminder of what it was that I drew. However, I'm looking at that picture now and have decided to re-title it *Notre Dame, As Seen From Germany Through The Black Forest*. Overall, the picture would have looked a heck of a lot better if I had drawn a few more trees over it and if I had drawn those trees way taller. In the end, I'm simply glad that I took a photo of that same view with my camera, so I at least have a somewhat decent documentation of what that view truly looked like when I stared at it through that window.

The trip that I took to France in 1999 was the first European journey that I did all by myself, and it wasn't until I traveled solo that I really realized just how much I tended not to pay attention to my immediate surroundings. I had grossly underestimated my personal ability to occasionally look up every once in a while to determine whether or not I was going in the right direction, and it was during this particular trip that

I made two wildly avoidable yet memorable mistakes that caused me to berate my own negligence.

Laon

I had only been in France for two days before I managed to accidentally board the wrong train that I feared wasn't going to stop until it reached the darkest depths of Siberia. I never kidded myself that I was good at either reading or speaking the French language, but I really had no excuse why I couldn't tell the difference between the words *Rouen* and *Laon*. I only noticed that I got on the wrong train when the arrival time that I wrote down for Rouen had passed, and it appeared as though the train had no intention of stopping any time soon. When I looked out the window and saw nothing but fields and cows, where the train was actually heading greatly concerned me. I started to worry that the train would roll into Russia for fear that someone would demand to see the passport that I wasn't currently carrying. I didn't necessarily come to Europe with a burning desire to spend some quality time in an airless Moscow prison, so I was naturally overcome with relief when the train came to a stop somewhere within the borders of France. I almost didn't care that I didn't know where I was when I elbowed my way to be the first passenger to leap off the train and land on some solid French concrete.

It only took a matter of minutes for me to recognize where I was when I spied some cows perched on a pair of bell towers way off in the distance. The city of Laon was the only place that I was aware of that peppered their cathedral with oxen, and it was a cathedral that I was planning to see on this trip, just not on the day that I accidentally wound up there. I had initially carved out an entire day for Laon because I wanted to explore the city in minute detail, so it bummed me out to learn that I only had three hours to spend if I wanted to avoid getting stranded there overnight. Thus, the gauntlet was thrown, so I hit the city running. However, my legs quickly encountered the longest set of stairs that my body had ever seen, and they instantly slowed my pace down. I swiftly came to learn that there was no such thing as doing Laon fast because the whole city was one enormous labyrinth of winding cobblestone streets. Of all the cities that I could have mistakenly ended up in, I was really pissed that I ended up in the most adorable one. It was fairly evident that walking around Laon in three hours was going to be the outdoor equivalent of trying to see the entire Louvre in a single hour. I quickly acknowledged that there would be no way I could experience the city as fully as I initially intended and that I would have to miss some little out-of-the-way things. However, I was super reluctant to miss anything, so I decided to tackle Laon the most efficient way I knew how: the American way – super rude and super fast.

The city of Laon was exquisitely delightful, and I wanted to stop for a coffee and a croissant at every single cafe that I reluctantly whizzed by in a frazzled blur. The main highlight of Laon was its cathedral, so I made it my goal to spend the majority of my time there. However, getting to the cathedral was going to take some time as it was located at the very top of a hill that was itself littered with a thousand different distractions. The city was too adorable for its own good, and it pissed me off that I didn't have the right amount of time to appreciate it properly. I kept cursing to myself that the city was too freaking hilly and the views were too goddamn beautiful. I lamented that I didn't have enough time to stop and soak in the scenery with a nice glass of wine and a ham and butter sandwich. Internally, I was crabby with myself, and I had no time for pleasantries when some poor sap made the mistake of asking me what time it was. I totally heard him, but I pretended I didn't because I knew all too well what time it was because I was chasing the clock that was running way ahead of me. Besides, he asked me the question in French, and I didn't know how to answer him back in the same language, so I figured that he'd get his answer way better if he directed it toward pretty much anybody else. Also, he probably wouldn't have liked it if I yelled the time at him in English, which was probably what I would have done because time was a bone that I wasn't in the mood to have picked.

I can honestly say that I barely remember what the cathedral looked like on the inside because I can only recall what it looked like on the outside. No one can really say with 100 percent certainty as to why the builders decided to place cows on the bell towers in the spots where gargoyles would typically be, but my hunch was that the construction was directed by someone who was an early medieval version of Antoni Gaudí. Every generation is entitled to at least one eccentric artist that they can claim as their own, and Laon Cathedral was evidently the product of one of the 13th century's quirkiest creators. I loved looking up at the cathedral and seeing full-sized cows gazing back down at me. The cows looked so happy poking their little necks out and watching the centuries march on by underneath them. I desperately wanted to get up there and pet them and tell them what good stone-carved animals they were standing there all nicely.

I really enjoyed the little time that I had in Laon, and I would consider going back there again someday and spending a night. I wouldn't doubt that gazing at the cows under floodlights in the evening while under the influence of a good wine buzz would be a very fine thing to do as that would have been the exact thing that I would have done had I missed the return train to Paris, but I didn't. I was so paranoid about missing that train that I got to the station at least 20 minutes early, which meant that I only got to spend a total of two hours and 40 minutes in Laon, and I spent most of that time walking up and down cobblestone streets and stairs. Man, that little city made such a good impression upon me. I fell in love with it. Not that I could ever afford to move to France, but I just now looked up what the real estate market looked like in Laon. There are definitely a few houses there that I could easily see myself living in. I, of course, am leaning toward pretend purchasing a 19th-century house across from the cathedral that boasts ten rooms and a small walled garden for the tune of €445,000, but it wouldn't take much to persuade me to pretend buy the sunny loft with a gutted kitchen and no bedroom for a mere €47,000. Either way, I'd be pretend living in Laon, and I could always get drunk and talk to the cows in English because they would be the only ones who would pretend understand me.

Beauvais

When I returned to Paris, I promised myself that I would make an effort to pay attention to where I was going, but I failed to promise myself that I would also pay more attention to the entire world around me. It was a promise that I should have made, but it would not have been a promise I would have kept because I committed another travel blunder less than 24 hours later. No doubt, I probably still would have managed to get myself locked inside a church even if I had promised to pay more attention to my immediate surroundings, for it's almost a given that I still would have tuned out the lady that yelled about something in French. I don't believe that I would have keyed into the fact that she was announcing that she was closing for the day and locking the door behind her, for I don't think that I would have expected the church to close at three in the afternoon. Okay, fine, it might have been closer to 4 p.m., but it was definitely nowhere near 5 p.m., which was when I typically expected most random places to close. Regardless, it was still relatively early when she abandoned me in there, even though I admittedly lost all track of time myself.

I traveled to the city of Beauvais specifically because I was interested in visiting the medieval era's most grandiose unfinished building, Beauvais Cathedral, but that wasn't where I wound up getting locked inside. Thinking about it now, I think that I would have preferred to have gotten locked inside Beauvais Cathedral instead of the church down the street because the drafts inside Beauvais Cathedral probably indicated that there were holes in the building that I could've crawled out of. The constant drafts made it absolutely freezing in there, but I totally loved it and wanted to stay for as long as I could because that was where I wanted to be. I came to Beauvais Cathedral because I was curious to see what humanity looked like when it carved its hubris into stone, and I was curious to see what that same hubris looked like when it transformed into humble.

The 13ᵗʰ century were boom years for cathedral building, and nearly every major city in Europe vied to build the biggest and prettiest one. The clergy of Beauvais took the challenge to heart and endeavored to create the loftiest and most attractive cathedral of them all. They actually succeeded in doing just that until a large section of the ceiling came crashing down before the cathedral was completed. The dramatic ceiling collapse caused the builders to lose their nerve, so they constructed a wall where the building was meant to continue and called the cathedral done. The stubby unfinished building was consecrated as a place of worship in the year 1272 and has remained in use for nearly 750 years despite its unstable and stunted condition. I always love me a good cathedral, and had I been told that I was allowed to see only one more cathedral and then I would be banned from seeing any more, Beauvais Cathedral would have hands down been the one that I would've chosen to see.

Every cathedral's sole purpose is to give humankind a proper space to focus on the divine, but Beauvais Cathedral caused me to ponder secular thoughts rather than spiritual ones. There was something about its unfinishedness that struck me as being very human. It was evident that she needed humankind's assistance to keep her standing. Massive wooden trusses were installed at critical junctures inside the cathedral to prevent it from collapsing in on itself, and steel tie rods were placed between the flying buttresses on the exterior to hold them steady. It was almost as though there was a general feeling that if Beauvais Cathedral fell, some part of humankind would fall along with it. So, aesthetics didn't matter so long as the cathedral remained standing.

Cathedrals are never meant to fall down, but Beauvais Cathedral has always teetered on the precipice. Most cathedrals seem to defy the ages, but Beauvais Cathedral didn't, not in the least. She was a relic from another age and the weight of time pressed heavily upon her shoulders. She was old, and she wasn't afraid to admit that she was frail and needed someone to guide her through the centuries. She didn't strike me as weak, but she did strike me as a visual for humankind in general. Beauvais Cathedral was essentially us, and humans don't always grow gracefully. We get old, we get wrinkled, and we struggle to stay warm. Most other visitors didn't spend a whole lot of time inside Beauvais Cathedral when I was there because the cold inside was very biting, and I couldn't help but feel like I was abandoning her the moment I decided to walk away. I felt like apologizing to her when I left, but I also wanted to explain that I couldn't stay in there forever. I wasn't comfortable inside that cathedral, and it reminded me how I sometimes wasn't even comfortable inside my own skin. I sometimes feel like leaving myself just for a moment, but that is not something that I can ever physically do. Walking away from Beauvais Cathedral was surreally satisfying in a way that I've only ever imagined because it felt like I was walking away from myself.

Down the street was St. Etienne Church, and it was a charming Romanesque sanctuary that I stumbled into when I was looking for somewhere to get warm. Soft music filled the space with a soothing sound which paired nicely with delicate glowing light and a pleasantly warm temperature. Being in there was a pure delight, and I took my time admiring the stained glass windows and stone carvings that were tucked way in the back of the Flamboyant Gothic choir. I had only really started scrutinizing things before the music came to an abrupt halt and all the lights suddenly turned off. I heard the lady up front make an announcement, but I admittedly ignored her because I always ignore French whenever I hear it spoken somewhere in the background. To me, her words were ambient noise, but I should have at least keyed into what she was saying, given that the lights just turned off and the music stopped playing. I didn't necessarily hear her say the word fermé (closed) as that would have been one of the only French words that my ears would have genuinely heard. Still, I also don't think that it would have mattered if I heard her say that because I was located so far in the back of the church that I probably wouldn't have made it to the door before she closed it behind her anyway. I was going to get locked in there no matter what because she didn't do a sweep for visitors who might have been lurking somewhere inside the building. Then again, I do believe that I was dilly-dallying. I might have just moseyed to the front thinking that she announced a ten-minute warning rather than the, "I'm closing right now, so you better get your butt out of here before I lock you in over the holiday weekend" spiel that she probably gave.

I caught wind of what happened when I walked to the front and saw no one sitting at the entrance. I immediately didn't think that it was that big of a deal to be by myself inside a church as I had wandered into plenty of churches before without another person in them. I never, in all my life, managed to get myself trapped inside one. Usually, there was always a door left open somewhere, so I simply assumed that would be the case this time, but I would soon discover that I was sorely mistaken. I reached for the front door and became immediately perturbed when the door resisted my attempt to open it. I didn't instantly think that the door was actually locked, but when I looked up to see what was preventing the door from opening, I noticed that it was securely locked with the aid of a key.

"Nonsense," I thought to myself. "No way was this door locked with some stupid key." Only, it was.

"Seriously, no way!" I decried out loud to absolutely no one but myself.

I thought that maybe the front desk lady was still in there somewhere, so I started to yell.

"Bonjour!" I screamed. "Hello! Don't leave me in here! Bonjour!" I heard my voice echo.

No one replied.

"Crap," I said to myself. "Crap, crap, crap, *crap!* This is not good."

I didn't immediately assume that I was stuck in there as I was pretty sure that I didn't try hard enough to open the front door. I went back to that door, tried it again, and became instantly deflated when I still couldn't get the unwieldy thing to move. My inability to open the door set me off one of those panic circles where I ran around and checked absolutely everything, including stained glass windows.

"Agh," I said to myself, "why is every window a stained glass window around here?" Normally, I'd appreciate such things, but right then, I did not.

I saw that there was a phone, but my non-existent French kept me from picking it up and dialing anything. I had no idea what number I would even dial if and when I had to finally break down and call someone for help because I wasn't entirely sure if 911 was a thing in France. I wasn't looking forward to being blamed for being inside a church when I wasn't supposed to be, and I most definitely did not want the French fire brigade to break a stained glass window on my behalf. Also, I was afraid of potentially being arrested for trespassing, even though it technically wasn't something that I intended to do. I ultimately decided that if I couldn't get out of there on my own that I would be stuck in there until someone opened the front door, possibly a good three days from then. The thought of being stuck in there over a holiday weekend caused a chill to run down my spine and sent me off searching for the communion wine because I needed a drink to calm down my nerves. I figured, what with it being a French church et al that there had to be a wine cellar in there somewhere. However, my search for the elusive cache ultimately proved futile. I was only disappointed for so long, though, because my frantic search for wine did lead me to discover a massive pair of medieval doors that looked like they hadn't been opened in at least 500 years.

The doors were seriously huge, and they were latched shut by a series of locks that I saw could be maneuvered if only I could reach them.

"Great!" I thought to myself, "I just need to find a chair to stand on."

I did a quick once over but came up empty-handed when I discovered that every single seat in the building was in the form of a pew that couldn't be moved.

"You have got to be kidding me," I said to God directly. "You have got to give me at least a bucket to stand on."

I did another once over and again came up with nothing.

"Bibles, maybe?" I thought about stacking those but only found one or two. "What kind of church is this?" I wondered.

The only thing left that I could do was jump as high as I possibly could and try to unlatch the locks with my arms outstretched way above me.

"This is gonna take some serious skills," I told myself and took a running head start for my first leap of faith.

I amazed myself when I got the first latch opened and was even more amazed when I got the second latch free after only taking the two highest jumps that I had ever taken in all of my life. I didn't analyze the locks all that closely before I started jumping, and I honestly thought that I was done after I got those two locks open.

"Thank you, God," I said out loud. "Guess you're not so against me getting out of here after all."

I grabbed my backpack and reached for the door, thinking that I was going to waltz on out of there. However, I was taken aback when all the door did was wiggle.

"Son of a b*tch!" was what I wanted to say but didn't because I was inside a church, so I said, "God freaking dammit!" instead. High above the other two locks was a third one that looked impossible to reach.

"How the heck am I supposed to get *that* one open?" I asked God and myself simultaneously. "There is no way that I can jump that high."

I had no choice but to try, so I tried and tried and tried and tried and failed with every single attempt. That third latch was just too high for me to get to, so I did another scavenger hunt for something to stand on. I forget now what I found, but I remember that whatever it was nearly killed me when I leaped off of it. I tumbled so hard that I had to lie down in a pew for about 30 minutes to regain my composure.

That long rest apparently did me good because once I got up, I put my backpack back on and told myself that I had no choice but to get that third latch open. I channeled my inner Olympian, took the biggest leap of my life, and majestically reached the third latch with my fingertips, which was just enough to flick the thing open. All my previous shaking of that door must have pried it relatively loose because once I released the third latch, the door instantly swung open, and I tumbled out of it like an alien from outer space and surprise-landed on some vagrant man taking a pee. It was pretty darn funny because that guy probably thought that he was perfectly safe peeing where he was, considering that he likely never in all of his life had ever seen anyone use the door that I just fell out of. I literally landed right on top of him and his being there gave me a much softer landing than if he hadn't been there taking his illicit piss. Hilariously, neither of us could tell who was more shocked at what just happened, and we both took off immediately in two different directions. I had absolutely no idea what time it was at that point, so I didn't stop running until I made it to the train station. Once there, I found that I had over an hour left in Beauvais to spare, so I decided to wait the hour out at the train station. I killed time by writing the lengthy experience down in my journal and happily contended with people staring at me like I was a crazy person when I couldn't stop laughing to myself as I wrote the story down.

Paris Sewer Museum

Before I returned home from France, there was one thing left that I wanted to do, and that was to spend some quality time at the Paris Sewer Museum. I had never been to a sewer museum before, and just the idea of such a place made me want to vomit and smile simultaneously. I almost couldn't believe that such a museum existed when I read about it in a guidebook because most cities don't tout their sewers as tourist destinations. Heck, I don't even know where the sewer entrance is in Phoenix, where I live, because it's not somewhere that I would ever think to swing by and spend an afternoon in. Actually, I have to correct myself and say that I *have* been to a sewer museum before. However, it wasn't a sewer museum, per se, but it was a sewage treatment plant. When I was in high school, in like eleventh grade or something, our class was split into two separate groups and got sent off on two entirely different field trips. Half the class got to visit the Kikkoman Soy Sauce Factory, and the other half got to visit a sewage treatment plant. I just assumed that both groups were sent to a sewage treatment plant and got to come back to school smelling like they just swam in a toilet for two hours, but, nope, that was just our lucky group. When we returned to school, my half had to tolerate the other half's smug looks as they ran around the hallways smiling and waving their little packets of soy sauce and demanding us to show them what we brought back from our trip. Our group came back empty-handed, aside from the story about how we learned that there were bugs that ate poop, and we saw hoards of them in large cisterns at the sewage treatment plant and that they could smell our shirts if they wanted to. Needless to say, the Kikkoman group was not nearly as jealous of us as we were of them.

That sewer treatment plant tour stuck with me for years because it was a rare view of the underbelly of how a city genuinely functioned. When I read about the Paris Sewer Museum, my first thought was that it was such a great idea that I couldn't believe that the city didn't also offer garbage dump tours or visits to a crematorium. There is so much about what makes a city tick that I only have vague notions about, and I was really hoping that Paris would peel back its skin and reveal itself to be a transparent jellyfish, but, alas, it kept most of its inner workings tightly under wraps. Paris exposed only a small portion of its historic sewer system for prying eyes to see, and what they revealed only made me want to see more. The museum succeeded in making the story of Paris' sewers fascinating. They were rightfully proud to show off their underground system because Paris allegedly was a horrible city to live in before proper sanitation. I tend to romanticize the past, but I probably shouldn't. When I think about life with no running water, no deodorant, no showers, no toilets, dim lighting, and roomfuls of smoke, I really appreciate the modern life that I am currently living.

The Paris Sewer Museum had a gift shop, and I totally regret it now that I didn't think to come home with a souvenir to immortalize that visit forever. I don't believe that they sold little packets of soy sauce with The Paris Sewer Museum logo printed on them, but if they had, I'm pretty sure that I would have bought a crap ton of them.

CHAPTER SEVEN:
Alaska, the American Northwest, and Freedom,
1998-current

Alaska

As much as I loved my jet-setting lifestyle, I couldn't survive on just cereal and toast forever. I needed to find a job that would pay me some actual money, so I landed a new position at a corporate travel agency. Gone was going to be my ability to jump on an America West airplane whenever I wanted, and in its place was going to be insanely discounted air, car, and rail travel instead. I was itching to open myself up to the wider world because I had exhausted all the possible day trips that I could reasonably muster. So, I was pretty okay with giving up my America West flight benefits if the trade-off meant that I could finally afford to take some genuine trips. I was ready for a change; however, there still remained one elusive travel destination on my bucket list that I wanted to cross off before leaving my sweet little gig.

When I grew up in Wisconsin, I thought that I hated the idea of Alaska. I despised the long Wisconsin winters and would constantly complain that it felt like we lived inside a gigantic freezer. I would frequently say that I would prefer to live inside a refrigerator instead of a freezer, and my only consolation was that I at least didn't live somewhere even colder, somewhere like, oh I don't know, say, *Alaska*. I could never understand why my dad would frequently say that his biggest dream in the world was to go to Alaska for some grandiose hunting and fishing trip. In my mind, Alaska was perpetual winter, so I thought that he was positively nuts for wanting to go there. My dad was a navy man, and he saw many exotic parts of the world, but the one place that he never got to see was America's 49th state. A massive stroke prevented him from achieving his dream vacation, so when the opportunity arose for me to travel there, I did so with the thoughts of my father weighing heavily on my brain. I didn't necessarily want to go to Alaska for me; I wanted to go to Alaska for him. He was still alive and residing in a nursing home, so I wanted to be able to describe the state's beauty to him with the best firsthand account that I could reasonably muster. With that premise in mind, I intended to see the Alaska that my dad always wanted to see, but the Alaska that I ended up seeing wasn't nearly as beautiful as I initially imagined.

The flight I came in landed at 9 p.m., but I only knew what time it was because I saw it displayed on a ridiculously large clock that hung in the center of the airport terminal. Outside, it looked like it was the middle of the day, and had I asked someone what time it was, they could have told me that it was noon, and I would have believed them had I not already seen the time displayed on that super ginormous timepiece. Indeed, the land of the midnight sun really did exist, and it felt surreal to step straight into it. Seeing the sun that bright at that unexpected hour filled me with supreme giddiness, but that giddiness quickly waned when I attempted to fall asleep in my el-cheapo hotel room that sported paper-thin curtains. I went to Anchorage poor as dirt, and I barely scraped up enough money to splurge on a hotel room. It was money that I justified was worth spending, though, because the alternative was to wander around Anchorage aimlessly for the duration of the night.

Personally, I would have thought that every window in

Alaska would have sported thick blackout curtains, but I soon discovered that my assumption was wildly incorrect. The sun penetrated through my eyelids until well past 11 p.m. and only gave me five hours of respite before it burned through my eyelids once again and determined for me that I was officially awake. It was only 4:30 a.m., but the world near the Arctic Circle evidently didn't care how early it was. I took the sheet off the bed, threw it over the window, and told the sun to bugger off. Doing that achieved absolutely nothing, though, because the sun still managed to shine through bright as shit. Since the sun and I were both wide awake, I decided to give up on sleeping and went outside to hunt down some much-needed coffee.

One would think that a town where the sun rose at 4:30 a.m. would cause people to start their days super early, but 30 minutes worth of wandering around Anchorage and finding nothing open confirmed that I was the only one awake. It was a pure stroke of luck when I finally did stumble upon a 24-hour coffee shop. I remember sitting down and looking for raw seal on the menu and feeling extremely disappointed when I didn't see that item on offer. "Okay, fine," I told myself. "Reindeer, maybe?" Ah, nope. "Walrus, caribou, fish, whale?" Nope, nope, nope, and nope. All my choices were limited to the usual suspects, so I settled for bacon, eggs, and toast, which I thought to be incredibly boring. A sushi plate of seal would have been better, but then again, it likely wouldn't have been because I have never known myself to be an adventurous eater. I think that I just liked the idea of ordering something traditional to the area to get me in the proper mood. I was in *Alaska*, I kept telling myself, but the bacon, eggs, and toast didn't put forth much effort to convince me of that fact. I was in *America* was basically what my breakfast point-blank told me.

The idea of America was pervasive and inescapable while I was in Anchorage. As much as I thought that I was somewhere foreign or exotic, there was some little reminder that showed me just how much in America I actually was. Anchorage looked like any other American city, for there was nothing particular about it that stood out as being that much different from anywhere else I had been to before. If someone had told me that the plane actually dropped me off in Toledo, Ohio, I might have believed it had it been cloudy enough to obscure the string of mountains that hovered over the horizon. I initially thought that I was going to be jealous of the people that lived in Anchorage because they lived so far away from the rest of the country. However, once I was there, I realized just how near to America they genuinely were. I have never been to an American army base in a foreign country before, but I gradually got the feeling that Anchorage felt akin to one. I suspected that both places had to be somewhat similar and ultimately concluded that where a person lived was analogous to a state of mind.

After I ate my breakfast of not seal sushi, I puttered about and watched the early birds fish from a local bridge over a river that didn't look all that romantic to me. What I wanted Alaska to look like and what it did actually look like were two entirely different things. The river that the men were fishing from looked like the most utilitarian river in the entire world. It was merely doing what any river was expected to do, and for some odd reason, I felt a tad disappointed with its ultra-typical appearance. In my mind's eye, that river was supposed to be wild. It was supposed to have salmon leaping into the air and grizzlies perched on its bank, but the river that flowed through Anchorage was piled with rocks and mostly devoid of trees. The river did not seem to be anything that would remotely grace the pages of a nature magazine as I mistakenly thought that every inch of Alaska would. I didn't see anyone catch anything, but if they were catching trout or salmon in that river, I concluded that it didn't matter how barren the scenery looked. The possibility of catching fresh fish for breakfast made me want to grab the nearest fishing pole, and it was right then that I realized what the magic of Alaska was all about. Alaska was about a quality of life that one doesn't get anywhere else. I got the sense that I was getting an accurate impression of what the Alaskan experience was all about right there on that nondescript riverbank. One thinks that one goes to Alaska for beauty, but, really, one goes to Alaska for bounty. I slowly came to realize that not all of Alaska was astonishingly beautiful. The people who make Alaska happen do so because there exists a motivation for them to be there. Standing on that bland riverbank got me wondering about how beauty truly was in the eye of the beholder. I was beginning to understand how different pairs of eyes interpret the same landscape in entirely different ways. I took it for granted that we all saw life in the same vein, but I saw right then that we all certainly did not. Everyone who looks at the world sees a different agenda written upon it, and everyone has their interpretation of how the world relates to them. Those that were fishing saw the world one way, and I, who was not fishing, saw the world another way, yet we were all standing in the same landscape together.

I spent a total of 24 hours in Anchorage, and during that

time, I managed to do three things: I visited their Arctic History and Culture Museum, I rambled around their 1964 Earthquake Park, and I got hopelessly lost walking around their massive public-use general aviation airport without really knowing how I wound up there. That last bit I could have done without, and it doesn't make me happy that getting all tangled up at that ridiculous airport happens to be what I remember most about my trip to Anchorage. I can't recall a whole heck of a lot about what I learned at that Arctic museum or at that Earthquake Park, but I can sure tell anyone who wants to know that seaplanes are as ubiquitous as pickup trucks in Alaska. In fact, I can officially sum up Anchorage in three simple words: one: trucks – because everyone had one, two: airplanes – because everyone had one (or at least I assumed that everyone knew someone who had one), and three: dogs – because everyone had one (or four) of those too. I kind of regret it now that I didn't keep count of how many dogs I saw in pickup trucks while I walked around that wickedly massive aviation lot that was choked full of airplanes, as keeping count of how many dogs that I saw would have given me something productive to do. What I did do, though, was look for the top of Mount McKinley that was supposedly looming over the mountain range far off in the distance. Even though I really tried, I couldn't determine which white blob was specifically Mount McKinley because all the mountains looked like clumps of low-hanging clouds to me. Although it didn't appear that any individual mountain stood out taller than the rest, I nevertheless checked off viewing Mount McKinley from my bucket list after I convinced myself that one of those cloudy blobs had to be it.

145

My not being able to distinguish Mount McKinley seemed to rather appropriately fit within a developing theme of my not being able to put my finger on the whole concept of Alaska itself. Even though I technically went there, I still kind of feel like I didn't, and I'm saying this even after I've been to Alaska twice now since Ryan (my current husband) and I went on a cruise there a few years ago. Alaska is one of those places that is so vast that it is nearly impossible to grasp. I don't believe that anyone can fully understand the complexities of that state, for it is way more than what any person can possibly understand. Alaska is bigger than who we are as a people, and it demands more respect than what we humans are capable of delivering. We are likely doing Alaska all wrong, and it is unknown if time will take kindly to our errors. All that Alaska asks from us is nothing, but that may simply be because the state has no voice with which to speak. We need to learn how to read the landscape and adhere to its requests as indicated in nature. No forest would ever ask that it be cleared, no river would ever ask that it be dammed, no tundra would ever ask that it be drilled, and no water would ever ask that it be polluted. Nature is a delicate thing, and it does its best when we leave it alone.

Climate change is affecting Alaska in negative ways, for environmental alterations are occurring at a faster rate than nature can adapt. Ryan and I watched environmental conditions outpace habitat right before our very eyes when we cruised the Tracy Arm Fjord in 2013. It was there where we observed huge chunks of Sawyer Glacier drop into the water, and we watched it make one unreal beautiful splash after one unreal beautiful splash in a grotesque display of wonderfulness. Neither of us particularly wanted to see the glacier shed off beautiful blue pieces of itself because its doing so meant that those parts of the glacier were dissolving forever. As awe-inspiring as it was, it was hard to call that glacier shedding pieces of itself as being an act of nature. That glacier would not have been calving so early in the season (we were the first cruise of the summer), or even calving at all had not that glacier been so intent on disappearing altogether because of environmental conditions. What we were witnessing was an act of humankind, not an act of nature, and it was a disturbing display of human negligence. The only reason why we went on that cruise at all was to see that glacier, so we weren't too excited to watch bits of it disappear before our very eyes. Most people go on their first Alaskan cruise when they retire as it seems to be the requisite thing that people do when they no longer have to go to work every day, but neither of us thought that the glacier would be there for us if we waited that long. We made what we figured was the wise decision and sought out our requisite retirement glacier early and pocketed the experience for future age-appropriate reminiscing.

I generally don't harbor good feelings about the future health of our planet. I am not a fan of the fact that Earth's fate does not lie in the hands of scientists, environmentalists, conservationists, or even artists but rather lies in the hands of the powers that be. I have a saying that there only exists one answer to every question, and that answer is money. In the future, that answer may change to water when there is no more fresh water left to drink, but for now, the answer is always money, for money is the root cause of everything. There is no escaping the effects of the mighty dollar as its influence surrounds us in ways that no one even sees. The power of money is inside all of us simply because we all have to breathe. It is the particulates that have been allowed to dance in our atmosphere that bind us all as victims of the same kind of evil. It is not pollution that we breathe; it is the by-product of someone else's wealth that we inhale deep into our lungs.

Sometimes it's just easier to not think about such things, and, indeed, most people don't. It would be much too easy to become a paranoid hypochondriac if one allowed oneself to mull over all the crap that one constantly gets exposed to; hence, it's simply safer to avoid dwelling on the negative aspects of our lives. One of the fortunate things about modern life is that it offers plenty of distractions to prevent us from worrying about how much pesticide was used to grow the cucumbers that we hurriedly buy in the store. Overall, it's much easier to worry about the stuff that one has a semblance of control over, but even then, daily life often seems daunting. I don't dare think about what the world will look like 1,000 years from now simply because I can't even keep pace with how much the world changes on a yearly basis. I don't even know what the latest statistic is regarding how much the planet has heated up recently, but it has gotten to the point where I don't even need to know anymore because whatever the statistic is, it's not going to be good. Climate change is depressing, and I hate the feeling of hopelessness that it causes. I don't have a good feeling about our planet's future because I don't think those who can make a difference actually will. We're all steering our planet into becoming our Solar System's next Venus, and we don't seem to care that we're doing it because we who are here now won't be around when the Earth eventually tips into that realm. Something needs to save us from ourselves, but unless another dinosaur destructing sized meteorite blasts through our atmosphere or a nuclear war decimates us all, there ain't nothing that's gonna shake us off of Earth's back and prevent the inevitable from happening.

Travel Agent Perks

Ignorance is bliss, and in 1998, I wasn't remotely thinking about the potential end of the world as I knew it. Terrorism wasn't even a by-word at that time, nor were the terms Y2K, 9/11, Axis of Evil, Taliban, Ground Zero, Guantanamo, Patriot Act, recession, lay-offs, housing bubble, foreclosure, bailout, 1%, surveillance, fake news, Black Lives Matter, Me Too, QAnon, Antifa, insurrection, quarantine, social distancing, vaccine, or pandemic. The last years of the '90s were America's final years of so-called innocence, but that was only because the majority of Americans chose not to look at what the rest of the world was doing. America lived in its own naive bubble up until 2001, and until that bubble burst, life was relatively straightforward. I wouldn't necessarily say that life was simpler back then, but maybe I would say that life was far less stressful. Life still had a normal trajectory in the '90s. One could reasonably expect to go to school, get a job, buy a house, and start a family without thinking that they would have to declare bankruptcy somewhere along the way to achieve the same sort of things that their parents did. Sure, interest rates were high in the '90s, but the housing prices weren't all out of whack back then, so those two things balanced each other out. I'm no economist, and maybe I'm talking out of my league here, but I do recall the '90s as being financially easier to live in compared to now. I lived off barely minimum wage in my own apartment by myself for years and never needed to file for governmental assistance, which is not something that I think many people could successfully pull off doing today. The cost of living is more expensive now, and the majority of that cost goes toward the basic need of putting a roof over one's head. Alas, I could go on and on about how the housing market pisses me off, but I shouldn't allow myself to go off on a tangent about that because doing so will cause me to lose focus on whatever the heck I was talking about, and I did already kind of forget what I was saying. Oh, yes, I was talking about the '90s. Those years were good to me. I traveled a lot and won a bunch of prizes.

The travel benefits at my new job were absolutely insane. If I thought I was a travel fiend before, I hadn't met my future self yet. I didn't know it at the time, but being a travel agent in the 1990s and early 2000s were going to be the last great years of travel agent discounts and freebies. I made out like a bandit during those years with free flights, free hotel stays, Eurail pass discounts, and a company-provided $1,500 yearly travel bank to spend on expenses. I put my name in a drawing to win a kayak one Christmas and surprisingly won it. I don't even know why I wanted to win a kayak because I didn't live near any water, nor did I own a large enough vehicle to transport such an unwieldy thing. It was a comedy of errors trying to get the kayak out of the building and into my friend's borrowed truck, and even more of a comedy when we took it inside my apartment and got it tightly wedged in the hallway. The theme song from Benny Hill ran through my head throughout the entire process, and I heard that song again when I had to get the kayak out of the apartment after I sold it to someone who had a more justifiable reason to own such a thing.

Years of traveling on a shoestring had taught me to be a savvy traveler, and I always found ways to make my $1,500 travel bank last the entire year. Lucky for me was that I've always been a total cheapwad, so it was easy for me not to spend a whole lot of money on any of my trips. I had made the decision years before that traveling was what I wanted to do with my life, so I taught myself early on how to budget appropriately. The less I spent per trip meant that I could afford to go on more trips than would typically be considered reasonable, and after a while, people knew that I was the go-to person when they needed to interrogate someone about the particulars of travel. In an office full of travel agents, I was the travel agent that other travel agents went to when they needed help planning their own family vacations.

It didn't take me long to develop a travel pattern that I pretty much stuck with until a global health pandemic put the kibosh on most leisure travel. Throughout the year, I used to take small jaunts to places in America that I had never been to before, and then in either March or October, I used to take a sizable overseas trip. The world is huge, and I always knew that I would never see it all, but knowing that never stopped me from at least trying to see as much of the world as I possibly could. I understand now that my travel habits likely left behind a sizable carbon footprint, and for that, I do feel terribly guilty. For years, I took airplane travel completely for granted, but I am more cognizant now and will henceforth make a concerted effort to travel less and stay at a destination longer, that is, of course, assuming that I will someday travel internationally again.

With my new job came the two biggest game-changers that

altered the way that I traveled. With my corporate discounts, I could finally afford to rent a car and stay overnight in hotels, which combined, meant that I could finally break away from city centers and venture off to farther-flung destinations. I already had it in mind where I wanted to tootle off to first, as I had long been curious to see what Mount St. Helens looked like in person. That incredible volcano blew itself up when I was seven years old, and I remembered it being a big deal when it happened, but I also remembered that I struggled to understand why. I think my child-sized brain just assumed that volcanoes were meant to blow up. It probably wasn't until the Space Shuttle Challenger blew up six years later that I realized that big things blowing up like that were not supposed to be normal occurrences. In my very near future, something else big was going to explode, and that explosion was going to be a bigger game-changer than those two other explosions put together. However, the falling of The Twin Towers wasn't anything that I needed to concern myself with quite yet.

Mount St. Helens and Portland

I don't suppose that I was necessarily expecting to see anything too terribly exciting when I drove from Portland to Mount St. Helens, but having nothing good on the radio to listen to caused my mind to turn into instant mush. Having no decent radio options didn't help make the ride go any faster, so I opted to listen to silence, which made the suffering drive even worse. There was nothing about the landscape to keep my mind engaged, and the weather outside was so horrid that I contemplated turning around on several occasions. I persevered, though, because I was determined to see that famous mountain. Yet, when I finally got there, I almost didn't know where to find it. Mount St. Helens was a blob of a volcano that lacked a distinctive top, and the landscape surrounding it was so shapeless that I wasn't sure what I was supposed to take a picture of. Mount St. Helens didn't look like anything specific at all, yet it was surprisingly attractive in a lunar landscape kind of way. Unfortunately, it was so freaking miserable outside that I only managed to stay out long enough to regret that I didn't bring along any mittens. I, therefore, spent the majority of my time admiring the volcano from the confines of my toasty warm car. Doing so suited me perfectly fine, though, because I just wanted to see it. I just wanted to see that famous volcano with my very own eyes.

The rain never stopped, but unfortunately for all the men planting trees throughout the National Park, it wasn't an excuse for them to stop what they were doing. It looked to me that they had an impossible job to do, which seemed to be nothing short of reforesting the moon. The Weyerhaeuser Timber Company had their signs up all over the place indicating what forests were planted when, yet many of the forests struck me as looking way older than whatever date was indicated on a particular sign. The whole reforesting effort was incredibly impressive, but also incredibly odd. Here nature destroyed itself, and here was man putting nature back together. I was having a hard time understanding why humans weren't just letting nature heal itself, and all I could think was that man was just too impatient of a creature to allow nature to take its own course. It's not that I thought that tree planting was a bad thing because I always think that tree planting is flipping fantastic, but it was just that I wasn't expecting to see tree planting at all, and especially not on such a massive scale. The planted forests had a surreal look about them, though, because they were all planted in way too perfect rows. The forests lacked a natural ad-hoc appearance and driving by them row after row gave me the sense that they were all part of a secret forest militia. I was careful not to piss the forest army off for fear that the trees would come after me in a surreal military battle that I wouldn't know how to fight.

I couldn't believe the weather difference between Portland and Mount St. Helens when I discovered that Portland was having a perfectly fine spring day while I was shivering my butt off on top of the volcano. I went to Mount St. Helens totally naive about volcanoes, but by the time I returned to Portland, I fully understood that volcanoes didn't mess around. That volcano made its own weather up there, and it didn't give a damn about what the rest of the world was doing. I have to say that Mount St. Helens definitely intimidated me and made me feel that humanity was just a small part of a much greater whole. Nature fascinates me in ways that I'll never fully understand, and I will always remain in awe of nature's supreme majesty.

There was something else that I always heard about as a kid that made an impression on my juvenile psyche and made me think that I was born in the wrong era. The stories about the Oregon Trail captured my imagination and caused me to think that I would have been the sort of person who wouldn't have thought twice about making that great leap into the adventurous unknown. The Oregon Trail was the greatest American adventure this country has ever seen, but it is not something that anyone will get to experience today simply because there is no modern-day equivalent. There is nowhere left for Americans to start from total scratch anymore because our country is now thoroughly claimed. The Oregon Trail was a short-lived once-in-a-lifetime phenomenon that was seized by many but experienced by few, for many people died on that treacherous overland route.

I never gave much thought to where the Oregon Trail actually ended. I suppose that I just figured that people tumbled into Oregon willy-nilly and made a homestead for themselves wherever they happened to land. I never really envisioned the pioneers all gunning for the same end destination, but I have since learned that most emigrants ended up in one big clump at a place coined "Oregon City." Before I headed out on my Mount St. Helens trip, I researched Oregon City and learned that it still existed as a functioning suburb of Portland. I channeled my inner pioneer spirit and told it to get ready for a day of some serious reminiscing once I learned that an "End of The Oregon Trail Interpretive Center" was to be experienced there.

I want to bring up Lewis and Clark right now because I had brought along *The Journals of Lewis and Clark* with me to read. I was particularly interested in reading about their experiences in Oregon because I was aware that they spent an entire winter on the Oregon coast. It only took me a couple of paragraphs to figure out that they didn't care for Oregon very much. The Corps of Discovery members constantly complained that they were wet, cold, and sick most of the time. Overall, I got the impression their experiences there left them with a bitter taste in their mouths, and I imagined that they must have counted the days until the moment they could leave.

They obviously hated the weather, and I kept reading journal entries such as "cloudy with rain all day," and "rain as usial" (Clark's spelling), and "we are all wet and disagreeable." The turn of phrases went on and on like that, and nothing that they said remotely spoke of "seens of visionary inchantment" (Clark's phonetic spelling again), which was a phrase that Clark used to sum up his impressions of Montana. Lewis ended up dying before the Oregon Trail phenomenon became an actual thing, but Clark lived until 1838, which suggests that he might have heard about the first Oregon pioneer wagon that headed out in 1836. I don't know what his opinion might have been regarding anyone's decision to settle there, but I'm pretty sure that if anyone would have asked him, he would have point-blank told them that the Oregon Trail would be way more tempting if it ended anywhere in Montana.

I found Oregon City to be a cute little town, and it didn't take much imagination to envision what the place must have looked like when the pioneers first saw it. The location was definitely appealing, and I especially liked that the city was positioned right beside a nice fat river. I could totally see how the emigrants deemed this location to be a sort of paradise, what with its water, land, trees, and squeaky clean air. I was kind of thinking to myself, "to hell with what Lewis and Clark said, this Oregon City place is really nice and has tons of potential." Part of me was seriously thinking of moving there, but then the words of Lewis and Clark started bouncing around my brain. Their lamentations made me afraid of liking Oregon too much. I've never lived in a place where rain was such a constant companion, so I had my doubts that I had what it took to make me a good Oregonian. That thought made me wonder how many pioneers ended up being disappointed by the weather. Surely, they all had to know what they were getting into, but then again, the lure of adventure might have conveniently glossed over all the rainy bits and left them completely unaware.

Whatever the case, most emigrants probably moved to a climate that was different from wherever they had come from, and I'm sure that over time people just got used to the crappy weather simply because they had to. The rain evidently didn't scare people away because enough people moved to that part of the country to cause Oregon to become a state roughly nine years after California did. The California Gold Rush had already happened by the time most people were rolling into Oregon, so I imagine that those emigrants were on the hunt for the next best thing. Indeed, not everyone was born to be a miner, so it probably didn't matter that most of them missed out on their chance of getting rich quickly. For what it was worth, Oregon became the place to have a different life and have a shot at becoming something more than what one was expected to be. The emigrants went there in search of a life that wasn't stagnant, and they yearned to gain something more than what they were initially given. I'd like to think that those who settled in Oregon were actually anti-settlers because they chose not to settle with the status quo. They wanted to live in a changed world, and they wanted to be the ones to change it.

The country that they were living in was still relatively new, and they had the chance to mold it into whatever shape they desired. America was putty in their hands, whereas America today is a lump of hardened clay in ours. There is no running to virgin land anymore and forming a whole new society.

Metaphorically, when anyone moves to Oregon now, one does so carrying a slingshot, whereas, in 1850, one got to roll into Oregon armed with a full-blown cannon. Oregon was theirs for the taking, and those people certainly took. They took it away from the native tribes that already lived there, but that's, unfortunately, a familiar story for this part of the world. Stealing land from native peoples was and is how America has always functioned, and if someone wants to dispute that fact, they can go talk to any Sioux native at the Standing Rock Reservation and ask them about their opinions regarding the Dakota Access Pipeline. I am not a fan of America's past transgressions, but I am also not a fan of its current transgressions either. I am well aware that the past can never be changed, but it would be nice if we could amend the errors of our ways moving forward. Alas, America is not famous for its apologies, so it surprises no one that it does nothing to change how it acts, so the topic is a rather mute one.

After I strolled around Oregon City a bit, I made it over to the End of The Oregon Trail Interpretive Center, and it proved to be every bit as interesting as I anticipated it was going to be. I left the Interpretive Center wanting more, and lucky for me, the whole area around Oregon City was one big historical extravaganza once I knew how to look at it. I left the museum armed with a driving tour map, and I spent the rest of the afternoon driving the last leg of the Oregon Trail in the direction opposite from whence the pioneers came. It felt a little wrong to drive what was known as "The Barlow Road" essentially backward, but, hey, this was Oregon, and their salmon swam against the current, so in a sense, I was doing a very Oregonian thing. I'm used to doing things backward anyway because being left-handed means that I do most things weird anyhow. For example, when I flip through books, I invariably start from the back and flip to the front, which means that I always know how a story ends before it even begins.

One of the sites mentioned on my map was something called "the wagon lift," which marked the spot where the pioneers lowered covered wagons down a large hill. I got out of my rental car and hiked that section of the trail and searched for the wagon lift thing but only after not finding it did it dawn on me that the actual lift device probably disintegrated ages ago. I didn't even know what exactly I was looking for, but it felt good to step on the actual Oregon Trail itself and do a bit of daydreaming. It was a crisp spring day, and I listened to the sounds of trees rustling in the breeze and the cheerful chatter of birds filling the air with their pleasant babble. When I stopped moving, the whole world was still, and I was able to think. Think about what? Think about everything. Mainly, though, I thought about them, whoever all those pioneers were.

The American Dream

I know that I idealize the Oregon Trail experience. I am perfectly aware that the actuality of their lives was a lot less romantic than what my fantasies make them out to have been. Knowing that doesn't bother me, though, because it's less romantic to know that there is hardly a place left anywhere today for the modern Thoreau to theorize a new philosophy. The world has gotten too busy, and the din of traffic noise will invade one's thoughts and ruin one's concentration if one even so much as tries to invent a new philosophy. There is nowhere to escape to in the modern world, for land is not cheap. No one can just go out into any random forest and build a Thoreau-style cabin anymore because they will be slapped with a hefty fine and a trespassing lawsuit if they even try to. The cost of living has made it too expensive to be a philosopher anymore. Modern life is heavily regulated, and there is no more slipping through the cracks because Uncle Sam has drones, and he will find you. America is entirely owned by somebody else, and that somebody else is never anyone you remotely know. Big Brother owns America, and he is definitely not your sibling even though the name implies that he is. The only reason why I know any of this is because I have looked into dropping out of society many times before because I, for a very long time, have been wanting to get away. However, I have yet to figure out a successful way to do so.

I want to hide, but I can't afford to. The rich have it easy, for they can go anywhere and block the rest of the world out for as long as they desire. However, for us regular folk, a simple cabin beside a river or a cute little beach hut are nothing but pipe dreams because those are luxuries that we will never be able to afford. At best, we might be able to scrape up enough money to buy a crappy mobile home in the wilderness somewhere, but the odds are pretty good that some freaked-out Doomsday prepper would be right beside you and annoy you enough to make you want to move back to the city. I'm being sarcastic, of course, but only to a certain degree. What I personally want to do is get away from everyone, but doing so would put me out on the periphery where there is zero access to water and where the next major forest fire would likely burn

160

my dream cabin away. I know that I sound incredibly negative, but it seems to me that America is already taken, at least all the good bits of it are. What's left are all the places that no one really wants or the places where most people cannot afford. The days of free land in Oregon are over and have been over for quite some time, and from the Native American perspective, those were days that probably shouldn't have even happened to begin with. Nevertheless, the shape of America was carved out long ago, and all the leftover scraps have already been grabbed. The only things left are the new luxury condos that keep getting built on land that gets gobbled up by faceless big corporations.

Certainly, our forefathers knew how good they had it. They were running away from that which this current generation can no longer escape. The New Europe is here and has been here since the rich got richer and the poor got poorer. History has repeated itself, and class distinctions have returned. In my eyes, modern America looks a lot more like how old Europe used to look. Revolutionary America is not the America that I currently live in, and I, quite frankly, don't even know what to call this America that I live in now. Times are changing quickly, and I am often under the impression that my vote never really matters.

I did go to Washington, DC once and waited in a long line to get inside the darkened room that housed the United State's most hallowed yellowed piece of paper. The Declaration of Independence was displayed under a smoky sheet of plastic inside a bulletproof glass case, and those two materials combined made the document rather difficult to discern. When I first approached it, I was disappointed at how hard it was to make the thing out, but once my eyes adjusted to it, all kinds of thoughts rushed into my head at once. It was for this piece of paper that America was born. All those signatures on that document were signed by men who were not afraid to fight for a new country. They were determined not to be subjects of the British Empire anymore. It was highly possible that they already saw themselves as Americans even before a single drop of ink dramatically hit that page. They knew what they were, and they were ready for the rest of the world to see them the same way they already saw themselves.

I already said once that the answer to everything was money, but I'm going to say it again here because money was one of the reasons, if not the main reason, for the American Revolution. It all boiled down to taxes and the fact that they disagreed with paying many of them, especially when they considered that they had no representation in the British Parliament. I'm debating with myself right now if I should bring up my opinions regarding taxes and have decided that I'm just going to blurt some things out. I don't like paying taxes mainly because I don't have a say where I want my hard-earned money to go. I know that most of my tax dollars are used to buy military equipment and that knowledge greatly irritates me. I want my money to go toward environmental things or to healthcare and education. Why can't I request all of my tax dollars to go toward cleaning up rivers? I wouldn't even mind working overtime and handing over more tax dollars if I could choose where my money would go. As it is right now, I don't ever want to work overtime because I hate paying more taxes. Again, it goes back to that lack of control and the feeling like my vote never matters. It's that circle of futility that I always encounter when I try to make any sense of our government. I find a lot of things wrong with the American political system, but it's not something that I will elaborate further upon because there really is no point in doing so. It suffices to say that the topic of politics is futile because the only direction that it goes in is circles.

I had grand ideas about getting into thoughts about what it means to be an American, but I lost my mojo to do so after I just finished watching the Brett Kavanaugh confirmation hearings. As I edit this, things on the Supreme Court have only gotten worse now that Ruth Bader Ginsburg died and became replaced with her exact antithesis. My fear of where America is heading has grown even more concerning now that Texas passed draconian laws regarding abortions and guns. All of this doesn't bode well for democracy, let me tell ya. I just don't get it, I don't get it at all, and it hurts my head to think about it. This is what I am talking about when I say that I don't know what to call this America that I'm living in anymore. "Amer-wreck-a," maybe? We are living in a cold civil war.

There used to be this thing called "The American Dream," and maybe that's all it is anymore, just a dream. I can close my eyes and see it, so I definitely know what it looks like. However, the world I see when I open my eyes doesn't come remotely close to matching that vision. I think that what used to be The American Dream has changed today, but we haven't entirely redefined what it is just yet because we are still in the process of figuring it out. When I close my eyes, I can see the original American Dream – the dream of success and happiness, but that dream may as well be in black-and-white because it is so out of date. Success and happiness are hard to achieve nowadays, for it's more like success or happiness now, and there's no dream in not having both. No, The American Dream has to be something else now, and it has to be something that we can all strive for. Maybe the physical action of treading water is the new American Dream because that's what we're all doing anyway. We're all simply trying to stay afloat here and not let our heads go underwater. So, maybe that's what the dream's been reduced to – the dream of not allowing The American Dream turn into a drowning nightmare.

CHAPTER EIGHT:
Native America, 1998-2011

Native Americans

Geronimo. Everyone knows that name, and everyone knows that famous picture of him kneeling with a rifle. That photo is arguably one of the best images ever taken of any human being, and there is no denying the indomitable fierceness that stared out of his eyes. He was a man that was pissed off, and he was going to remain pissed off for the rest of his life and for the rest of forever. Crazy Horse. He was a man that was not afraid to die. He fervently believed in his people's way of life, and he fought to his very end to protect it. The Crazy Horse Monument that is being carved in the Black Hills is a sad tribute to the great warrior that will likely forever remain unfinished, just like how his own life will forever remain undone. Sitting Bull. He was a spiritual leader of the Ghost Dance. He believed in the power of ancestral spirits and the spirits' ability to fight off the encroaching white man. His Ghost Dance movement was the last-ditch grasp that the native people had on who they were as a people, but they lost their grip when the white man pried their fingers off their spiritual rope. Sacagawea. She was absolutely critical to the Corps of Discovery's survival. It was because of her intimacy with the land and her native skills that Lewis and Clark were able to make it all the way to Oregon and back. She crossed some of the land's most difficult terrain, and she managed to do so while carrying a newborn baby on her back. Cochise. He was a heroic warrior who fiercely defended his people, his homeland, and his way of life. He was a man who only wanted peace, and he was willing to murder every single white man if he needed to in order to achieve it. Red Cloud. He was a man who spent much of his life fighting. He fought soldiers, and he fought government agents, but always, he fought for his people. He said that the white man made many promises, but the only promise they ever kept was the promise to take their land away from them. Chief Joseph. He resisted the forced relocation of his tribe and fought until he could fight no longer. When he said the words, "I will fight no more forever," the spirit inside all native peoples died. The fight for their survival was over when they were told that a new age was beginning – a new age that didn't really see them in it.

Those people mentioned were the few Native Americans that I actually got to learn about in school, but they were not the only Native Americans to have ever mattered. There were centuries of wonderful, creative, brave, and noble native peoples that preceded those that lived after the Plymouth Rock landing, but who any of those people were didn't remotely concern any of my teachers. According to the educators, the only America that I needed to learn about was the one created after the pilgrims arrived in 1620. No mention was ever made of America's rich and fascinating pre-history, and I suspect that my teachers shied away from talking about early Native American history because doing so would have made standard American history seem terribly dull in comparison.

I've always loved history, but I didn't always love American history because I typically felt that my teachers took the lessons they taught way too seriously. It was always my opinion that American history tasted bland and needed a little bit of spice to make it more palatable. Our nation's history needed the spice of our nation's native peoples, but the American public education system didn't stock that vital ingredient in its metaphorical pantry. No doubt, it was good of my teachers to share some information about certain Native Americans with us, but it was also an abysmal oversight to withhold from us the story about Native America itself. I would have liked to have learned about North America's ancient past when I was younger because maybe then I would have grown up with a better understanding of this country's bona fide history. The native peoples shaped the United States in more ways than any of us can feasibly comprehend, and it is their stamp that is marked on the country that modern Americans currently live in. I essentially grew up not fully understanding what my home country was genuinely about, so it became my adult mission to figure out where it was exactly that I lived.

Cahokia

I started reading books about ancient North American history in my early 20s, and it came as a complete surprise to me when I learned that I apparently lived in a country that boasted a bona fide pyramid. Actually, it's more accurate to say that it more than pissed me off to learn that we had a legitimate pyramid here in the United States because my not knowing about it proved to me that I was never exposed to the more interesting bits of America's actual past. There definitely was an America before the Colonial Americans that I knew nothing about, and there could not have been a better structure than a pyramid to represent the mysterious past that lurked somewhere below the depths of this country's staid and sanctified history. It didn't really matter to me that the humongous grassy flat-topped mound pictured in the books didn't exactly look like a traditional pyramid, but a pyramid it undeniably was, and it must have held a certain power over the Native American's psyche. Pyramids never just happen, for they always need a reason to be created and a collective force to bring them into existence. Judging by the pyramid's massive size (the base was nearly equivalent to that of the Great Pyramid in Giza), it seemed pretty apparent that the structure once loomed large in Native America's earthly universe. I was curious to know what that universe used to look like a thousand years ago when they saw it from the top of that mound, and I especially wanted to know what sort of people were privileged enough to earn that specific view. Indeed, that view must have been exceptional, and whoever got to see the world from that vantage point must have seen more of the world than anyone else. Naturally, I couldn't help but to wonder what that same view looked like today, so one gray day in November, I made a pilgrimage to Native America's ancient homeland to try and obtain a glimpse of the universe that they used to see.

My journey to Native America's ancient past started at an archaeological site known as Cahokia Mounds State Historic Site, which was located near the border between Missouri and Illinois. To get there, I flew to St. Louis, which was a city that didn't convince me as being all that great after I tootled around some badly worn-out neighborhoods. The year was 1998 when I went, and the car tour that I gave myself was one of decrepit architecture depressing-ness. I drove by one grande dame building in disrepair after another in Old North St. Louis, and I got the impression that the city's better days were long behind it. Granted, I intentionally went to the worst side of town because that was where the more interesting buildings were situated. However, I left sooner than I wanted to because the city kind of scared me. I checked out a few other historical neighborhoods after that, but I couldn't shake the impression that Old North St. Louis was a good section of town to get shot in. I decided to abandon my joy ride early and made my way over to the Cahokia Mounds Park much sooner than I anticipated. I originally wanted to wait for the sun to get a little higher in the sky to burn off the nip that was putting some frost on my windshield, but I said, "Fuck it," to myself when my tootle around St. Louis wasn't as fun as I thought it was going to be.

The fact that Cahokia Mounds was a UNESCO World Heritage Site was a curious detail that wasn't promoted to unsuspecting travelers who casually drove right past North America's largest pre-Columbian earthwork without realizing that they did. I wasn't expecting to blow right by the pyramid myself as I was specifically on the road to find it, but then again, I wasn't exactly looking for it when I mindlessly drove along a very nondescript thoroughfare. However, blow right past it, I totally did, and I drove ten miles deeper into Illinois than I intended to before I realized that I didn't know where I was going. I vaguely recalled seeing a blur of green whiz over my left shoulder several miles back, so I made the wise decision to turn around and investigate the hunch that I might have missed it.

My suspicion proved correct, and it was indeed the pyramid that I traveled 1,500 miles to see that I had driven right past without the slightest bit of fanfare. I was thoroughly

169

baffled about how I initially missed it, and I remember exactly what my first impression was when I finally saw it: disappointment. I wasn't disappointed in the pyramid itself, but I was disappointed to learn that a humongous road was placed directly in front of it. The mere existence of a major road at the base of the pyramid proved to me that our nation didn't value the cultural monument enough to protect it from sooty exhaust fumes. The road being there told me all that I needed to know: Americans perceived the pyramid as being in the way.

I had only read the littlest bit about the pyramid's creators before I set off on my trip because I intentionally wanted to learn about the Mississippian culture in situ. My goal was to immerse myself in the historical landscape and mentally envision what their world looked like based on whatever my eyes presently saw, and what my eyes presently saw was a whole lot of green. Cahokia Mounds was a sprawling 2,200-acre site, and it filled my eyeballs with massive amounts of grass. Grass, grass, grass, as far as the eyes could see, grass, grass, and more grass. There was so much grass all around that it made me wonder if grass was a modern man's creation or if it was something that the natives had to manicure and mow as well. Five minutes into Cahokia, and all my thoughts were centered around grass and about how utterly strange grass really was. All around me were mounds of various shapes and sizes, and all of them were covered in heaps of the green stuff. I started to wonder whose job it was to mow all that grass and if that job was akin to painting the Golden Gate Bridge. I've heard that painting that bridge was a never-ending task that had to be started over the moment it was finished, so I imagined that whoever mowed Cahokia had to start over from the beginning as soon as the final acre was clipped.

To say that Cahokia was a large city for its time doesn't eloquently describe just how large Cahokia genuinely was back in its day. At its height in 1100 AD, there was no other city in the Mississippi valley that rivaled the size of Cahokia, and its position on the confluence of three significant rivers meant that Cahokia held most of the power in the region. Its influence was vast, and one didn't need to physically live anywhere near Cahokia to know where it was, for Cahokia was everywhere and filled everyone. Unfortunately, much of Cahokia today has been plowed over, intentionally removed, or erased by erosion, but I found what remained to be insanely powerful. It was impossible not to feel the spirits of Cahokia all over the landscape, for it was their blood in the soil that was making all that grass grow. A total of 80 earthen mounds (out of an original 120) dominated the otherwise flat landscape, and it was haunting to know that many of those mounds were burial tombs.

I started my journey inside Cahokia's visitor center, where many burial objects were on display. In archaeological parlance, it is correct to say that the burial objects were excavated from the mounds, but in layman's terms, it's correct to say that the burial objects were looted from those graves. I often feel conflicted emotions regarding the acquisition of grave goods, and none more especially than when I encounter Native American artifacts. Yet, the items pulled from those mounds were some of the most wonderfully curious objects that my eyes had ever seen, and I found the displays wildly intriguing. One object, in particular, stood out as being more curious than the rest, and that was a stone tablet carved with a figure coined "Birdman." I could try to explain what that figure looked like, but any attempt at putting that beaked, misshapen, man-bird into words is a feat that I don't know how to achieve. All I can say is that whoever carved him must have been on peyote and that he most likely smoked it out of one of the many beautifully wrought figurine smoking pipes that were on display nearby.

Aside from the wonderfully dopey-looking Birdman, many of the objects in that museum could have passed as being fine art by today's standards. Seeing such high-quality art made me wonder if whoever created those objects saw themselves as artists in the truest sense of the term. It got me thinking that Cahokia's society must have been based on a class system because not just any farmer could have carved most of those wonderfully rendered pieces. Undoubtedly, artists of that quality needed to have been specially trained, and that insight alone gave me a small window into their values. The people of Cahokia valued beautiful things, and they must have been well enough off that they could allow certain people to dedicate their lives to mastering artistic skills. Theirs must have been a stratified society, and it got me wondering if the artisan class was something that one needed to have been born into. Judging by the appearance of Birdman, I assumed that one was born into their social orders because whoever carved Birdman evidently did not naturally possess any artistic skills. No doubt, some other naturally talented person could have carved Birdman way better, but that person was probably given a farming tool to hold instead of a carving implement.

I eventually learned that not everything in Cahokia was a

bed of roses, however, when I read the informative plaque regarding Mound 72. I will simply call Mound 72 "The Death Mound" because that was where archaeologists discovered evidence of human sacrifice on a massive scale. I can't say that I was disappointed to read the facts regarding The Death Mound, but I'd be lying if I didn't say that I was a little disheartened by it. To me, human sacrifice always seems wrong, but maybe it wasn't to those who gave their lives for a cause that they believed was greater than themselves. History is always a leap into the unknown, so to understand it, one must attempt to understand what historical people were thinking. The Mississippians had a culture that they fervently believed in and a system of values they were trained to uphold. Culture has everything to do about how a particular society happens to be raised. Had I been born then as the same person I am now, my life would have very likely ended at the age of 21 when I would have been buried in one of those tombs to accompany my chief in his eternal afterlife.

I carried thoughts about time and place with me when I climbed to the top of the pyramid colloquially referred to as "Monks Mound." The modern-day view that I was rewarded with was a landscape composed of traffic and grass, but it wasn't too hard to imagine what the view from there used to behold. Cahokia at its peak must have looked amazing when it unfurled itself beyond the horizon, but the passage of time took that Cahokia away from the world and left us with the outlines of where it used to be. The wheels started to spin in my head when I looked at what was left of Cahokia today, and it got me questioning the concept of human origins. From where do we come from, I wondered? Of what purpose are we born at the time that we are? How different would I have been if I was born in a different era? Would I have been a different person if I had no schooling and a wildly different set of beliefs? Would it have mattered if I didn't know that the Earth revolved around the sun? Perhaps ignorance is bliss and who I truly am inside is unaffected by education. What would be left of me if I took away all my present-day cognition? Who, I asked myself, was I? Who, in fact, was anyone?

I was tempted to ponder what the meaning of life was, but I decided against doing so because I knew it was a question that couldn't be answered. Instead, I simply asked myself what it meant to be human. What did it mean to be real? Was happiness a factor? Perhaps. Perhaps not. Emotions are subjective, and happiness changes. Happiness lasts but for mere moments, so happiness could not possibly be the meaning of being human simply because humans are not always happy. To be human, I ultimately decided, was simply to be alive. To be human was to see, to feel, and to simply be. The meaning of being human was nothing other than the meaning of not being dead. Once a person's dead, the meaning of being human is entirely over. The important thing is to be alive to life when one's alive to it because the whole meaning of being human means absolutely nothing once life itself is over.

I imagined the original inhabitants of Cahokia returning to their city and surveying the landscape from the top of their slightly eroded pyramid alongside me. What would an original Cahokian with an intact Cahokian mind make of the landscape, I wondered? The city itself would probably look abandoned through a pair of Cahokian eyes because all the domestic structures that once filled the city with so much life had long ago melted away. Indeed, many burial mounds were still intact, but many burial mounds were no longer there. If given the right materials, the ancient Cahokians could resurrect the city, but I wondered what the point of doing so would be. Cahokia would be nothing if it didn't possess power, and the city lost that when a flood probably took it away. Living by large rivers doesn't come without risks, and the Cahokian's gambled against nature until they likely lost their entire wager.

Ancient Cahokia holds absolutely no meaning to modern Americans today. A new city had risen on the horizon, and even that city has already passed its apogee. The skyline of St. Louis hovered off in the distance as if to say to Cahokia, "I understand well what your fate was." The city of St. Louis was not entirely unlike Cahokia with its decaying houses and abandoned factories. The ancient Cahokian would have to decide which city was more worthy of a resurrection, the one with an arch or the one with a pyramid, and I'd venture to guess that the Cahokian would say to resurrect whichever one had the better potential of succeeding. *The Spirit of Cahokia* should have been the name of the plane that Charles Lindbergh flew from New York to Paris because I suspect that he didn't fly that route alone but had a Cahokian ghost for a co-pilot. Cahokians loved to achieve great things; moreover, they loved towering far above everyone else, so they probably already knew their way around the clouds and successfully guided Lindbergh to his highest aspirations.

Canyon de Chelly

Personally, I am not a big fan of heights, and I'm actually always a little bit afraid to fly, but I do harbor a passion for driving my car, sometimes for hours on end and to nowhere in particular. There is something almost spiritual about America and her miles upon miles of wide open roads. Driving long stretches of highway across the continent with nothing but the pavement below and the sky above is very tantric to me. I adore how America's roads speak to the young, call to the wild, and haunt the lonely. There is a freedom like nothing else when one drives for hours on end in a landscape of sheer emptiness. It's odd to think about how young America's roads are because they feel like they have been here forever. I sometimes find it impossible to believe that there once existed an America before her many highways. I often wonder what this country used to look like before so much pavement painted large swaths of it a specific shade of black.

Arizona, in particular, is blessed with lots of open space. However, much of that space has lines running across it and way too many semi-trucks barreling through it. There is hardly a portion of this state that does not have a service road penetrating its interior, so to envision an Arizona before its many roadways is almost impossible. Yet, such an Arizona did once exist and had existed for millions of years. I sometimes catch glimpses of its former existence when I accidentally find it hiding in tucked-away corners, but those glimpses are rare. Arizona is a rugged landscape full of inaccessible canyons, harsh deserts, extinct volcanoes, massive mountains, and vistas that go on forever, which altogether conspire to make it a challenging state to grasp. The state's most precious resource is water, but it's a resource that I rarely encounter because it tends to flow in the hardest-to-reach places. I used to wonder why so many Native American ruins were located in such impossibly remote canyons, but now I know that Native Americans lived wherever the rivers dictated them to be.

The Native Americans saw themselves as being just one part of a much greater whole. They were one with their environment, and they lived their lives very organically. The ancestral Native Americans were human beings in their most natural state, and there is both beauty and horror when I pause to give that concept some serious thought. I don't believe that I would even know how to be the same kind of human being that they knew how to be. Humans today see themselves as being set apart from nature rather than set directly in it, and the modern instinct is to battle nature, not embrace it. Nature is nothing more than a mere afterthought in the modern-day mindset, and it only gets considerable thought after nature does something destructive to humankind. It used to be that we could read nature, but now nature reads us, and it doesn't seem too pleased with the stories that it regrettably reads.

Humankind used to know that arguing with nature was pointless, and we never used to fight to stay in places where nature decided it didn't want us anymore. If the rain stopped coming to where people lived, people abandoned their homes and followed wherever the clouds went. The weather was one thing that ceremony could never control, and it was the constant flux of wet and dry spells that kept many native peoples on the continual move. Arizona, in particular, evidently went through more than its fair share of erratic climatic events, for there exists a plethora of ancient Native American dwellings that seem to have been up and abandoned. The native world was one of constant flux, and life must have moved around slowly in geographic circles. Where one generation might have started, another generation might have ended, and all the generations in the middle might have lived somewhere else in between.

Typically, when one comes across ancient dwellings, it's often hard to tell what the structures used to look like because the weight of time usually presses the ancient structures down to a pile of stones. Some ruins, though, miraculously dodge the effects of time and find a way to survive into the modern era relatively intact. The White House Ruins at Canyon de Chelly National Monument was originally a village created in two separate parts, and it was the part tucked inside an alcove that managed to survive relatively unscathed. No photograph of those ruins does them proper justice, though, for it's almost impossible to conceptualize where they exist. A massive sweep of rock looms directly above where the ruins sit, and it dwarfs them to such a degree that they seemingly disappear straight into the environment from whence they sprung. If I stare at photographs of the White House Ruins for too long, I stop seeing the ruins altogether and only see the menacing sweep of rock that seemingly threatens to crush the ruins to smithereens. There was always something quite fearful about that looming hunk of stone that would cause me to think that it wasn't the safest place in the world to tuck a human life under. I always wanted a bit more context when I looked at photos of the White House Ruins, though, and I hoped to gain that larger picture with my very own eyes someday.

As soon as I was old enough to rent a car in 1999, I did, and I drove it over 900 miles to Canyon de Chelly, Mesa Verde, and Monument Valley in four speed demon days. It was the first full-fledged road trip that I ever took by myself, and I had brought along a huge stack of CDs to keep myself company. There is something about having an excellent soundtrack to accompany a road trip that makes a good trip even better, and for this journey, my stand-out man was a guy named Jason Molina. His band called Songs: Ohia only had two albums out at the time, and I listened to them both incessantly because they fitted my mood so perfectly well. Normally, I would seize the opportunity right now to segue into the topic of music and go on and on about how great Jason Molina was, but I shall resist the temptation to do so and will strictly focus my thoughts on ancient America. However, if I did allow myself to stray a little bit, I would mention that Jason Molina will forever be my most favorite musical artist and that I'll never get over the sad fact that he drank himself to death at the too young age of 39. If I were so inclined to allow myself to continue, I would then go on to mention how I thought that the world could really use a movie about Jason Molina right now because his melancholic art was something that we could all relate to in our modern time of crisis. I would also then throw it out there that I already had an entire movie script written inside my head and that I would be willing to work with anyone who wanted to make such a film. I would, of course, then have to warn that someone that I envisioned my Jason Molina movie to be an art project of a sort and that I saw it being a little bit blurry and a little bit messy but clearly focused in the end. Alas, I will refrain from mentioning any such things, though, for I don't want to distract myself away from the thoughts about ancient America.

I got my first real-life look at the White House Ruins from an extremely far distance at the park's overlook when I first arrived, but the canyon's vertical wall dwarfed the ruins so entirely that they were almost impossible to see without squinting. The overlook was meant to provide a glimpse of the ruins, but what it provided instead was a sweeping view of the canyon itself in all its barren beauty. What was before me was glorious native country, and it looked incredibly foreign to my eyes. I had been to the Grand Canyon before, but Canyon de Chelly in no way resembled it. This canyon was its own entity, and it had something entirely different to say. I needed to get intimate with its ruddy rocks and its sheer cliff walls before I could understand the language that it spoke, yet I wasn't entirely sure where to point my ears or cast my gaze. I looked down and saw teeny-tiny people walking on a trail directly below where I stood, so I took them as a hint and followed wherever they were going.

I had read ahead of time that the trail to the ruins was a little precarious in parts due to uneven terrain, but I soon found out that the most dangerous thing about that trail was me. At one point, I looked up to survey all the beauty that surrounded me and then almost stepped off a precipice. After I caught myself from nearly falling off a cliff, I became super aware of where I placed my feet and made doubly sure that every step I took wasn't directly into thin air. The climb down the steep rock escarpment probably took way longer than it needed to because of my heightened paranoia, yet my languid pace did allow me to notice all the scrubby desert scenery in much greater detail than usual. I saw a beauty in the desert that I typically tended to ignore, and there were times on my slow walk down that I actually stopped to admire something relatively mundane. The natives always knew what they were looking at when they peered into the desert, but I knew absolutely nothing about anything that I saw. I didn't have a clue what any of the bushes that I admired could have done for me if my life totally depended upon them, and I genuinely wondered how much native knowledge had been lost throughout the years. I took a moment to wonder how many generations it would take to gain all that lost knowledge back and concluded that humanity would probably need to start completely over again if we wanted to know even half of the things that the natives once understood.

I eventually reached the canyon bottom's riparian zone and enjoyed the dappled sunlight as it filtered through the modest forests of cottonwoods, mesquites, and tamarisks. It was late October when I was there, and many of the cottonwoods were dropping their leaves. The falling leaves made me feel like I was walking into the past because the autumnal atmosphere felt like home to me. I connected with the ancient ghosts that I sensed were there and everything around me, for just the briefest moment, looked utterly familiar. The time-space continuum did not exist every time a breeze tossed some leaves off the trees, but in moments when the wind didn't blow, I found myself very much in the present moment where I only half-heartedly wanted to be. I wanted to be there, wherever the spirits were, and when the leaves fell, I was among them, and it felt good, so very good.

It is in such moments as those when I generally prefer to be alone. I don't always need people around me, and I know myself well in silence. I sometimes think that I exist better with trees than I do with people, yet I also believe that it is the land that links people with each other. It was the land that I was walking on in Canyon de Chelly that connected me with the spirits that used to live there, and it was the land that was the portal that connected us all. I felt a sense of oneness with everyone around me, whether they were in spirit form or flesh, and my preference for aloneness lost all meaning when I felt that I was part of everyone. It was an epiphany for me to feel that way because I generally don't care to be around a whole lot of people, but while at Canyon de Chelly, I not only wanted to be around others, but I wanted to *be* other people as well. I wanted to feel what it was like to be everyone past, present, and future, and I wanted to physically touch the common thread that bound us all as one species.

I approached the White House Ruins with a sense that I was returning home to a life that I never knew I lived. If I didn't believe in reincarnation before I approached the ruins, I definitely believed in reincarnation when I was near enough to practically touch the ruined structures. The ruins, however, were not to be touched due to their fragile condition and were fenced off from visitor's pawing hands. One was only allowed to touch the ruins with a pair of eyes from a respectable distance and drink in the view with a metaphorical straw. From where I stood, I admired the appearance of the White House Ruins and mused about how I didn't think that the buildings looked real. The more than 1,000-year-old adobe structures were built into a cave and right to the very edge of a precipice high up in a vertical rock wall, and the tight collection of houses looked like a surreal Native American fantasy. The Ancestral Puebloans that once lived in those deftly perched abodes must have been an imaginary race because I found it hard to believe that they didn't know what vertigo was. The fact that they evidently had no fear of heights made me think that the ruins emerged out of a past that didn't seem to belong to the human race, and with that thought in mind, if reincarnation was real, then I must have once been an alien.

It was amusing to think that the Ancestral Puebloans were actually aliens from outer space, but deep down, I was fairly certain that they were bona fide human beings from planet Earth. The Ancestral Puebloans themselves never thought that they came from anywhere else other than Canyon de Chelly, and they even claimed to know who their creator was. They believed that their creator was an Earth Goddess known as the Spider Grandmother, and they believed that her spirit lived inside a tall sandstone spire formation known as Spider Rock which was located not very far from where they resided. The Spider Grandmother lived among the people she created, and she wasn't simply Mother Earth but was the very Earth itself. The Ancestral Puebloans believed that they emerged from the very same land that their goddess resided in and her being there meant that the earthly world and the spirit world were an integrated whole. Spider Rock rose like a sentinel in the center of Native America's version of Eden, and the question of their origins was never a mystery to them, for they never left the landscape from whence they sprung.

I was raised as a Christian, and the supposed location of my origins exists on the other side of the world in some mythical Garden of Eden that no longer exists. The fact that my origin's true location is forever lost means that the concept of Eden will never be anything more than just a fantasy. It actually doesn't matter that there is no Eden for me to go back to because even if Eden were a real place, it would be located somewhere far away and possibly in the center of a war zone. Christianity is a

Middle Eastern religion, and I always find that my mind has to travel to its farthest reaches to envision where many of its stories took place. It is not a religion that feels particularly close to home, and I have always felt a certain level of disconnect toward it. In comparison, the original inhabitants of North America had no reason to believe that they arose from anywhere other than where they already resided, and their creation stories placed their land and their people at the center of all things. Their creation story was never an imported myth created by a culture that was not their own, and John Milton would never have written his epic poem *Paradise Lost* had he been born a Hopi.

Human beings have an insatiable quest for knowledge, and we're desperate to know how we became the creatures that we've become. We all want to know what great event caused us to be born on this incredible blue planet, and the modern-day answer to the question of our origins is entirely determined by one's faith in either science or religion. It was while I stared at Spider Rock that I realized just how much we are all products of whatever time that we are born in, for no ancestral Native American ever gave thought to the possibility of evolution. It was there where I realized that my mind was not molded by my own creative force but was instead molded by all the available information that surrounded me. I was essentially nothing more than a creature of culture, and the thoughts that I believed were my own were really just thoughts that I was trained to believe in. I realized that all religions were simply products of their own place and time, but I also thought that maybe science suffered from that same predicament as well. Science was something that I assumed was unchanging, but then I acknowledged that even science changes with every new discovery. I decided right then that I didn't know what I believed in, and it felt perfectly fine to admit that to myself. All was flux, and what I believed in didn't actually matter because a thousand years from now, someone else standing on the same spot and looking at the same view would most likely believe in something entirely else. I do truly hope to be born again so I can be that person who will stare at Spider Rock a thousand years from now and contemplate humanity's story.

Mesa Verde

From Canyon de Chelly, I headed over to Mesa Verde National Park and drove through a desolate landscape of scrubby nothingness and mobile homes. The Navajo Nation occupied that corner of Arizona, and its unfortunate reputation for being one of the poorest places to live in the country was made evident by the plethora of tires I saw tossed on top of people's roofs. Mobile homes are notoriously noisy, and people discovered that throwing some weight on the roof helps alleviate them from rumbling in the wind. Apparently, someone got disillusioned with the effectiveness of the tires, though, and chose instead to toss a deer carcass on their roof. Seeing that lovely thing rotting up there was an arresting visual that logged itself permanently inside my brain. Yet, what I saw when I drove through the Navajo Reservation was poverty's exterior, and I didn't remotely get a glimpse of what that poverty looked like on the inside. Outsiders might think that they know what it's like to live on a reservation after a quick drive through one, but the fact that outsiders don't actually live on one means that they won't ever truly know. The modern-day road trip through America's poorest section reveals nothing to the casual traveler other than the realization that there exists a large portion of the country that they know nothing about.

There is something both lonely and appealing about wide-open spaces that seemingly go on forever. Much of the Navajo landscape was so utterly flat that it lulled my mind numb. I drove over a hundred miles without thinking about a single thing, and it was only when I got closer to Mesa Verde National Park that my reverie was finally shaken. The flat land of foreverness morphed into the distant past when I entered Mesa Verde's craggy world of mesa, canyons, and precipices. Suddenly, the world wasn't desolate anymore, and instead of looking at nothing, my eyes landed on some much-needed trees. Pinyon pines and junipers abounded and gave an otherwise gray world of rocks some lovely shades of green. It was apparent that time had done its bidding on the landscape at Mesa Verde for quite a long while, and there was something peculiar about that landscape that seemed older and more knowing. Nature was humankind's original mentor, and Mesa Verde was where man learned how to become the human being that he grew to become.

People visit Mesa Verde today because they want to know what it is like to step inside an image they've seen a hundred times before in countless magazines. Mesa Verde's famous cliff dwellings are highly photogenic and exhibit an exotic appeal that strikes viewers as being too surreal to actually believe. Indeed, there is nothing about the ruins at Mesa Verde that looks familiar to a modern pair of eyes, and it is precisely that unfamiliarity that draws most people to that park. The ruins at

Mesa Verde represent everything that modern cities are not, for most people today lack an intimate connection to the natural world. In comparison, the Ancient Puebloans lived very organically in anti-cityscapes that merged seamlessly into the environment, and their villages must have pulsated with an intensely feral vibe. The Pueblo villages at Mesa Verde were built above, below, and inside mountains. It was hard for me not to wonder if the ancient inhabitants were more animal than human because I had a difficult time figuring out where man ended and where nature began the more I stared at the remnants of the ancient Puebloan world.

The builders of Mesa Verde did not see the world in black-and-white but instead saw the world in circles and squares. It was shapes that dictated pueblo society and gave the communities a distinct appearance. Groups gathered in circle kivas and families lived in square abodes. Living in a pueblo village was visually obvious as well as incredibly convenient, for everything that the villagers needed was located either above, below, or in the center of where the community lived. Farming occurred above, hunting occurred below, and everything acquired was processed or consumed somewhere in between. Life didn't extend much beyond their immediate surroundings for the simple reason that life didn't need to. By all appearances, the cliff dwellings looked like they were built by a group of people who knew something about life that we today are no longer privy to. If I had to propose a theory as to what they knew then that we no longer know now, it would be that humans didn't need very much beyond what they could provide for themselves.

Again, being at Mesa Verde had me pondering the concept

of human origins. I was glad that I wasn't born at Mesa Verde because although it seemed like life was simple there, living there looked like it was very hard. Soot stains had blackened the walls, which indicated that Pueblo life was very smokey. Living there must have been cramped, smelly, dirty, and probably only as comfortable as always being slightly starving could have possibly been. More than anything, the landscape around Mesa Verde looked hungry to me. One bad harvest would have caused their lives to teeter on the very same edge that their cliff dwellings were built upon, and it's frightening to think about how much of their lives were lived on a precipice. I suspected that living on a razor's edge must have affected their perception of the world and likely caused them to see a thinner line separating life from death than we notice today. Life to them must have seemed very tenuous, but then again, maybe life just seemed perfectly natural. The Native Americans only ever knew how to live as active members in the natural world, so surviving in the wild was the only way they knew how to be. It's no understatement to say that they lived nearly everywhere that we no longer do now. Almost all their former cities in the American Southwest were abandoned centuries ago, and no one has since entertained the thought of moving into any one of the sheer number of ruins left behind in the Four Corners region. I suspect that their former cities remain empty simply because none of their villages strike us as realistic places to eke out a modern-day existence.

The community at Mesa Verde was just but one piece of a much greater whole, and the larger picture extended over an insane amount of geography. The Four Corners region was once densely populated, and there is hardly a canyon or a cave that doesn't hold some haunting reminder that the area was once known as home to many generations of families. Not a single nook or cranny was overlooked, and people lived their lives wherever they could fit themselves in. The natural real estate options were essentially endless, and it's not going out on a limb to say that the Four Corners region is probably where North America's first major metropolis was originally located. Surprisingly for how vast the Four Corners region was, most of the villages were well connected either by footpaths or smoke signals, which undoubtedly helped make the large distances feel much smaller. The entire Four Corners region used to be one super-sized community, and I supposed that it still technically was once I considered how many ghosts still probably resided in their former abodes.

Hovenweep

To describe what the Four Corners region looks like, it's best to imagine what the sound of nothing makes and allow that silence to paint a visual inside the head. The absolute quiet needs to be almost deafening, and that silence needs to melt the imagined landscape into a void. That void needs to hang suspended in the nowhere space that lies between past and present, and that void needs to have always been there. The Four Corners region is where limbo resides, and that limbo is filled with air, sky, and beauty. Lots and lots of beauty. The Four Corners region's landscape yearns to be seen, yet it only reveals itself to viewers gradually. One must become intimate with the landscape first before one can claim to know it well, and those who do know it well know that it is not a place for the timid. Survival is never a guaranteed thing in the high desert, and it is an excellent place to discover what it takes to remain truly alive.

When I started to learn about ancient North America, I came across a hundred photographs of Mesa Verde's famous cliff dwellings before I came across a single photograph depicting the lesser-known contemporary site of Hovenweep. I remember exactly what the first image of Hovenweep was that I saw, and it was a picture of a partially ruined tower perched on top of a boulder that had massive drop-offs on all four sides. The image was visually arresting, and it made me think that the Ancient Puebloan race must have been entirely composed of magicians because it looked as though one needed a pair of wings to reach the structure's door. Indeed, every photograph that I came across of Hovenweep was visually arresting, and it wasn't a stretch to believe that those who once inhabited that site were an inhuman race. Too many of the ruins looked as though they were put there by someone or something else, and the city overall looked entirely too impossible to actually believe. Naturally, I instantly wanted to go there and see that magical city with my very own eyes so that I could convince myself that it was a place that existed in the realm of reality.

The Ancestral Puebloan world was extensive, and it once covered an area that today resides within modern-day Arizona, Utah, Colorado, and New Mexico. However, the outlines of their ancient boundaries are now difficult to discern, and it's possible to roam over parts of their ancient homeland and not even know that they were once there. If someone wants to see where the ancient Puebloans used to reside, one has to go to the Four Corners region with that explicit intention in mind and go there prepared to do a whole lot of driving. The distances between the patchwork of ancient monuments in the Four Corners region are incredibly vast and frequently upon roads that are rutted and unpaved. Hovenweep is the main attraction at an extensive archaeological site known as Canyons of the Ancients National Monument. The dirt roads inside that 275 square mile Monument have a reputation for being particularly bad, but Ryan and I blatantly chose to disregard that knowledge in 2011 when we stupidly drove our rented compact car down a horrifically muddy stretch. Long story short is that we didn't see as much of the Canyons of the Ancients National Monument as we originally intended to because we spent the greater portion of our time there digging mud out of our car's wheel wells.

When Ryan and I arrived at Hovenweep on our Four Corners Road Trip Extravaganza, we pulled up under a bluebird sky that turned majestically sour in a matter of minutes. We didn't get very far on the interpretative trail before we heard a distant rumble of thunder that heralded to us that the time was ripe for a picnic in the car. Summer on the Colorado Plateau is notoriously unpredictable in a predictable way, and we had learned from experience that the sound of thunder, no matter how faint or how distant, meant that we were going to get wet in a matter of minutes unless we did something about it. We had been caught off guard in the high desert enough times before to know that storms had an annoying tendency to materialize out of nowhere, so it was no surprise to us that we found ourselves back in our vehicle within mere moments of our arrival. We also knew from experience that high desert storms tend to be intense but also very quick, so we busted out some snacks and waited for the entertainment to begin. Just as we expected, the rain came fast and furious. We pleasantly munched on trail mix as we watched helpless visitors get pelted by slanting shards of rain as they ran pell-mell in the parking lot in a glorious fit of pandemonium. Their surprised shrieks were a familiar sound, for we had made those same sounds ourselves before, and we both admitted to each other that we each felt a little schadenfreude. Much to our joy, everyone was under the impression that the raging storm was going to last for a while, and we took it upon ourselves to secretly wave goodbye to every car that high-tailed it out of the parking lot until we were the last car remaining. When the storm ended about an hour later, we emerged from our cocoon and reveled in the fact that Hovenweep was now solely ours to explore.

The summer sky after that storm was stunning, and the air was scrubbed so squeaky clean that it made the entire landscape look like an enhanced memory. It was almost as though the film of time was lifted, and there was nothing for us to forget and only things for us to remember. The ruins of Hovenweep after the rain were instantly familiar, and they gave us the strange sense that this was somewhere we had always known. Here was where many of our memories had disappeared to when we didn't know where most of our memories had gone.

So much of Hovenweep was in ruins, but then again, so much of it also wasn't. The entire landscape was littered with giant walls that held up nothing but the sky, and the first word that came to mind when we came upon the extensive collection of ruins was haunting. What was spread out before us was a ghost town in the truest sense of the term, and we didn't pause to wonder where all the ghosts had gone because we could feel them all around us. It wasn't hard to imagine what life must have been like there because there were plenty of ghosts around for us to spy on.

Hovenweep National Monument was created to protect six clusters of Ancestral Puebloan villages that were either ingeniously tucked into canyons or curiously placed on top of massive boulders. When Ryan and I were there, we couldn't resist a game of pretend house shopping, and we both picked a property that we wanted to pretend live in. We ended up choosing ruins that were located nowhere near each other which would have made our pretend lives rather inconvenient, so we decided to nix our choices and went pretend house shopping again together. We both ultimately agreed that we could pretend live in the ridiculously tall Square Tower but then decided against it when we realized that neither of us could figure out how the heck to get inside it. We then both settled on moving into Hovenweep Castle instead because it was an attractive building that offered plenty of space. I then read the brochure that I was carrying around and learned that we would be responsible for making astronomical observations if we lived in there. We really didn't trust ourselves to be the ones responsible for announcing to the village of ghosts when the time was ripe for planting or sowing the crops, so, in the end, we choose to move into some random ruin that was tucked inside a little nondescript alcove somewhere off to the side where no one would expect anything from us instead.

Most cities start with a center and then naturally grow outward like growth rings on a tree, but that exactly describes what did not happen at Hovenweep. Hovenweep lacked a definable center and grew out more like an octopus than it did a tree. The city sprawled out its tentacles across the landscape as if the canyons were an open-faced Mariana Trench without any water. Hundreds of former dwellings had receded into the canyons from which they sprung, and to recognize some of the former abodes required a discerning eye. Like the octopus that Hovenweep always was, the city had camouflaged itself into its surroundings and thus rendered itself nearly invisible, so it took some training to get the eyes to learn what it was that we were asking our eyes to seek.

Hovenweep felt like it was a city that we could understand because it was replete with suburbs and exurbs even. Indeed, Hovenweep was not just one village but was one village among many. To understand Hovenweep properly, one needs to take the entire landscape as far as the eyes can see and even beyond that into full account. We were curious to see what the rest of the area looked like, so we decided to go ruin house shopping in the outlying villages. We wanted to find a ruined property with fewer neighbors because where we ultimately chose to pretend live was a little too hemmed in for our tastes. We were fully aware that living in the exurbs would translate to a longer commute when we wanted to go back to the original hood and visit our ghost friends, but we were new to the area and wanted to consider all of our options. In a way, it felt totally wrong to superimpose our modern expectations regarding home buying onto that landscape, but we were having fun doing so, well, at least we were having fun doing so up until the moment that our car got stuck in the mud. The bad thing about schadenfreude is that it sometimes comes back to bite you in the butt, so we knew right away that no one was going to come to our rescue. We were in a rental car, so there was nothing in there tool-wise that would have helped us do any digging, so we scoured the landscape for the strongest sticks that we could find and solidly went to work. There were a few moments when we both thought that our ruin house hunting was actually going to pay off because the mud was caked into the wheel wells so thoroughly that it looked like we were going to be stuck there forever, but the fear of actually living in a ruin put a fire under our butts. I almost wish that someone would have seen us because I am sure that we looked ridiculous stabbing at all that mud with puny little sticks, but no one came by because we were in the middle of nowhere. Most of the dirt roads were mysteriously unmarked, and the monument map that we had was so positively useless that we didn't even know where we were other than "somewhere-ish." We were on the hunt for the pueblo labeled "The Horseshoe Ruins" before we spontaneously stopped to dedicate an hour of our lives to dig the car out of mud, but once we accomplished that feat, we allowed the hunt to continue, albeit we wisely chose to go it on foot.

I'm not even sure how we found the ruins because neither of us saw any signs that might have kindly pointed us to them. I do remember at one point that I said out loud that our search for the ruins felt a little like a modern-day version of Coronado's expedition for the Seven Cities of Cibola. I was half looking for a lost city made out of gold, but I knew deep down that we were really searching for an abandoned city made out of stones. When we did finally find the ruins, I liked the idea that we stumbled upon one of the cities that Coronado was looking for, but there was no way that would have been the case because most of the Four Corners region was already abandoned for at least 200 years before Coronado might have rolled up to them in 1540. History is full of all kinds of crazy stories, but the story of Coronado's expedition from Mexico to Kansas in a wild search for riches definitely ranks as one of the crazier ones, mainly because his entire journey ended up being a wild goose chase for nothing. I can totally imagine that Coronado had zero appreciation for knowing that he was seeing things and meeting people that no one else in the world knew even existed because all he wanted to see and meet was a big pot of gold at the end of a rainbow. Conquistadors, they totally baffle me. They were definitely the wrong people to unleash upon the New World because they were only in it for the money that they assumed was theirs for the taking, and they weren't averse to murdering native peoples to take what they thought was rightfully theirs to steal.

As I admired the delicately perched ruins that were dangling on the edge of a cliff, the thing that I most wondered about was how? How did they do it? How different was the world when they lived in it? There had to have been more water when they were there, and the loss of that water had to have been the reason why they abandoned their homeland. Looking at the ruins, I got a sense that the people who walked away from them did so reluctantly and left their homes with the intention of someday returning. The villages at Hovenweep were too beautiful to leave behind, and there was no possible chance that wherever they went to next was even half as dazzling as the villages they had to say goodbye to were. Hovenweep was their home, and if they could have taken their buildings and their landscape with them, they most certainly would have done so. The landscape around Hovenweep was who they were since time immemorial. How could they have walked away from the land they identified with unless there were reasons outside of their control that forced them to do so? Everyone talks about the rise and fall of the Roman civilization, yet no one ever mentions a word about the rise and fall of those who inhabited the Four Corners region.

So, what exactly *did* happen to the ancient inhabitants of all those marvelous ruined structures? The general consensus states that a prolonged drought forced all the inhabitants in the Four Corners region to migrate south, where they eventually re-established themselves to become the modern-day Pueblo, Zuni, and Hopi people. When I stopped to give the idea of mass migration some serious thought, it made me wonder how many years had to go by before the inhabitants had to concede that the rains were never coming back. How many people had to die before they were finally convinced that their way of life was permanently altered, and they all had to find a different place to live? At what point did they know that it was either leave or watch everyone around them perish? It was hard for me to imagine the heartache they must have suffered through when they finally decided to leave behind what took generations to build and not having any choice in the matter. The Hovenweep ruins were sentinels that stood guard over a silent trauma that left chilling scars upon that landscape forever.

Chaco Canyon

For as enigmatic as Hovenweep was, the UNESCO World Heritage Site known as Chaco Canyon was even more so particularity because of its sheer size and for the fact that archaeologists can't seem to agree whether or not people once permanently lived there. What archaeologists do agree on, though, is the theory that Chaco served as a special gathering place for ceremonies due to the undeniable amount of evidence that points to the fact that Chaco was no ordinary city. It seems as though the Chaco basin acted as a natural calendar for the ancient Pueblo people circa 900-1150 AD, and its unique location organically dictated how to align many of its buildings with solar, lunar, and cardinal directions. Chaco's extensive sphere of influence traveled far beyond its immediate surroundings, and the power of Chaco seemingly seeped deep into people's bones. Chaco drew people in like zombies and caused its visitors to venture over endless miles of challenging terrain. Many of the sacred paths that they traveled on faintly remain on the New Mexican landscape today and can be best appreciated in aerial photographs.

Our journey to Chaco National Historical Park officially started on the outrageously rough dirt road that was so badly washboarded that we could have channeled our inner Victorians and did our laundry on it. For 13 long miles, we debated over whose butt was getting more rattled, and our bottoms were only given a rest when we unexpectedly came upon a herd of sheep that were getting shepherded by a dog. There were no humans in sight, just a dog and his sheep, and seeing that most adorable dog working harder and happier than any human would caused me to fall instantly in love with the area around Chaco. Overall, the drive took us over an hour to complete, but it was totally worth it. Our achy bodies were redeemed when we exited the car and stumbled onto a desolate landscape that had us believe that we drove all the way to the moon.

The whole of Chaco Canyon was a massive barren place. The huge quiet landscape hosted a motley of ruins that seemed as though they sprouted from the soil like mushrooms after a rain. Yet, rain was not something that happened very often at Chaco, and there wasn't a single tree in sight to shelter under even if it did. In fact, there was nothing much to indicate that a whole lot of nature survived at Chaco at all, and the fact that there were so many ruins on the landscape really did kind of muck with my brain. I wondered how humans managed to survive in a place where not even plants or trees were crazy enough to plant their roots. It was hard not to wonder what motivated people to build an extensive community in a place that looked as though it had no interest in sustaining life, any sort of life, at all. What was it about Chaco Canyon that drew people to it and made people want to celebrate it?

Chaco Canyon was a place that the Ancient Puebloans believed in. People came to Chaco because their culture devised a belief system that was entwined with the Chaco landscape. Earth, sun, moon, stars, all of it spiritually resided there. Chaco Canyon was where the heart of the pueblo peoples resided, and it was not a place they were trivial with. The ancient peoples took their actions at Chaco seriously, for they likely believed that the very nature of their survival wholly depended upon the outcomes of the ceremonies they performed there. Unfortunately, the original believers of Chaco have long since disappeared, and Chaco proved to be a difficult place for me to wrap my head around simply because I couldn't see what it was that they saw. I just don't look at the world the same way that they did. I don't see the moon, sun, and stars writ upon the landscape around me. I don't personally *need* to see how a shaft of light falls upon a spot on a building at a certain time of year because my life moves according to dates printed on a calendar. I loved the idea of Chaco, but Chaco will never function as somewhere that I'll ever need.

The most famous ruin among the many ruins at Chaco Canyon was the great house ruin known as Pueblo Bonito. The multi-roomed structure was technically a ruined ruin because a sizable section of it got buried under a massive pile of boulders. Large rocks sheared off the canyon wall during a storm in 1941, and it was an event that the ancients always feared and tried to prevent from happening. Prayer sticks and support logs were found wedged between the canyon wall and the teetering boulders, which indicated that the ancient builders were well aware of the precariousness of their situation. Yet, the builders of Pueblo Bonito placed the great house where they did because the celestial alignments could not be defied, so they accepted their fate and put their faith in prayers as well as in some practical engineering.

Pueblo Bonito was a massive great house even by typical Puebloan standards. The unusual D-shape building contained several hundred rooms piled several stories high and possessed more kivas than what an average Puebloan village would typically know what to do with. Altogether, the entire structure was one gigantic and dizzying maze, and its craziness inspired me to keep an eye out for M.C. Escher's ghost the whole time I was there. Other visitors kept materializing out of rooms and off of staircases that I swore weren't there a second ago. Walls functioned as if their original purpose was always to hold the sky above them as a roof. Being in ruins suited Pueblo

Bonito's personality well, for it gave it a way to express itself creatively. Sheared corners, missing ceilings, and invisible floors altogether made Pueblo Bonito who it was now. Overall, she appeared at peace with her transformation and seemed quite willing to flaunt it. Pueblo Bonito was always meant to house hordes of people, and she still technically did despite her faded and crumbled beauty.

The great house was designed to shelter the hundreds of people who all came to Chaco to perform the ceremonies that were deemed necessary to keep their entire world in tune. Theirs was an entirely different mindset, and I spent the whole time at Chaco thinking that whoever once came there had to be something other than human. The reason why I say that was because there was a particular staircase carved into a rock that just didn't seem humanly possible to utilize unless a person had suction cups for feet, a zero fear in heights, and a penchant for dropping into an abyss. That staircase was literally carved into the curving edge of a cliff and seriously disappeared into a void. I assumed that there must have once been a ladder underneath that staircase to catch all the dangling feet, but if that was the case, then they indeed constructed the world's longest ladder to have ever graced this planet, and I lamented the fact that there wasn't a single thread of its former existence to prove that it was ever there.

Chaco exists in a league of its own as far as ancient sites are concerned in the United States, and the fact that the site was once so sacred made our modern-day pilgrimage there a profound one. More than anything, Chaco Canyon was a feeling, and we got the sense that Chaco was always meant to be experienced cerebrally. Chaco was a frame of mind, and once we left that site, our Chaco mentality came along with us. We left the physical Chaco exactly where we found it and filled our heads with Chacoan thoughts that stuck with us throughout our next Pueblo destination.

Bandelier

Bandelier National Monument was another ruin site that I was excited to visit. It took us three hours to drive the 135 miles to it from Chaco, but it would have taken us approximately 42 hours to walk to it had we chosen to hike an ancient footpath that would have led us there. Footpaths, might I mention, proved to be quite the theme at a Bandelier satellite site known as Tsankawi, and it quickly became my favorite place because it looked like an American version of Pompeii and Atlantis smashed together as one. Deeply rutted footpaths were scoured into the soft volcanic tuff so severely that it gave us both the impression that Tsankawi was occupied since at least forever ago. The abandoned caves, the worn-out trails, and the footpaths that doubled as staircases got my imagination rolling into directions that were being newly forged inside my head. I was desperate to know how many years had to go by before those paths emerged to look how they did. 50? 100? 200? 1,000? 5,000? 10,000? Any one of those numbers could have been the correct answer because there was no way of knowing how long that area had been visited or occupied by hunters and gatherers. The earliest Native Americans could have been the first ones to have started those paths, and everyone else since then likely followed their lead since time immemorial.

From how worn out the paths were, it was evident that life hadn't changed very much for a very long time, and I surmised that every generation must have looked relatively the same to a certain degree. As usual, it was easy for me to glorify what ancient life must have been like, but deep down, I knew that my glorification of ancient life was grossly misleading. I always think that life must have been simpler back then because it just wasn't possible for people to live beyond their means. There were no McMansions to maintain, there were no Joneses to keep up with, and there were no lawns to mow or hedges to trim. Life back then had boundaries, shared values, and modest expectations. There was a collective mindset that kept their world in some sort of order, and survival depended on everyone doing what they were expected to do. I enjoy idealizing what I think their values must have been because whatever qualities I think they possessed is what I strive to attain for my own being. I want to embrace nature more, I want to value the land I live on, and I want to exist very simply. Also, there was a wild side about the ancient Native Americans that appeals to my sensibilities, and I like it that they thought they were the only ones living on this planet. The entire world as they knew it was all theirs to enjoy, and I find their ignorant bliss enticingly appealing. My mind only rarely wonders about how uncomfortable life must have been. I rarely ponder about how often they coughed smoke out of their lungs or how many times a day their stomachs rumbled because there wasn't enough food to satisfy their stomachs. The only variable in life was the weather, and shamans could only do so much to make it rain before everything went to total crap and the entire village had to move somewhere and start anew.

The cities that the ancients left behind make it possible for us to deduce who they were as a people, but I fear that the same cannot be said of us when the day comes for someone in the future to sort through all our personal belongings. When our civilization dies, there will be so much crap leftover that it will be impossible to deduce who we exactly were. The cities that we will leave behind will be full of unnecessary clutter and stupid little things. We will essentially be uninterpretable and written off as wasteful beings that had no clear set of values. It is wishful thinking that we could leave behind nothing because we are too far gone now even to think that we could clean up the mess that we spewed all over the globe. Modern civilization is ugly, and I'd prefer to look at a domestic trash heap every morning if doing so meant that the rest of the nature around me was as pristine as it was 1,000 years ago.

Unfortunately, the America that Ryan and I wanted to see no longer existed, and what we saw instead were the shattered remains of the America that used to be. The ancient Native Americans were the last natural human beings that North America got to experience. We that live here today do not know how to behave naturally anymore, for we have lost our animal instincts. We outsourced our humanity to corporations and industrial farms and allowed capitalism to kill the beast that once roared inside of us.

CHAPTER NINE:
Mexico, 1998-2000

Mexico City

I knew that I was going to like Mexico City the moment I arrived and hopped on their metro that kindly catered to people who didn't know how to read. I genuinely appreciated that I didn't have to struggle with pronouncing any of their metro stop names when I saw that all of their stops were displayed with pictograms in addition to words. To get to my hotel, all I needed to know was that I was to get off at the pictogram of a church bell and that my stop would come after the pictogram of an eagle. What I didn't need to know was that my stop's actual name was *Insurgentes,* and the stop before mine was an unpronounceable word that had way too many letters in all the wrong places: *Cuauhtémoc.* Bell and eagle were images that I could deal with, so I got to save my sanity to likely lose on something else.

The view from my cheap hotel room was of nothing particularly special, but the view from my hotel's restaurant window was of absolute and total chaos, so that was where I pulled up a chair and took a perch for the evening. I ordered a beer and some tacos and stared like a cat out the window. From where I sat, I got to watch a live game of *Frogger* play out on the largest traffic circle that my eyes had ever seen. I deliberately chose to stay in a hotel that overlooked The Angel of Independence Monument because it was the one landmark that I had seen the most pictures of. However, none of the pictures that I saw of it even remotely hinted at all the chaos that occurred directly below its towering pedestal. If there was

205

a live Lucha Libre fight going on in the center of the restaurant's dining room, I didn't remotely notice it because I was way too enthralled with watching people almost die as they ran across multiple lanes of traffic. If there was a crosswalk somewhere on that traffic circle, the people that I watched run for their lives didn't bother to use it, and I more than once thought that I was for sure going to see someone get plowed over by a taxi. More than anything, though, I was actively doing research because I was at some point going to have to cross that traffic circle myself if I wanted to see the Angel Monument up close. However, I was losing the desire to do so the more I watched people almost perish in their desperate pursuit to reach it.

I started the next morning at that traffic circle, but the rush hour traffic convinced me that getting close to the Angel Monument was something that I would be better off doing later in the day, say, oh, perhaps sometime after midnight. I wasn't too hung up about getting that close to the statue, though, because I figured that I stared at it long enough from the window the night before, so I decided to save my life and pushed on with the rest of my morning.

I got on the metro and exited the stop that displayed a circular pyramid for a pictograph and started to hunt for an ancient round temple dedicated to the Aztec god of the wind that supposedly sat somewhere in the bowels of the Pino Suárez metro station. Once I located the Ehécatl Temple, I declared to myself that my trip to Mexico City had officially begun. I then performed a little internal ceremony at the foot of the ancient shrine to celebrate. The whole reason why I came to Mexico City was to visit pyramids, and that little round temple was just a small teaser of what brilliant sights were yet to come. The main purpose of my journey was to visit the archaeological site Teotihuacan; however, I wasn't running there straight away because I wanted to build up to that site first. I wanted to get my head in the right space before venturing off on my Teotihuacan pilgrimage, so I figured that it made sense to start my journey as close to the bottom as I possibly could. Yet, the true bottom of Mexico City didn't reside in the bowels of the Pino Suárez metro station, for Mexico City's true bottom resided somewhere well below the city's declining water table. However, that was a bottomless site that couldn't be reached.

I nevertheless saw what the true bottom of Mexico City looked like when I stepped inside their lop-sided Metropolitan Cathedral. The slanting interior was so dizzying that it caused me to wonder whether my eyes were crooked or if the Metropolitan Cathedral was. Judging by the amount of scaffolding that held up the cathedral's interior, I deduced that the crooked thing out of the two of us was decidedly not me. The massive cathedral that took 250 years to build was taking far less time to sink into the mushy ground that it was built upon, and its wavy appearance had a nauseating effect upon me. I felt drunk the whole time I was in there, and all the beautifully decorated yet considerably tilting chapels only intoxicated me more and made me want to vomit all over the gorgeous marble floor. I wound up exiting the building way earlier than I intended to, so I bookmarked it in my brain to go back to it later. However, I never made it back there because I had seen enough crooked buildings by the end of my four days in Mexico City that I didn't have a hankering to see any more. I slowly came to understand that Mexico City was a city that never should have happened because it was built upon land that used to be covered with water. The whole of Mexico City sat upon squishy ground, and many of its buildings were melting into the pavement as if they were sandcastles returning to the sea. Most of those buildings were not descending into watery graves, though, because there was hardly any water left in the aquifers to receive them. When a building sinks in Mexico City today, that building descends into an empty tomb.

Before Mexico City was Mexico City, it was the Aztec city, Tenochtitlan, and it was nestled on an island inside a lake. Conquistador Hernán Cortés and his military buddies were the first and last Europeans to see Tenochtitlan at its glorious height. When Cortés tried to describe what they saw in a letter to King Charles I of Spain dated October 30, 1520, he likely feared that his description of a wondrous city filled with canals, buildings, markets, and temples was too fanciful to be believed. Even as the conquistador's men looked at Tenochtitlan with their very own eyes, they rubbed them in disbelief and asked if what they were seeing was indeed a dream. (Bernal Diaz, "The Conquest of New Spain," c.1565)

Tenochtitlan was ruled by a man named Moctezuma II, and he welcomed Cortés and all the other strange-looking men into his city with surprisingly open arms. Cortés proceeded to grab those open arms and wrapped Moctezuma II with them and made him a prisoner in his very own realm. Less than a year after meeting Cortés, Moctezuma II was dead, and a year after that, the city of Tenochtitlan was besieged. The once beautiful Tenochtitlan was destroyed, chopped up, and drained as if it never existed, and a new Spanish city rose atop the newly wiped slate. The former Aztec Empire got washed out with the newly drained lake and was left to desiccate under the sun like a fish pulled out of the sea.

After I exited the dizzying cathedral, I disoriented myself even further when I walked around the chopped-up remains of what was once Tenochtitlan's religious precinct. Excavations were conducted in the late 1970s through the early '80s on the Metropolitan Cathedral's plaza where many Aztec temples were thought to have originally stood. Only the bottom halves of the temples were discovered, though, because that was all that was left of them after the Spanish quarried and whittled the formally imposing structures straight into the ground. Cortés and his men saw no reason to leave anything standing once they were aware of the Aztec's penchant for human sacrifice. In truth, the Spanish probably didn't seek to destroy the Aztec Empire purely out of disgust, but they probably sought to wipe the Aztec Empire completely off the face of the planet purely because they were enraged over the Aztec's particular thirst for *Spanish* blood. 68 of Cortés' own men had their hearts ripped out and their faces torn off by what they regarded to be the hands of heathens on top of what they deemed to be pagan temples. Yet, those men might never have been sacrificed at all had not the Spanish slaughtered thousands of unsuspecting Aztec nobles during a festival first. The Spanish fought the Aztecs with weapons, and the Aztecs fought the Spanish back with fear. In the end, weapons defeated fear, and fear got buried under the ground.

The Spanish pulled the stones off the temples that their comrades were sacrificed upon and reused that material to build the newly rising city's first major church. My mind pained at the irony of that, and it got me thinking about how religion was wrought with symbolism except for when it interferes with one's worldly needs. Symbolically, I would have thought that Aztec temples would have been tainted in the eyes of the Spaniards, but I guess that they chose to look the other way when they picked off the stones and walked them over to the new building site. The one thing that they did not pick over, though, was a sizable Day of the Dead-looking altar, for that was left sitting there fully intact for future archaeologists to discover in all its disturbing glory. Seeing that altar of carved skulls really put things into perspective for me, and I tried really hard to see what Cortés and his men must have seen when that altar displayed racks of rotting heads. The more I looked at the truncated ruins of Tenochtitlan, the more I tried to understand what the Spanish were thinking when they buried that Aztec city under the ground. There were definitely things that the Aztecs did that the Spanish didn't agree with that probably led them to believe that destiny brought them to the New World for them to eradicate the native peoples and their way of life utterly and completely. Certainly, the Aztecs were too brutal for their own good, but so too were the conquistadors. Had either culture been born on the other side of the world, they both would have ended up looking exactly the same, for their natures were very similar. A conquistador born in an Aztec's loincloth would have seen him performing human sacrifices, and an Aztec born in a Spaniard's full set of armor would have seen him cutting that Aztec worshiper down. It was pure chance that determined which side of the world each man was born on, and it was that same chance that determined which weapon each man ultimately held. No

Spaniard was afraid of an Aztec skull rack when he had muskets, lances, swords, and armor to protect him from gaining a spot upon one.

Another thing that Cortés and his men possibly saw was the now-famous Aztec Sun Stone that was likely displayed somewhere near or upon Tenochtitlan's main religious temple. How that massive and intricately carved basalt object survived relatively unscathed probably had everything to do with the fact that it was just too intriguing of an object to physically destroy. When the time finally came for the Spanish to officially purge all pagan images from the new colonial city, the Aztec Sun Stone was oddly not broken into pieces and thrown into history's trash heap. Instead, it was carefully inserted face down into a hole and covered with dirt. I surmised that the object was given a proper burial purely out of superstitious fear that if it wasn't properly buried, the Aztec spirits would come back and haunt those who lived on their former stomping grounds. Weapons may have won the war against the Aztecs, but fear undoubtedly retained a certain measurable hold.

I had seen plenty of photographs of the Aztec Sun Stone before, and I gathered that the object was big, but not as big as it actually ended up being when I saw the intricately carved monstrosity in person. The Sun Stone was perched on a pedestal and stood at a height well above my head. Maybe it was because I had to bend my neck practically backward to look at it that the object appeared extra massive to me, but even if it had been hanging at eye level, there would have been no denying its extraordinary dimensions. Looking at it got me wondering who exactly the Aztecs were because the carvings left no doubt in my mind that they possessed insanely creative imaginations. Every Aztec object I saw inside The National Museum of Anthropology revealed that theirs was an imaginative culture, although I had to admit that their choice of subject matter was highly disturbing.

At one point, I went back to the Sun Stone to take a second look at it because I didn't think that I quite sank my eyes into it well enough the first time around. The Sun Stone was pure eye candy to ogle at, but once my eyes got adjusted to seeing it, I saw that the figure in the center sported a knife for a tongue and held a human heart in each of its clawed hands. In a nutshell, that object epitomized all Aztec art, for most of the art in that museum struck me as looking rather mean. After a few hours in that museum, I half-expected to come across an exhibit case full of children's dolls in the shape of demons, baby rattles made out of actual rattlesnakes, or pacifiers in the shapes of human bones because my mind was slowly turning Aztec on me. Even though I found no such display cases, I didn't rule out the possibility that such objects were hiding in storage bins somewhere in the museum's basement to avoid arousing the inner Aztec that might have lingered inside of everyone.

For me, the Aztec Sun Stone is the image that I most associate Mexico with, but that's not the image that most people associate with Mexico, for that honor goes to the Virgin of Guadalupe. I'd even venture out on a limb and say that most people don't even know what the Mexican national flag genuinely looks like and probably think that the famous image of the Virgin of Guadalupe graces the very center of it. The image of the Virgin Mary standing on a crescent moon with her hands folded in prayer and enveloped in an aura of light is the most iconic Christian image to have come out of Mexico and land straight into tattoo parlors. If anyone gets a tattoo of the Virgin Mary, it's almost always some version of the image that was divinely imprinted on a cloak worn by a man named Juan Diego in 1531, and no visit to Mexico City is complete without seeing that renowned relic in person. For many Catholics, the journey to the Basilica of Our Lady of Guadalupe is tantamount to a religious pilgrimage, but since the only pilgrimages that I typically do end in archaeological ruins, the journey for me was more akin to an excursion. I was more curious to see what the experience of viewing that cloak would look like than I was curious to find out what that experience would feel like. I was raised as Lutheran, so I wasn't taught to worship Mary. It suffices to say that I wasn't as interested in seeing the actual Virgin of Guadalupe cloak itself as I was interested in seeing what the Catholic faith looked like in the eyes of those who believed in the power of that religious relic.

Honestly, I don't know if I truly believed that the image imprinted on the cloak was indeed created by a divine hand or not, but I did know that I could *choose* to believe in its miraculous origins if I wanted to. People believe what they want to believe, and the thing about faith is that it never requires any proof. Religion comforts people with the thought that someone or something else is always enveloping us with its presence to the extent that we genuinely believe that we are never truly left to our own devices. We believe that another hand is always guiding us, but really, that other hand might be nothing other than our very own hearts. One can believe in anything, or one can believe in nothing, but either way, it is the heart that does all the actual bidding. Actions are more powerful than thoughts, and it's how one behaves that is the true testament of one's core beliefs. Whether or not I believe in religion and all its trappings does not matter in the grander scheme of things because what matters is how I treat myself, how I treat others, and how I treat the planet. Abraham Lincoln gets the credit for saying, "Actions speak louder than words," but I want to rephrase that and say that actions speak louder than thoughts. A person can say anything out loud to satisfy the status quo, but it may not accurately reflect what that person truly thinks. Words can be construed into facades for ideas to hide behind. For example, it wasn't the word "Helter-skelter" that caused the Manson murders to occur, but rather it was the *idea* of chaos that the word represented that caused random people to die at the hands of violent strangers.

In the end, I barely looked at the Virgin of Guadalupe's cloak. I had to wait in a long line for a turn to view the relic, and once I finally did approach it, the person behind me thought that it was her turn to view the relic as well. Not two seconds later, the person behind her joined our little viewing party and piled on top of the both of us, and I got weighed down to such a degree that I had to untangle myself and step away. I think I saw the cloak for all of 60 seconds before I bowed out and left the church altogether because it was just way too crowded in there for me. I grappled with trying to figure out what I gained from that experience, and all I could think of was that I learned that people were impatient, as if that was something that I didn't already know. I went to the church because I wanted to see if the people that went there were anything special, but they ultimately proved to be just like everybody else. I wish that I had something more enlightening

214

to say about the Virgin of Guadalupe relic, but I really can't comment on something that I didn't have the proper chance to appreciate.

Teotihuacan

I was lucky that the locals were generally nice people, though, because had they not been, I would have definitely missed getting off the bus at the unmarked Teotihuacan stop that came up way quicker than I expected. I honestly thought that the ride to Teotihuacan was going to take a longish time, so I was kind of shocked when everyone pointed to the exit and urged me to get off when the bus stopped in the middle of nowhere just barely outside of Mexico City. The fact that I was a tourist was painfully obvious, and it made my destination easy for everyone on board to deduce. I took it on faith that they knew where I was going better than I did, so I willingly got off without knowing where the heck I was. When the bus pulled away, I looked over the treetops for the tippy tops of pyramids and got slightly worried when I didn't see anything pyramid-looking looming overhead. I have zero recollection of how I physically managed to get to Teotihuacan from that bus stop because I don't remember seeing a single sign that might have helpfully pointed the way. It's probably safe to assume that I must have followed my nose and sniffed my way to the pyramids like the archaeological bloodhound that I am in times of dire need.

Even though I wound up spending at least seven hours at Teotihuacan, I didn't nearly see all that I wanted to. I grossly misjudged the size of the site and dilly-dallied away the first couple of hours exploring the Pyramid of the Feathered

215

Serpent and the Citadel complex in way more detail than I really had time to do. I didn't notice until several hours in that I wasn't budgeting my very time wisely when I realized that I allowed myself to get sucked in by the curious sculptures of serpents and googly-eyed monsters, all the while neglecting the fact that I still had several square miles yet to cover. It wasn't until I pulled myself away from the Citadel complex and walked the insanely long Avenue of the Dead that I realized how grave my mistake was to squander so much time in such a little section. I looked everywhere for a reset button that would allow me to restart my day and lamented when no such button was anywhere to be found.

The ruins of the largest city to have ever existed in pre-Columbian Mexico sprawled over the landscape without a single hint of stopping. As far as Teotihuacan was concerned, the city could have easily gone on forever, and the question that I most wondered about was why it didn't. From its zenith between 100 BC and AD 650, most of Mesoamerica was under Teotihuacan's spell, and it's probably not a stretch to say that Teotihuacan was indeed Mesoamerica itself for the majority of its existence. To call Teotihuacan a former mega-city is an understatement because it was more like a former mega-world, for both earthly and spiritual delights were equally experienced there. It was impossible to look at the incredible ruins of Teotihuacan and not muse about the meanings of all its pyramids and temples as they stood as lonely testaments to a world that vanished thousands of years ago.

No one knows who built Teotihuacan, but given its size and an estimated population of upwards of 200,000 people at its peak, the city was most likely a conglomeration of several different cultures. Not even the Aztecs knew what mysterious culture built Teotihuacan, and when they stumbled upon the deserted ruins in the early 1300s, they asked many of the same questions that we still ask today. The Aztecs only knew how to answer their questions with mythology, whereas we today know to answer those same questions with archaeology. However, there are no wrong answers to any of the questions posed to Teotihuacan, for Teotihuacan defies all that is true or false. Teotihuacan is a place that just is, and the Aztecs were just as awed by the ruins as we are today. Thoroughly perplexed, the Aztecs had no idea what to make of the mysteriously abandoned site, yet they couldn't resist falling under its spell. They ultimately concluded that Teotihuacan was where all their gods were born and from where their deities created the universe. It was from Teotihuacan's two largest pyramids where the Aztecs believed the Sun and the Moon were thrown into the sky. The Aztecs scampered all over the site and incorporated everything they saw there into their own legends and creation myths. They revered Teotihuacan as a sacred place worthy of pilgrimage, and I came to regard it as the Mesoamerican equivalent of ancient Delphi.

I initially had plans to climb to the tops of both large pyramids, but I only got as far as halfway up the Pyramid of the Sun before I noticed how incredibly hot it got in Mexico. From the ground, climbing the Pyramid of the Sun looked totally doable, but from the pyramid's mid-level platform, climbing the rest of it looked like it was way too much to tackle under the searing sun. I stopped to ponder the pyramid's impressive dimensions and seriously wondered how anyone could have possibly piled up such an incredible mountain of stone under such unrelenting conditions. The only answer I could tell myself was they must have used slaves – lots and lots of slaves – to build not just one massive pyramid, but two and even three when I tossed the Pyramid of the Feathered Serpent into the equation. I never understood why cultures in some of the world's hottest climates were motivated to build some of the world's most massive structures and mused that pyramid building would have been more something that I would have thought the Scandinavians would have done. The whole pyramid building thing baffles me to no end, and I'll never be able to wrap my head around how or why any of them were ever created.

I am embarrassed to admit that I didn't make it to the top of the Pyramid of the Sun, nor did I even so much as put a toe upon the Pyramid of the Moon. Teotihuacan overwhelmed me, and I saw as much of it as I could from my vantage point on the ground. The whole place was absolutely fantastic, but I'm having a hard time right now finding the right words to aptly describe it. It would be much easier for me to open my head and dump my memories of Teotihuacan across the page and allow those images to be interpreted as some kind of Rorschach Test. Teotihuacan remains an enigma to me even though I physically experienced the place in person, but that's mainly because I honestly still don't know what it was that I truly saw. The ruins of Teotihuacan were left to the elements just as much as they left to the imagination, so my experience of the site was personal and unique. Teotihuacan ranks as North America's greatest unknown, and it's highly doubtful that many of its mysteries will ever be unraveled. I'd say that its mysteries are part of its allure, but I'd also say that its mysteries are part of its tarnish. I couldn't shake the feeling of wanting to know what Teotihuacan was like before the Aztecs arrived and thoroughly stamped their own interpretations of it all over the place. I felt like all views I saw of Teotihuacan were seen through a pair of Aztec-laden eyes, and I genuinely wondered what the vistas would have looked like from an original Teotihuacano's point of view.

Villahermosa

Teotihuacan whetted my appetite for pyramids and set me off on a mini obsession for many months thereafter. I checked out so many library books about ancient Mexico that I couldn't realistically read them all. I did, however, manage to look at all the glossy pictures of nearly every pyramid ever photographed in that country, though. Some ruins were more photogenic than others, so I eventually gravitated toward a handful of favorites, but after a while, I found myself solely obsessed over a Mayan site called Palenque because it stood out as looking more romantic than all the rest. Palenque was almost too enchanting with the way its ruins emerged out of the jungle and sat under a perfect layer of beguiling mist. The ruins looked magical and seemed more like an apparition than a reality. The city looked like it would evaporate into vapor the moment anyone tried to touch it, so I convinced myself that I needed to feel the ruins with my very own hands to make myself believe that the place was actually real.

I mused about visiting Palenque for two years before I decided to bite the bullet and figure out a way to get myself down there. I was already pretty well versed on how to find Palenque on a map because I had looked it up 50 times before, but I was a tad bit disappointed when I looked it up again during the planning stages of my trip and saw that Palenque still hadn't moved like I secretly hoped that it magically would. I do believe that I was waiting for Palenque to pick up and relocate itself to somewhere more safe and convenient for travelers to get to, but Palenque was apparently quite content to be where it already was – in the heart of the Zapatista rebels territory in the region of Chiapas. I was able to overlook the whole Zapatista rebels bit, though, after I read that they didn't generally meddle with tourists because their beef was with the Mexican government. The rebels had their last major uprising in 1994, which didn't sound all that long ago to me in the year 2000. However, 1994 also sounded like it was far enough in the past that the odds of an all-out war happening right when I'd be rolling through their region was relatively slim. What I was more concerned with, though, was the logistics of how I was going to physically get to Palenque because it was inconveniently located nowhere near Mexico City.

Not flying into Mexico City was going to mean that I'd have to fly into some other Mexican town which, in turn, was going to mean that my total inability to speak Spanish was going to be exposed. At least with Mexico City, I could get around by pointing and looking at pictures, but anywhere else in Mexico would require me to spit out a few Spanish words every so often, which wasn't something that I was confident I could do. I would have to fly into whatever major airport was located closest to Palenque, and that city turned out to be a place called Villahermosa. Before I bought the ticket to fly there, I wouldn't have been able to rattle off its name if someone had asked me to name as many cities in Mexico as I possibly could because Villahermosa was not somewhere that I had ever heard of before. Other than Mexico City, most Americans can only name cities in Mexico that are either on a beach or immediately across the border, so I felt like Christopher Columbus when I discovered Villahermosa and internally acted as though I sailed halfway around the globe to find it.

For the most part, people know that there are two versions of Mexico: the one dolled up in heels and make-up for the tourists, and the one that walks around unshaven in its pajamas for the locals. Villahermosa, I immediately found out, fell into the pajama category. I had never been inside a supermarket that played trumpet, tuba, and accordion music so incredibly loud before that it made my ears want to bleed as they did when I went inside a supermarket in Villahermosa. I totally lost my concentration when I walked around that market and completely forgot that I was in there to buy some bottled water. I left the store holding three different types of bread and not a single bottle of the one thing that I specifically went into the store to buy. Truthfully, I people watched more than I shopped because I was enthralled with how nonchalant everyone was with the music blaring louder than any death metal concert would have deemed a reasonable volume to crank the music at. What I was most enthralled with, though, was the children. Kids, toddlers, babies – they were all perfectly fine with obscene instruments honking into their ears. The fact that they were so nonplussed with it fascinated me and made me want to interview them about their currently unfolding childhoods, but I knew that they wouldn't have heard me if I tried.

From the supermarket, I made the long trek over to the archaeological/zoo combo park known as La Venta. I had read quite a bit about La Venta ahead of time, so I was excited about seeing the colossal Olmec heads that were scattered throughout the park. Also, I was excited about the prospect of seeing some wild coatimundis (a raccoon-type animal with a long snout and a long tail) that were rumored to run all over the park as if they were regular squirrels. To get there, I had to walk along a sidewalk that skirted a busy road, and it only took me two steps in before I realized that I needed to pay close attention to where I was placing my feet. Not only was the street littered with way too many random piles of dog poop, but it was also littered with way too many random potholes that looked way too eager to twist both of my ankles and snap them off my feet. I also had to be super careful not to trip on any sections of uneven pavement that conspired to make me accidentally tumble into oncoming traffic that I sensed wouldn't stop for any falling pedestrian. Additionally, I had to be hyper-aware not to step on any loose manhole covers that appeared to be the only barriers between the Earth and a bottomless pit. I, at one point, shouted down one of the many sidewalk black holes and asked if anyone needed me to drop them down a roll of bread because I figured that was what I would have wanted someone to do for me had I been the one stuck somewhere in the bowels of Villahermosa.

Ah, yes, the bowels of Villahermosa. Little did I know that gaping black holes were going to be the theme for that day, but I'd be lying if I didn't say that I might have had my suspicions. I actually don't like to make fun of Mexico because it's a country that somewhat tries to do its best, but it's that lack of effort at critical moments that I find to be utterly comical. Copious amounts of dog poop and precariously placed manhole covers are easy fixes that Mexico puts in no effort toward fixing, so it's just easier to laugh about such things than it is to bitch about them, I suppose. Mexico is a funny place in a myriad of ways, but it's also serious at times, and it was its serious side that was on show at La Venta.

The park presented an impressive collection of archaeological artifacts that harked back to the time of the mysterious Olmec culture. I channeled my inner Indiana Jones and excitedly stumbled upon colossal stone heads, ancient tombs, and mysterious statues on paths that wound through a dense layer of jungle. I still don't know much about who the Olmecs were as a culture because not much is really known about them in general, but I did admire their penchant for carving gigantic heads with curiously flat faces and voluptuous lips, though. The Olmecs were possibly the most influential culture to have lived in early Mesoamerica, and they were most certainly one of the earliest cultures in that part of the world to have thought monumentally. There was something in the Olmec's psyche that caused them to want life to be bigger than it was and spurred them to build what is believed to be Mesoamerica's first bona fide pyramid. Unfortunately, the pyramid they built has since heaved under the weight of time and currently sits on the landscape like an eroded memory. I didn't bother to make the 75-mile trek to the original pyramid site because the objects in the archaeological park were all moved from that location, so context-wise, I was already as close to the Olmec's former homeland as I needed to be. However, the distance between now and 2,500 plus years ago was a gap that couldn't be bridged, and there was nothing about any of the stone monuments that struck my sensibilities as being remotely familiar. I tried tapping into any latent thought processes that might have been lingering inside that might have helped me understand what I was looking at, but I had to concede that no ancient Olmec thoughts were lurking inside me.

Psychologically, the objects in the park and I existed on two separate planes of existence. There was no amount of staring that I could possibly do into the eyes of a gigantic head that would make me understand why a statue was carved the way that it was. The Olmecs were an enigma, and they were not going to tell me anything that they hadn't already told everyone else. The lips on all the statues stayed resolutely sealed despite my best efforts to pry them open. In the end, I conceded to respect their silence. The Olmecs already said everything that they had to say when their contemporaries were around to listen to them speak. I mused that every pyramid in Mexico today was likely a visual expression of the words that once fell from the tip of an Olmec's tongue.

Many things in La Venta park managed in some way or another to sufficiently elude me, and that, of course, included the coatimundis (also called coatis) that rushed around and made a constant blur of themselves somewhere in the background. I could always tell that the coatis were there, but every time I tried to look at them, I would only see the leaves they kicked up as they scampered away. After a while, I started to think of coatis as cartoon characters and determined that my chances of seeing real coatis would be much better if I moseyed on over to the zoo.

When I got to the La Venta zoo, the first thing that I did was look at the park map for where the coatimundi exhibit was. However, my search was stymied when I failed to find anything labeled as such. Right when I resigned that I wasn't going to see any real-life coatimundis, I walked through the zoo entrance and was greeted by a pack of them expecting me to hand them some food. The coatis proved to be just as darned adorable as I thought they were going to be, and their antics provided an admission's worth of animal entertainment. I almost didn't care what the rest of the zoo had to offer because the coatis were what I came to the zoo to see, but the cute little creatures eventually grew bored of me and quickly made off in a cartoon character hurry. I took their departure as a hint that I probably needed to get beyond the zoo entrance and see what other animals I could befriend.

I honestly don't remember what other animals I saw there because all I remember were the ones that I wasn't able to see. I particularly don't remember what animals I didn't see housed in the nocturnal animals building because the glass on the display cases was so fogged up and filthy that I couldn't even see past my own smudged-up reflection. Actually, I don't even remember seeing my reflection because I recall the building being so pitch black inside that I couldn't even see my hand when I put it in front of my face. The only lighting that I saw was whatever red glow managed to escape from the insides of the fogged up display cases, and I used that little bit of light to grope my way for the exit door that I assumed had to be around there somewhere.

I don't remember now if I had to go up a flight of stairs on my way into the building, but I do remember going down a flight of them in total darkness on my way out. At the bottom of the staircase, I remember going through one of those metal exit turnstiles and then having my eyes immediately assaulted with some insanely bright daylight. My eyes were still in the process of dilating when I tried focusing on an exit sign that pointed directly toward a specific door. Even though the room was intensely illuminated, I still couldn't quite see where the heck I was going. However, the exit sign was pretty straightforward, so I simply followed to where it was pointing. I don't know where I went wrong, but I knew that I made a mistake when I opened what I thought was the exit door and took a giant step into thin air.

My foot literally dangled over an abyss and had I not caught myself in the door frame, I would have fallen straight into an inferno that apparently also functioned as a generator room in what looked to be a time capsule from the Cold War era. The cacophony of ancient equipment buzzed so loudly that I thought I might have entered a portal into a Villahermosa supermarket where the ghosts of Salvador Dali and M.C. Escher did all their grocery shopping for the underworld. That room was the strangest, deepest, and most dangerous place my eyes had ever seen, and I was suspending directly over it. To say that I was dumbfounded doesn't even describe how I felt when I hovered over that Dante's Circle of Hell of a pit that, by all appearances, didn't seem to possess a floor. It was the umpteenth time that day that I almost got swallowed into the bowels of Villahermosa, and I was starting to believe that I needed to spend some time down there and see what I was missing. I couldn't believe that the door that I opened wasn't even locked. That door definitely needed to have been locked, but of course, it couldn't have been locked because it was a goddamned swinging door. The swinging door that led to the bottomless pit was located right next to the actual exit door and how the heck anyone was to know which door led to Earth or which one led to hell was not remotely obvious. Once again, all I could do was take stock of the fact that I was definitely in Mexico, so I laughed about it to myself. Nervously.

Palenque

From Villahermosa, it was a two-hour bus ride to the modern city of Palenque, and I somehow managed to complete the journey without having everyone on the bus point and stare at me when my stop arrived. The hotel that I checked into was nestled on the very edge of a jungly neighborhood that was delightfully coined *La Cañada* even though there was nothing about the scenery that invoked images of Canada (the country) in any way, shape, or form. I have since learned that the word la cañada means glen (a secluded narrow valley) in Spanish, but that was not something I was privy to at the time. However, had I known, I wouldn't have bothered keeping an eye open for a moose that I was never going to see as I strolled around the little neighborhood. Frustratingly, I was made painfully aware that it was supposedly not safe to walk La Cañada all by myself when every person I encountered told me to hurry back to the safety of my hotel for some imperceivable reason. From what I could tell, most of La Cañada was overgrown and abandoned, but overall relatively benign, so I stubbornly walked the entire two-block circuit by myself despite everyone's protestations. The majority of La Cañada was a genuine ghost town in the truest sense of the term, and it gave off the feeling that it was disappointed in itself. However, that was precisely what I liked about it, and the feeling of forlornness drew me in and made me want to experience it all the more. It was pretty apparent that an obscene amount of money was once spent on the idea of creating the perfect little hotel and entertainment district in the middle of a jungle, but all the hotels, restaurants, and nightclubs had long since morphed into trees. Nature was La Cañada's best-paying guest, and I voyeuristically watched nature heedlessly enjoy itself as it slipped its tentacles across fragmented walls, broken patios, rotted fences, busted windows, and lonely dance floors.

I wasn't quite sure why the hotel I was staying in was still in business when all the other hotels around it had mysteriously shuttered, but I lumped the hotel's mere existence into the "this is Mexico" category along with all the other little things about Mexico that made absolutely no sense to me. I initially walked around the neighborhood because I wanted to find somewhere local to eat but inevitably found myself in my hotel's on-site restaurant, where I toyed with the idea of ordering bananas stuffed with cheese. The view from the restaurant's patio was of an abandoned field filled with waist-high jungle bramble, and I watched a child squat down and take a dump there while I casually dined on a delicious bean and cheese burrito. I continued to watch the child not wipe himself before he mad dashed back inside a dingy cinder block house that I wouldn't have noticed was even there had he not run inside it. Watching that whole production got me thinking about what life was like without indoor plumbing and doing so made me realize just how far away I was from an original human condition. I've never lived anywhere that didn't boast an indoor bathroom before, so I had to concede that the field child was essentially more human than I was. Although watching him didn't inspire me to drop my drawers and poop in front of the restaurant, watching him do that did make me wonder what primal instincts were still lurking inside of me. I ordered another beer and pondered whether it took being born inside a hovel to make a person understand what it meant to be a genuine human being. By the time I finished my second beer, I concluded that the level of one's economy was indeed a major deciding factor that determined the level of one's genuine humanness in the absolute basest sense. There's always a hidden cost to everything, and the cost of having more money comes at the price of giving up a certain amount of one's natural existence.

I got up super early the next morning because I had a wild hair to walk the six miles to Palenque ruins like some sort of Victorian explorer. However, I had to abort the idiotic jaunt less than one mile into it because I grossly underestimated how insanely muggy Palenque got at six in the godforsaken morning. All the visions I had of myself of being a Victorian adventurer were dashed when I decided that it would be a much better idea to allow the 8 a.m. bus to whisk me to the archaeological ruins instead. I was a little bit peeved at myself for waking up so stinking early in my eagerness to see the ruins before they were awake that I pouted and dragged my feet for the first several steps on my way back down the muggy hill. I wasn't too excited about knowing that I now had two hours to kill, so I decided that I didn't have a good excuse not to explore a set of abandoned buildings that I had noticed on my early ramble out. I really should have stopped making bad decisions while I was ahead, though, because poking my head inside an unfinished cinder block building in the middle of an overgrown jungle was a good way to almost get bit by two humongous spiders hiding in the corner. My god, those spiders were freaking huge and seeing them definitely put a zip in my step when I hurried back down the hill to the safety of my hotel room. Once I was back, I was more than willing to patiently wait out the two hours for the wonderful, convenient, and I assumed spider-free bus to safely drive me to Palenque ruins like I should have planned to have done in the first place.

I arrived at the UNESCO World Heritage site of Palenque just as it opened, and I approached the ruins right as the very last breath of the morning mist lifted like a curtain in a theater. The ruins assumed the role of actors on a stage, yet they struck me as looking more like deer that I feared would run away once they noticed that I was watching. The stone monuments looked skittish, and I was afraid that they were going to retreat into the forest the moment I got too close to them, so I carefully tiptoed toward them and hoped that they wouldn't notice me. The scene that sprawled out before me was almost too beautiful for my eyes to take in, so I paused for a moment to allow my eyes to catch up to my brain, or maybe allow my brain to catch up to my eyes, as I wasn't quite sure which one was ahead of the other. I closed my eyes and listened to the haunting calls of the howler monkeys reverberating against the stone walls and giving a voice to the structures that had otherwise lost their ability to speak. The ruins had volumes to say, but they could only communicate in sounds that howler monkeys understood because humans had stopped communicating with the buildings well over a millennium ago. Inwardly, the buildings were infused with a human spirit, but outwardly, the ruins were feral.

There was an elegant beauty to the ruins of Palenque that tempted me not to wonder what the city once looked like when it was new. A beautiful sadness hung over Palenque that I found to be rather attractive, and I followed that sad emotion as it wafted through all the empty palaces, lonely pyramids, deserted temples, overgrown fields, broken canals, and uninhabited homes. Following the sorrow allowed me to experience all the other emotions that the inhabitants left behind and gave me a sense of their haunting presence. I could *feel* who the inhabitants of Palenque were when I breathed in the same air that they used to breathe.

Palenque was no longer just a place in pictures to me anymore when it became a place that I could physically and mentally be a part of. Palenque seeped through my pores and became something that I could feel like a tear welling up under my eye or like a butterfly fluttering in my stomach. This was an archaeological site that I could become one with, and it was a surreal awareness that I had never experienced before. For the rest of my life, I will always say that Palenque is my most favorite archaeological site in the entire world if ever someone feels compelled to ask me because I don't believe that I'll ever feel those same feelings again. Time didn't matter when I was there, for the whole concept of time seemed arbitrary. The Mayans struck me as being contemporaneous of our time, even though they existed 1,500 years before any of us were born. The fact that the city looked so modern was something that my eyes took for granted, and it only took a few minutes of walking around before I felt like I was somewhere very familiar.

Palenque didn't look like it was someplace that was meant to be abandoned, and there was an apologetic look written all over the pyramids' facades for having suffered a fate that they didn't seem to deserve. An underlying creative force still pulsated through the pyramids' veins, but the reason for their existence stopped coursing through their blood centuries ago. It seemed to me that all the rose was sucked out of the pyramids' cheeks, and the entire city appeared to be suffering from a prolonged existential crisis. Still, the air above Palenque hung heavy with a weight of importance just as it had for the last 1,500 years because the Mayans forever infused the site with a strength that was never going to wane. This was the city where the famous Mayan ruler named Pakal sat on his throne for a long 68 years from 615 to 683 AD, and it was also where he was laid to rest in one of Mesoamerica's most spectacular tombs. Much of Palenque's power was due to the achievements of this one single man, and when visitors look at Palenque today, what they are seeing is him and the long shadow that he will forever cast.

The original Mayan name for Palenque was *Lakam ha* which translates as "Place of the Great Waters." The name only made sense to me after I stood next to one of the incredibly energetic rivers that the site was named after, and the water was so raging that I couldn't hear myself think. Palenque's vigor was undoubtedly imbued with the same power of the rivers that once surrounded it. The Mayans that lived at Palenque mastered the art of taming wild rivers, and they built canals to divert the flow of the water to go under the city. Time has since eroded many of the lids that once covered those canals, and I found those exposed waterways to be Palenque's most charming feature. I spent a good amount of time looking down on the city from atop a very tall structure, and I remember thinking to myself that I was admiring the most beautiful city to have ever graced planet Earth. That thought was officially solidified when I saw a toucan fly over a patch of trees because the sight of a wild toucan confirmed to me that I was indeed sitting in the center of absolute paradise.

A large portion of Palenque remained unexcavated, and I at one point ventured down a little-used path that meandered around an overgrown collection of disintegrated abodes. Walking down that path allowed me to imagine what the 19th-century explorers John Lloyd Stephens and Frederick Catherwood must have felt when they were the first Europeans to scamper around the ruins of Palenque in all its smothered and overgrown glory. I knew that I was only getting a teeny-weeny taste of what those two actually felt, though, when I got nipped by annoying ants after I accidentally stepped on one of a possible thousand ant hills. I was highly aware that Stephens and Catherwood felt far worse things when the jungle took a sizable chunk out of them, so my ant incident was minor in comparison. Stephens recounted the problems that they had with ticks, mosquitoes, stinging flies, bats, and mice when he wrote his seminal book titled *Incidents of Travel in Central America, Chiapas, and Yucatan.* He made particular mention about how racked with malaria Catherwood was and how that awful illness didn't stop him from drawing amazing pictures with the aid of his camera lucida.

I was right in the middle of thinking about those two

explorers when I heard the footsteps of someone coming toward me. My mind immediately thought that I was hearing the ghost of either Stephens or Catherwood, yet, as the person got closer, I started to see the clear outlines of a man wielding a machete. Under normal circumstances, I would have been alarmed to see a strange man walking around a forest with a machete slung over his shoulder, but I figured "normal" by Chiapian standards probably meant that the man was simply on the hunt for some bananas to hack down and sell at one of the 50 gazillion banana stalls that dotted this portion of the country. I had never in my life seen as many banana stalls on the side of the road as I had already seen in my two days so far in the region of Chiapas, and the stalls were notable for the fact that they all looked exactly the same. Other than bananas, the only other thing I saw for sale was dresses that also looked exactly the same, which solved the mystery for me why all indigenous women dressed identically. With the power of deduction, I figured that the machete-wielding Mayan was probably not on the hunt for dresses but was likely searching for bananas, yet something inside me really didn't want to be inadvertently murdered that day. So, I took the initiative to be uber friendly to the stranger as we passed.

"Hola!" I beamed and startled the crap out of him.

"Hola," he said in return and almost dropped his machete.

And with those words, we both managed to live to see another day. Little did I know at the time that he was not going to be the only person that I'd see in Chiapas wielding a machete. Indeed, I was going to see another such person the very next day who was going to look like he intended to use his weapon on something a little more substantial.

Chiapas

I had two full days to spend in Palenque, and I originally planned on spending both of them at the archaeological site. However, I got tempted away from spending a second day there because a hotel brochure convinced me to take a gander over to the turquoise waterfalls of Agua Azul instead. The photographs in the brochure made the waterfalls look like it was the sort of place that I'd regret not seeing if I chose against going there. So, I justified it in my head that it was worth giving up a second day at Palenque ruins for them since the odds were that I would never make it to this part of the world ever again.

I boarded the bus with nine other tourists, all of them young and European. The ride to Agua Azul was going to take about two hours, and we were going to traverse through some of the hilliest and most rural Mexican countryside that most of us had ever seen. Actually, it wasn't Mexican countryside that we ended up rolling through but rather Zapatista Mayan countryside, which looked to be a grade below even the lowest grade of poverty that the Mexican countryside typically offered. The bus rambled past numerous cinder block shanties that looked hot as hell to live in, and their appearance brought to my mind photographs of the Appalachian mountain shacks that people resided in during the depression. In actuality, the Appalachian shacks looked like mansions compared to the poor Mayan dwellings because at least the Appalachian shacks were bestowed with decent-sized porches for people to sit on. Such a porch was something that a meager Mayan hovel could only dream about if only it knew that such a thing even existed. Looking at the Mayan houses reminded me of the kid that I watched poop in the jungle the other day, and thinking about him helped me humanize the people that I wasn't seeing because they existed somewhere behind closed doors.

In truth, there probably wasn't anyone behind any of those doors because we encountered an entire Mayan village on the side of the road when they pulled a rope across the highway and made our bus come to a complete stop. Our driver was relatively nonplussed over the occurrence and seemed quite used to opening the door and letting in a pair of men holding machetes. The two men gave a brief speech which our bus driver obviously knew by heart because he didn't wait for them to finish talking before he translated for us what the men were saying.

"These men are from a poor village," our bus driver explained. "They request that you each donate some pesos into the money jar."

A glass jar the size of a Vlasic pickle container got passed around, but it was already full to the brim. It was impossible to squeeze any more pesos into it, so as the jar got passed around, we all just pretended to shove some money into it. I feared that the men would accuse us of cheating, so I braced for a whack in the head with a machete. I felt sorry for them, but also not, because it pissed me off that they presented us with an already full money jar which caused us to endure a psychological conundrum. Part of me wanted to argue with them about how counterintuitive their actions were because I thought that if they were going to terrorize us bus passengers, the least they could do was terrorize us correctly. After the men disembarked, a pair of six-year-old girls got on with a handful of bananas, and a German couple in the first row of seats bought them all and spared the rest of us from the hassle. The banana purchase apparently released us from our hostage situation because we were allowed to go on our way immediately after the banana transaction was complete.

I was fully expecting the water at Agua Azul to be a beautiful shade of blue, but it was the rainy season, so stirred up sediment caused the water to be a murky shade of brown. The waterfalls were still undeniably attractive, but their incredible beauty didn't stop me from calling the cascades Agua Chocolate to myself. Nevertheless, the landscape was nothing short of paradise, and I had to remind myself to occasionally blink when I couldn't stop my eyes from staring. I walked the entire length of the riverside path a few times over because it was stubby and didn't go very far, but I soon found myself looking for other trails in which to explore. I thought I stumbled upon an interesting hiking path when I saw one that descended into a lush tropical jungle, but I had to do a speedy about-face when I came upon a sign that read: "Warning. It is not recommended that you go any further. This trail has been the site for many dangerous assaults." Visions of more machete-wielding Mayans came rushing into my head, and it didn't exactly put me in the mood to see any more.

Since my hiking options were extremely limited, I knew that the next logical thing to do was go shopping for bananas and dresses. Several ramshackle shops and residential shacks were huddled together in a designated area near the water's edge, which tempted me to do a little perusing. I was honestly more curious to peek inside the homes than I was interested in doing any actual shopping, so I stealthily managed to get a glimpse inside a couple of hovels. I saw no furniture, only empty rooms with mats on the floor and maybe a hammock or two strung up between the walls, and the sight of the poverty-stricken interiors seized me with supreme pity. Just when I was feeling the glummest that I had ever felt, I noticed two little girls lying on a dirt-encrusted mat under a table in one of the stalls. The girls were entertaining themselves by tickling each other and acting silly. It was super sweet but super sad. The parents were manning their banana table with permanent marks of dejection etched across their faces. It was probably going to be another day of not making a whole lot of money, so I contributed to their cause and bought a bunch of bananas.

On the bus ride back to Palenque, everyone asked each other if they wanted a banana because we all had so many. It was painfully obvious that every one of us had experienced the exact same day.

CHAPTER TEN:
Germany, November 2000

Ancestry

My father's history was always somewhat of a mystery to me because he ended up in a nursing home well before I thought to ask him any personal questions regarding his past. I was only 14 years old when he suffered a debilitating stroke that landed him in a nursing home. I didn't immediately realize it right away, but any questions that I might have wanted to ask him about pretty much anything needed to have already been asked. He remained severely brain-damaged for the remaining 18 years of his life, and it bothered me how often I would think of some random question to ask him but couldn't because there were just too many things that he couldn't remember. After a while, I realized how pointless it was to think of questions that he would never be able to answer, so I suppressed my curiosity and accepted his situation for what it was.

My parents never once gave my sister and me the lowdown about what their lives were like before we were born, for they made it seem as though their lives only started when we all became a family. It really amazes me now that my sister and I never thought to ask our parents any questions regarding their past, but I suppose that we just didn't register that there existed a time in their lives before they had the two of us. It wasn't until I got the bright idea to write to my dad's sister and ask her some questions that I finally got some answers about my dad that I was curious to know.

My aunt probably wasn't all that surprised to receive a

239

letter from me because she was well aware of my dad's unfortunate situation. I started the letter with an apology for my intrusion and then followed with a bombardment of questions. I asked her where in Germany their parents were from and why and when they came to America. I asked her to tell me what my dad was like when he was a kid and what our neighborhood in Milwaukee was like when they were growing up. I admitted that I knew next to nothing about my father's background, but I don't remember if I admitted that I was embarrassed by my ignorance even though I was. In short, I told her that I was desperate to learn anything about my dad's side of the family because it was all terra incognita to me. I thanked her in advance for a reply and then impatiently waited for her response.

Much to my relief, my aunt kindly wrote back. She answered all of my questions and generously tossed in a few childhood photographs of my dad for good measure. It was super weird to see my dad as a child, and I struggled to recognize where any of the pictures were taken because none of the backgrounds looked remotely familiar. I grew up in the same house that my dad did, but it was obvious that none of those photographs were captured there. I had no idea where any of those pictures were taken, and it seemed almost as though those weren't really images of my father at all, but rather pictures of someone else entirely. The concept of my dad ever being young seemed oddly foreign to me, and I struggled to wrap my head around the notion. Additionally, she thoughtfully included an old postcard of my grandparent's village. The postcard was from a city called Munderkingen, and it showcased seven different scenes that presumably summed up the entirety of the place. One of the images was of an impressive triangular building with the handwritten words "Grandma's house" scribbled next to it, and the sight of those words threw me for a loop.

"Why in the world would my grandma walk away from a mansion?" I wondered to myself. "That place looks like it was a castle."

I honestly didn't know what I was looking at because it didn't make sense that a postcard would display my grandmother's ancestral home. I should have been suspicious when I recognized the writing to be in my mother's unmistakable script because she wasn't exactly the authority of where her mother-in-law formerly lived. Still, I figured that my dad must have pointed out his mother's house to her when he must have shown her that same postcard in some convoluted scenario.

"Apparently, my grandma was royalty," I thought to myself and immediately started planning a trip to Germany to reclaim my throne and reinstate the monarchy. I fully anticipated that my coup would ultimately fail, but I figured that it was worth a shot to go there and at least see my grandparent's village with my very own eyes. I always knew that my dad was a first-generation immigrant, so I figured that a trip to Germany would help me better understand where my father's influences originated.

Germany was never a topic when I was a kid. That country was so out of sight and out of mind that I never heard it brought up in any conversations. Heritage didn't mean much to us because we just considered ourselves as being plain 'ol Americans. Just like how I never thought too deeply about my parents, I never thought too deeply about my American-ness because both things just were. It wasn't until I got that postcard that I looked at a map of Germany for the first time in my life. I didn't even know where Munderkingen was, much less how to pronounce it. It took me nearly forever to find the darn place on the map, and once I did locate it, it took me another forever to figure out how to get there without renting a car.

Flying from Phoenix to Germany was going to be a cinch in the year 2000 because Lufthansa offered non-stop flights to Frankfurt at that time and travel agents only had to pay the taxes for a stand-by ticket. However, getting from Frankfurt to Munderkingen would involve a few extra steps because only one city in Germany offered trains to Munderkingen, and Frankfurt wasn't it. I needed to get to a city called Ulm, but so did the friend I invited to join me from England. Unfortunately, my English friend couldn't find any flights to Ulm from London, but he did find flights to Munich, which was the next closest city. No doubt, taking a train from Munich to Ulm would make the journey to Munderkingen a little more tedious, but it was something that I was more than willing to do. Overall, I was just happy that any train at all went to that little podunk town on the edge of nowhere in particular. However, my English friend wasn't nearly as thrilled as I was about going to a small German village that barely registered on a map, and he struggled to figure out if it was even an endeavor that he wanted to tackle.

Graeme, or whatever his name is

"Tell me again, where did you say that you wanted us to

go?" my English friend asked me for the umpteenth time when we were still in the planning stages of the trip.

"Munderkingen," I told him for the zillionth time, "but it looks really small, so we won't be spending all of our time there. If you come with me, I promise that we'll do whatever you want to do for the majority of the time in Munich."

Now, before I go any further with this conversation, I will introduce who this English friend was that I was asking to come to Germany with me. He was one of my international pen pals that I met through an advert in an English history magazine. I made a few decent friends through that pen pal service, and I took a couple of them to the Grand Canyon when they flew to Arizona to visit me. However, the one I was inviting to Germany was my favorite because he was the most artsy. I have long ago lost communication with all of them except for this one, and I recently told him that I would be writing about our Germany trip. I asked him if he preferred that I call him by his real name or if he rathered that I call him by a pseudonym. Without skipping a beat, his response to me was that he wanted me to call him "Sir Charles Darcy." I haven't broken it to him yet that I wasn't writing some highfalutin Jane Austen style novel, so I've taken the initiative to take the name that he wanted me to use down a notch and will refer to him as Graeme. However, I did toy with the idea of using his real name, which happens to be Gary.

I was apparently treading into unfamiliar territory when I asked an Englishman to join me in Germany for a vacation. I was totally ignorant of English people's traveling habits, and I was completely unaware that they would sooner go to Spain, France, or Italy ten times over before they even considered the idea of stepping a single foot inside Germany. It took some serious arm twisting on my part to convince Graeme that Germany was indeed a place that people sometimes went to when they went somewhere for a vacation.

"Stop calling it a vacation," Graeme told me, "and call it a holiday. Also, stop using the word Germany with it in the same sentence."

"Okay," I complied, "I will rephrase my question then. Would you like to go on a *holiday* with me to a beautiful *Teutonic country*?"

"Well...," Graeme hesitated, "since you put it that way..."

"Great!" I exclaimed. "So, you'll go!"

"I guess so," Graeme sighed. "When?"

"November!" I announced.

"November?" Graeme bemoaned. "You can't be serious. Why not in the summer?"

"It has to be November," I explained, "because that's when the flights have a better chance of being empty. I'll be flying stand-by, so I have to be sure that there will be open seats."

Graeme tried his best to persuade me not to go. "Perhaps you should take the empty seats as a hint that maybe going to Germany in November is a lame idea."

"Bah," I poo-pooed. "You live in England. You should pack a swimsuit because Germany will probably feel warm to you in November."

"Well, if that's the case," Graeme countered, "then you should pack a parka."

Graeme agreed to meet me in Munich on the dates that I selected in November, but how the flights worked out from the US caused me to arrive in Munich a day before he did. I had 24 hours in Munich all to myself, and I spent most of that time just wandering around outside admiring all the pretty buildings. I wasn't entirely sure what Graeme had selected to do in Munich, so I didn't want to risk accidentally spoiling anything. I purposely avoided going inside any significant buildings and instead just soaked in the gorgeous autumn light. The sun hovered low on the horizon and cast a warm golden hue on everything that it touched. There was something about that horizontal light that reminded me of the finest fall days I experienced growing up in Wisconsin. I lamented about how I didn't get to see that kind of northern light very often anymore. It was the kind of light that I instantly miss when I see it because I know that the warm glow never lasts for very long. Sure enough, that light didn't linger, for it was gone the very next day when Graeme arrived and unpacked his suitcase.

"Excuse me," I said to Graeme as he unpacked in the dim steel light that barely penetrated through the window, "but why did you bring England with you?"

"What do you mean?" he innocently responded.

I walked over to the window and threw open the curtains. "It was sunny here yesterday, but now look at it. It's all England-y out there!"

Graeme instantly went on the defensive. "Well, you can't blame me for that!" he exclaimed. "I told you that Germany in November was a lame idea."

"Well, Munich did remind me of Wisconsin yesterday, so I guess that it still will," I said in reference to the generally cruddy Wisconsin-like weather.

"What?" Graeme asked. "I don't understand what that means."

"Nothing," I said.

"What?" he asked again.

"Never mind," I said and brushed the conversation aside. "So, what's on the agenda for today?"

"Museums!" Graeme exclaimed, much to my pleasure. He was definitely the museum buddy I had always wanted to have. However, we had already discovered a few years ago that the only thing we had in common as far as art was concerned was our mutual dislike in the exact sort of art the other one greatly admired. It didn't take me long to realize that Graeme was not only born in the wrong century but that he was also born in the wrong gender. His inexplicable penchant for Sèvres porcelain and Wedgwood pottery greatly concerned me and left no doubt in my mind that if he could choose to be reincarnated into any person in any era that he would definitely choose to be reborn as Madame de Pompadour just so that he could poop bouquets and invent the color pink. I, on the other hand, abhor pastel colors. I generally gravitate toward the darkened tones of Old Master paintings or the tonal grays of ancient carvings. Graeme once sent me a postcard in the mail of a pile of bricks displayed on the floor at the Tate Gallery in London, and when I visited him there, he dragged me to the display to see it. I seriously thought that he was joking when he, the guy who greatly admired old grandma stuff, said that he honestly appreciated the static display of construction material. We naturally got into a row about what art was because I declared that a stack of bricks on the ground wasn't art, and I threatened to kick it.

We spent the greater part of our first day together at The Glyptothek and The Pinakothek Museums, and it is safe to say that we saw wildly different things inside each of those places. I could tell pretty quickly that The Glyptothek wasn't going to be Graeme's cup of tea when we walked in there and saw that all the Greek and Roman statues were in the same pale hue as the colorless sky that we just escaped. Of course, all that gray meant that it was going to be precisely the sort of place that I was going to enjoy. However, that being said, we both soon concluded that viewing identical-looking statues over and over again did get quite repetitive after a while. However, nothing in there stopped us from looking at every single display, and doing so gobbled up a lot of precious time when we still had two museums to go. We recognized the error of our ways when we entered The Alte Pinakothek (The Old Art Museum) and instantly realized that we needed to budget our time more wisely if we wanted to visit the Neue Pinakothek (The New Art Museum) as well. The only way we could tackle both art museums efficiently was to split up, which was what we organically ended up doing after one of us kept lingering too long over a painting the other person didn't remotely care for. Graeme didn't care to know what I saw in Albrecht Dürer's self-portrait any more than I cared to know what he saw in one of Cezanne's bazillion still life paintings. However, the one artist we did agree on was J.M.W. Turner, and we both got lost in his painting titled *East End* together. I don't remember what Graeme's opinion was regarding his seeing one of Van Gogh's famous *Sunflowers* paintings, but I'm pretty sure that he liked it because it was one of the few Van Gogh paintings that I've never particularly cared for. He would probably think that it would be an absolute sin if I didn't mention the deep appreciation that he had for Gainsborough's painting of *Mrs.*

Thomas Hibbert, just as I would think it would be utterly blasphemous for me not to mention the admiration that I had for Caspar David Friedrich's painting, *Giant Mountain Landscape with Rising Fog,* and just those two titles alone demonstrate what kind of different people Graeme and I are.

We built up massive appetites after we spent the entire day on nearly empty stomachs, but we definitely weren't hungry enough to justify the dizzying amount of food we got served at an authentic German restaurant that we stumbled into when we exited our final museum. We each placed an order for a German meal of some sort before I spoiled my appetite by eating most of the bread that was plopped onto our table. I have never been one to say no to bread, so I couldn't resist putting my hand into the breadbasket way too many times and gorging on the delicious carbs before my huge jägerschnitzel meal arrived (which I ate all of). I never felt like such an ancient Roman glutton before, and had The Glyptothek not been closed, I would have moved our table into there and eaten my meal among my marble contemporaries.

Ulm

I could have easily slept all the next day away because I woke up the following morning still feeling incredibly full. However, being lazy wasn't an option because there was a marathon train ride out there waiting for us, and I didn't want to miss it. We forced ourselves out of bed and moseyed our way to the train station through a steady blast of wind whose only purpose was to make our walk to the train station that much more miserable. It was a relief when we got onto a train, and I wasn't sure if it was a good sign or not that we watched the season change right before our very eyes as we rode straight into a billowy snowstorm. We left Munich in fall and arrived in Ulm over an hour later in winter. When we exited the train, we genuinely thought that we might have accidentally got dropped off somewhere near the North Pole. I had set aside a couple of hours to spend in Ulm before our onward venture to Munderkingen, but I could tell right away that I should have allotted more time. My first impression was that the city was too adorable not to be a real-life Christmas Village set inside a city-sized snow globe. It uncannily felt as if we walked into a Grimm's Fairy Tale story that was already in full swing, and I braced for the ground to rumble from someone turning the page that I thought we were standing on.

I remember what we did in Ulm distinctly because climbing up Europe's highest church spire during a snowstorm was an experience that was impossible to forget, especially while it was happening. I honestly don't know why I bothered taking pictures of the scenery that supposedly unfurled below the spire because what the snow didn't obscure, layers of scaffolding most certainly did. Unfortunately, work on Ulm Minster will never be finished because the race is permanently on to save it from eroding from all the uric acid that has accumulated at its base due to its unenviable reputation for being a gigantic piss magnet. A big plaza sits in front of the church, and the correct portable restroom-to-festival ratio has yet to be divinely revealed. So, until that magic ratio is ultimately determined, Ulm Minster will remain under some form of scaffolding.

There might have been more to do in Ulm than just visit its massive church that I kept wanting to call a cathedral even though it technically wasn't, but I intentionally didn't do any research about Ulm in advance because I didn't want to know what I'd be missing when we didn't have enough time to see anything besides its most massive building. It turned out that it was a good thing that I was blissfully unaware that the world's most fascinating prehistoric mammoth ivory sculpture was housed inside Ulm's Museum, for had I known that the 40,000-year-old artifact known as Lion-man was there, I would have sacrificed a good amount of Munderkingen time to go over there and see it. As it was, I didn't even know what to expect in Munderkingen either because I couldn't find a whole lot of information about the village in advance, and I suspected that was likely because there wasn't a whole lot to say about it.

When Graeme asked me what we were going to do for the rest of the day in Munderkingen, the only answer I could give him was, "just be there," which wasn't exactly the most satisfying answer to his expectant ears.

"Is that just another way of saying that there's going to be nothing to do there?" Graeme asked with a hint of sarcasm in his voice.

"Nah," I scoffed. "Don't worry. There will be plenty to do."

Munderkingen

Right as I said that, we pulled into the Munderkingen train station. The buildings around the station were of the quintessential German utilitarian caliber, which is a fancy way of saying nothing particularly special. By all appearances, my grandparent's hometown looked like it was the kind of place where the surrounding village people went to when they needed to utilize the nearest transit station. My gut instinct was that my ancestors were certifiably blue-collar well before the term was even invented. I had to admit to myself that it might have been a mistake to drag a guy all the way there from England, but then I had to remind myself that I dragged myself all the way there from America, so either way, I needed to make the best of it.

"Well, shall we go explore?" I asked not only Graeme but also myself.

"You say that like you don't know if we should," Graeme half surprisingly replied.

To say that the weather was far from beautiful doesn't quite describe how gloomy the weather truly was. The ground under our feet was wet and sloshy, and the sky above was watery and gray, and together those two things made us feel like we were the uninspired ingredients inside a bad weather day sandwich. Both of us questioned what the heck we were doing there, and it wasn't until Graeme noticed a bridge over a river that we discovered that there was something worth aiming for.

"The medieval portion of the town must be somewhere on the other side of that bridge," I said to Graeme, to which he replied that I'd better hope so.

Indeed, that bridge separated the old Germany from the new and crossing it was like stepping over a threshold. Both of my grandparents must have crossed that bridge at least a hundred times during the course of their young lives, and I wondered if they looked back at the medieval village one final time before they never saw it again. I wondered if leaving the village was something that both of them wanted to do or if leaving it was something that they both *had* to do because there was nothing on either side of that bridge for them. I was told that my grandfather came to America (alone? with someone? I don't know) in the late 1920s and then sent for my grandmother to follow a couple of years later, but other than that, I know nothing else. Heck, I didn't even know if theirs was a love story or not, but I like to imagine that it was, and I am sure that they must have sent a few love letters to each other across the ocean before she arrived. If that was the case, then they must have been the originators of the pen pal gene that got handed down to me, and Gary, oh, I mean, Graeme, was an incidental benefactor of my genetic inheritance.

"So, what's the plan?" Graeme wanted to know.

His question was my cue to pull out the postcard of the ginormous building labeled *Grandma's house* and show it to him.

"What's this?" he asked.

"It's a postcard," I told him. "We have to find where this house is."

I handed Graeme the postcard for him to scrutinize.

"That's not a house," Graeme declared, "that's a public building. You just took a pen and labeled it as your grandma's house."

"No, I didn't," I defended. "My aunt sent me this."

Graeme wasn't buying it. "Why would she send you that?"

"She sent it to me after I asked her to tell me about my grandparents," I explained. "Supposedly, that was my grandma's house, so I want to find it."

Graeme still wasn't believing me. "No way was that your grandmother's house."

We went round and round for a little bit, but I couldn't

convince him that it was, so we agreed to disagree and together went in search of the monstrous building. Of course, we found the place immediately because it was impossible to miss the most conspicuous structure in the whole entire village.

"There it is!" I said and gawked at the building that boasted nine chimneys, nine bells, and a large clock plopped in the center of it.

"That is not a place of residence!" Graeme said and started to look all over the building for a plaque that would announce its true nature. Unfortunately, all he managed to find was a doorbell.

"Well, are you going to ring it?" Graeme asked me.

"Oh, I don't think so," I said. "I have no idea who any of my relatives are."

Graeme was getting slightly frustrated with me that I thought I had family living somewhere inside that building.

"This is not someplace where anyone lives!" Graeme said and investigated the building once again for any signs that would identify what the building actually was.

"Why don't Germans label their buildings?" Graeme said and grew frustrated.

Meanwhile, I, too, started to question why the postcard was labeled how it was, especially since the words were written in my mother's unmistakable script. She had no way of knowing where her husband's mother once lived in Germany no more than my dad would have known where his wife's parents once lived in The Netherlands. It wasn't a mystery that was going to be solved that day because we eventually walked away from the building without figuring out if it was indeed my ancestral home or if it was the village Town Hall, which I found out years later that it was.

I liked hanging out with Graeme because there was nothing that I could say or do that could baffle him any more than how much I baffled him already. My whole entire being often made little sense to him, and we both stopped trying to explain ourselves to each other once we realized that we both had our own ways of looking at the world. The trip to Munderkingen was simply par for the course, and I didn't need to explain why I wanted to go there just so that I could walk up to what I thought was my grandmother's house and not knock on the door because all he needed to know was that I had my reasons. Graeme didn't necessarily know that I was unaware of what my own reasons were for wanting to travel all the way to my grandparent's hometown. I was sure that he sensed my cluelessness when I stood in front of that building and started to question my very own existence.

"What are you thinking of?" Graeme asked me.

"I honestly don't know," I said. "I guess that I'm thinking that I don't have much of a connection to Germany after all. I don't even know what I'm looking at."

While it was true that I didn't come to Munderkingen with any grandiose intentions, I did at least want to vicariously experience what it was like to live in that tiny out-of-the-way village. Had my grandparents never immigrated to America, this was where I could have been born, and I wouldn't have been born the same version of me. I guess that I never realized just how American I truly was until I made the trek to my grandparent's hometown. Half the reason I was even American at all was because my dad's parents decided to get on a boat and permanently leave behind the city that I was currently standing in. I'm looking back on that trip now, and my overarching thought is that I think that I went to Munderkingen too soon. I hadn't seen the poster of Munderkingen that was stuffed deep inside the attic yet, but had I seen that poster beforehand, my Munderkingen experience would have had a lot more perspective.

My grandparents used to live in the same house in Milwaukee that I grew up in, so they were likely the ones who placed a large framed poster of Munderkingen deep inside the attic. Someone from Germany apparently sent them a poster that depicted their hometown, and I assume that it was sent to them with the thought that doing so was a nice gesture. By all appearances, it seemed as though my grandparents gratefully received the gift and thought to wonderfully preserve it by not letting it see the light of day. I'm really curious to know why someone thought that it was perfectly okay to send my grandparents a Nazi propaganda poster just because it had an image of that big Munderkingen building on it. If anything, receiving a propaganda poster might have been a final nail in the coffin for my grandparents to say that they weren't Germans anymore. Just seeing the words *Heil, Hitler* at the bottom of the poster was probably enough to make them glad that they never had to utter those words out loud. Overall, I think they were glad that they left Germany when they did because they got out of there before WWII started, and I can only imagine how painful it was for them to watch their home country crumble from afar. If anything, that poster might have been a reminder that they made the right decision to come to America when they did, and had I seen that poster before I traveled to Munderkingen, I would have understood their perspective quite a bit more. The building pictured on the poster wasn't an image of my grandmother's house, as my mother mistakenly interpreted it to be, but that building was simply a picture of home. The country of Germany itself was probably what my grandparents saw when they looked at a picture of that building and had I known that, I wouldn't have thought that anyone related to me lived in there when I was afraid to knock on that door.

There wasn't a whole lot to do in Munderkingen, mostly because Munderkingen wasn't the kind of place where tourists generally flocked to in the chilly month of November. We only saw a few restaurant options, and none of them were open. We essentially crushed the whole town after we visited a church and walked around the village a few times over. We probably spent the same amount of time standing on the bridge and looking at the river as we did wandering around the pocket-sized village, and had we known that the river that we were staring at was the Danube, we might have admired it even more. I always thought that I wanted to see the Danube, and I left Munderkingen not knowing that I did.

Dachau

We only had one last day to spend together, and we chose to spend it at the Dachau Concentration Camp Memorial Site because the weather was just too miserable to want to spend it anywhere else. In truth, we still would have gone there even if the day ended up being sunny, but I was glad that the sun stayed behind clouds because the last thing that I wanted to do was walk around a former concentration camp in beautiful weather. No sun should ever be allowed to shine upon a place where horrible atrocities were carried out because sunshine implies hope, and hope was not something that most Dachau prisoners had.

Neither of us wanted to leave Germany without exploring its Nazi history in some way, shape, or form, so visiting a concentration camp was something we both felt equally compelled to do. "Those who do not learn history are doomed to repeat it" is a famous maxim said by the philosopher George Santayana, and though I know nothing about the man who said that, the phrase that he uttered is one that I have taken straight to my heart. I am a firm proponent of learning from history's mistakes, but society in general never seems to want to look back and see what has already come before it.

Once again, neither of us consulted a map ahead of time to determine where we needed to go. I don't know why we both assumed that the Dachau concentration camp was located within walking distance from the Dachau train station because we soon found out that it wasn't. Our assumption slowly eroded after we trekked along nondescript surface streets for nearly an hour with nary a sign that we were even heading in the right direction. I, for some reason, insisted that the concentration camp had to be near and implored that we continue our walk just a little bit further, but Graeme proved to be the wiser of us two when he said that he was going to ask the pair of cops that he just spotted at the end of the street for directions. The gray sky opened up and started to rain, so I stayed behind under an awning and watched Graeme talk to the police. I could immediately tell by his body language that the cops were telling him that we were nowhere near where we wanted to be. Graeme waved me to come over, and together we hitched a ride to the Dachau concentration camp in a cop car which was an irony that wasn't lost on any of us.

The pair of cops looked to be about our age, somewhere in their mid-twenties, and they were a male-female team, just like Graeme and I, so I suspected that they would be easy to talk to. I was going to start the conversation first, but they beat me to it and threw out the first question when they asked us if this would be our first time visiting the Dachau concentration camp.

"Yes," we said, "first time for the both of us."

I was under the assumption that the ride over there wasn't going to take very long because I was still relatively convinced that we had almost reached it on foot. I didn't want to squander any precious talking time with polite but meaningless chit-chat, so I jumped straight in with some hard-hitting questions.

"So, what's it like living in a city that's best known for having a concentration camp?" I blurted out and heard Graeme make an audible gasp.

The cops, much to our relief, were totally unfazed by the question.

"That camp belongs to our grandparent's generation," both cops started to explain. "Our generation had nothing to do with it."

"Right," I agreed, "but does it bother you to live in the shadow of that history?"

The cops, much to their credit, were very open to answering my uncomfortably blunt questions while Graeme tried his best to disappear into his seat.

"No," they started to explain, "no one can change the past.

The only thing that we can do now is not let those kinds of things happen again."

That was pretty much the extent of what they had to say about the topic. They were both very pragmatic about it, and I found their perspectives to be very insightful. How else could successive generations deal with the evils of the past but accept the past for what it was and allow the present to be what it is? Sure, they could have chosen to hold grudges against their forebears, but I doubted that doing so would have made their own lives any better. They were the inheritors of a past that they didn't personally choose, and that was going to be the case for every single German for ad infinitum. They will never be able to escape their history, for it will always be there lurking behind them. It is unreasonable to think that exorcising the same demons over and over again would do their nation's psyche any amount of good. The reason why places like the Dachau Memorial Site are important is that they don't erase the past but instead expose the past for the whole world to see.

After a ten-minute cop-slash-taxi ride, we arrived at the Dachau concentration camp under a gray sky that was nothing short of dismal. The overall color palette of Dachau was gray. Gray sun, gray clouds, gray walls, gray floors, gray everything. I arrived there not knowing much about what happened at Dachau specifically and was completely unaware that there was a difference between a concentration camp and an extermination one. I was under the impression that all Nazi camps were pretty much the same in that they were all equally horrible, but I soon learned that some camps were marginally more horrible than certain others. Dachau, it would be revealed, fell somewhere toward the more horrible end of that spectrum.

Dachau was the first concentration camp that the Nazis established, and it set the model for almost every concentration camp that followed. The Nazis were inspired to build this camp because they needed somewhere to imprison dissidents (those who opposed the Nazi regime). The camp then grew in size when they needed somewhere to imprison those they considered undesirable (Jehovah's Witnesses, Jews, gypsies, gays, mentally disabled, clergy, Germans of mixed race, the list went on). The Dachau prisoners basically became slaves, and they had to see the taunting words "Arbeit Macht Frei" ("Work makes one free") emblazoned on the iron gate that they had to walk through on their daily march to manual labor. For many, the work that they performed did indeed set them free when they eventually died from exhaustion, starvation, disease, or execution. If the work they performed didn't kill them, then the deranged medical experiments performed on them frequently did.

I tried to wrap my head around what life must have been like for those imprisoned at Dachau. I vicariously tried to conceptualize what it would have meant to have everything taken away from me. First, I would have lost all my material possessions, then I would have lost all my freedoms, then I would have lost my dignity, then I would have lost my hope, and then I would have lost all my faith in absolutely everything. I would eventually be reduced to nothing. I would become no one. I would feel done, but I wouldn't be done because I would have to continue to suffer. I would have to continue to starve. I would have to continue to be cold. I would have to continue to survive. "Survive?" I would have asked myself. "For what reason?" I would have nothing to live for. The world would offer me nothing other than a bottomless pit of bleakness. Somehow, I would have to believe, not in God or in humankind, because both would have forsaken me, but I would have to believe in myself. Every prisoner that survived Dachau survived solely because they never gave up on who they were as an individual. After all, that was the only thing they had left to hang on to in this world.

I wasn't sure how anyone managed to survive Dachau or any other concentration camp because they made the prisoners feel so dejected and dispirited. As I walked around the site, I couldn't help but wonder how I would have fared, and I was fairly convinced that I would have easily succumbed to death. The damp and the cold alone would have done me in well before illness, starvation, overwork, experimental testing, or bullet would have gotten to me. The place was tragic in every possible sense of the word. So much about Dachau was about sadness, mainly because there was nothing there to be happy about. Neither of us particularly enjoyed the time we spent there, and I think that was because we were not supposed to enjoy it. No one goes to the Dachau Concentration Camp Memorial Site because they want to walk away happy. People go there because they want to see what humanity looks like when it ceases to appear human anymore. There were no humans at Dachau. The prisoners weren't any more human than the captors were because both of them were reduced to parodies of themselves. The prisoners lost their humanity when they lost their spirit, and the guards lost their humanity when they lost their ability to feel.

The framed poster of Munderkingen that was stuffed in

the attic currently resides under my bed because I, for some reason, volunteered to take the thing home with me after my mom passed away. I don't even remember now how much the airline charged me to lug that oversized thing back home, but I do recall that I wasn't excited about paying the hefty fee, especially when I considered that I was bringing back something that I had zero intention of ever hanging on a wall. The poster has seen the light of day only once since it left its home in the attic, and that was when I took it to a military pawnshop to have it assessed. I asked the guy behind the counter if the poster had any value, and he basically told me that it more or less did not. He said that only someone who lived in Munderkingen would be remotely interested in owning that poster and only on the condition that all the propaganda nonsense was wholly whited out. He then excused himself, dipped into a back room, and reemerged with three mint condition Nazi posters that colorfully advertised the newly built autobahn.

"I've had these posters forever," he lamented. "No one wants them."

So, in short, he told me that I was stuck with that poster forever unless I was willing to whitewash the past and hawk the adulterated poster at some random flea market in Germany. I thanked him for his time and walked out of there thinking that I was now not only the official owner of that poster but was also now the official guardian of a very specific slice of history. No way was I going to erase anything printed on that poster, and I found it hard to believe that anyone ever would. It wasn't as though history could magically be absolved of its wrongdoings with the simple act of erasing some words on a propaganda poster because the damage that those words inflicted had already been done. That poster was a testament to a past that had already happened, and defacing it now wouldn't retroactively alter the entire course of history. I believe that it is essential that we as a society preserve some artifacts from history because once all the artifacts are gone, there will be nothing left to remind us who we used to be. Yet, it's hard to look the past in its eyes when it burns a hole straight through you, so most people avoid making eye contact with history and look the other way.

CHAPTER ELEVEN:
America/France, Sep-Oct, 2001
The Day the World Changed

I wasn't entirely sure who would be calling me at six in the morning, but my hunch was that whoever it was had something terrible to tell me. I was scheduled to leave for Paris later that afternoon, so my immediate thought was that Lufthansa Airlines was calling to tell me that my international flight to Frankfurt was canceled for some bizarre reason. Either that, or I thought that it was maybe my mom calling to tell me that my dad passed away because that was unfortunately what I usually braced for whenever the phone rang unexpectedly at some godforsaken hour.

Surprisingly, when I picked up the phone, I was greeted with neither of those scenarios. Instead, I was barked at by my friend, Cathy, to "hurry up and turn on the TV."

She was talking a mile a minute, and the only words I caught her say were, "airplane, New York, and World Trade Center," in no particular order.

"A plane crashed right into it!" Cathy exclaimed.

"Crashed into what?" I asked her.

"Into the building!" she said.

I honestly couldn't understand what the heck she was talking about, so I turned on the TV and saw images of a smoldering skyscraper.

"What the hell happened?" I asked.

"I have no idea," she said. "The news is saying that it was an accident."

The idea of a plane crashing into one of the world's tallest buildings seemed super weird, but it didn't strike me as being entirely implausible considering how much space those buildings took up in the sky.

"That's so horrible," I said. "How big was the plane?"

"They're not sure," Cathy said, "but they think that it might have been a commercial jet."

"Holy crapola," I said. "Are you serious?"

"I knew that you were supposed to be leaving today," Cathy stated, "so that's why I called you. I wanted to make sure that you were still home."

Cathy and I were co-workers, and we always knew what the other was doing whether we wanted to or not because we sat right next to each other at the travel agency. We were often the only person that the other had to talk to, and it's safe to say that we both knew way more about each other's lives than either of us truly wanted or intended to know. She and I were good friends, though, and I appreciated her calling me to give me a head's up on the currently unfolding drama because she knew that I wouldn't have gotten wind of it on my own since I was famous for never watching TV.

"Thanks so much for calling me," I said to her, and then we each sputtered out something that sounded like a goodbye.

I kept my eyes firmly glued on the TV for the entirety of the morning and watched in disbelief one catastrophic event unfold after another. The day started with the assumption that it was a freak accident that some plane hit the World Trade Center, but it soon became apparent that it wasn't an accident at all when a second plane intentionally flew into the other building. Those were kamikaze pilots flying those planes, and I cringed when the news announced that there appeared to be two more such pilots still up in the air and heading for unknown destinations.

As news of the other planes was being told, live footage of people jumping from the burning buildings flashed across the screen and made the horrific scene look even worse. Knowing that people were having to choose between being burned alive or free-falling over 1,000 feet to their imminent death seemed too surreal to believe. It seemed extremely unfair that those people were forced to make such a decision on a day that they thought was going to be just like any other.

About 30 minutes after the second plane hit, the news announced that a third plane was heading for Washington DC. The city braced for it to hit The White House, and it wasn't exactly a sigh of relief when it instead crash-landed into The Pentagon. For about 20 minutes, most of the news focused on The Pentagon, but then all the cameras went back to New York because the South Tower at the World Trade Center started to crumble. Humongous barrels of smoke filled with reams of paper and debris soon began to cascade down the street and outpaced nearly everyone who tried to run away from it like some modern-day Vesuvius eruption. The dust cloud was so thick that I could practically smell it through the TV, and it caked people from head to toe, making them look like walking plaster cast molds.

Not more than four minutes later, the news announced that a fourth hijacked plane crashed in some random field in Pennsylvania, and most reporters interpreted that crash as a hijacking gone awry. Footage of that scene showed nothing but an empty crater of billowing smoke because there was nothing physically left of the plane to even show. The aircraft had obliterated into absolutely nothing, and that scene contrasted very sharply with the visual display that was unfolding at the World Trade Center site. It was almost as though the two scenes were not even related because they looked so wildly different, but both scenarios were equally horrific for every person that was inside each of those planes. Not much time was spent dwelling on the Pennsylvania crash, though, because not less than 20 minutes later, footage of the North Tower collapsing made its debut upon the screen. More dust, more paper, more deaths, and more people screaming and running. I didn't realize it at the time, but in three short hours, the entire world as I knew it irreversibly changed.

I eventually did get that phone call from Lufthansa Airlines later that morning, and they told me that the plane that I was supposed to be on had emergency landed somewhere in Canada. For the next several days, no flights were allowed in or out of the United States, and the only sound that I heard above my apartment was the occasional swoosh of fighter jets going I didn't know where. I lived near the Phoenix airport at the time and was incredibly used to the constant sound of airplanes. The sheer quiet between the fighter jets was noticeable, and the silence really bothered me. I never noticed how loud all the planes were until they were completely scrubbed from the skies. The lack of noise kinda mucked with my head and made reality more difficult to recognize.

I couldn't shake the feeling that this country had gotten duped into believing that we were something that we were not. My gut instinct was telling me that everything was bullshit. Bullshit and assholes. Me, us, the world – all of us were lied to. There had to have been a reason why America got attacked, but like most American citizens, I didn't know what that reason was. I was pissed. Pissed at us, pissed at them, pissed at the world. It pissed me off to see Bush standing on the rubble pile like some kind of cheerleader as if he had nothing to do with the reason why that building was in crumbles under his feet. All that was left of the World Trade Center was a skeletal ribbed corner section of one of its buildings, and it stood defiantly on top of the ruins. There was something about that imagery that looked eerily similar to the photographs I had seen of dead trees left standing at the Battle of Verdun. Our country was already at war and had apparently been at war for a while, but no one in our government ever bothered to tell us that we were. The only people that were blindsided by those planes were us, the people that lived in America. Everyone else in the world, though, probably anticipated those planes coming toward us for quite a long while.

The World Trade Center towers might have been so incredibly tall that they blocked America's view from the rest of the world. We had cocooned ourselves in a blissfully unaware bubble, and it was only when those towers came crashing down that the bubble popped, and we got our very first glimpse of what the rest of the world genuinely looked like. The world looked bad, the kind of bad that caused some people to think that only terrorism would make it better. It was the kind of bad that was perpetuated by ignorance, poverty, fundamentalism, greed, violence, and war. It was also the kind of bad that permitted iconoclasm to thrive in certain parts of the world. Six months before the planes were flown into the World Trade Center towers, two monumental Buddhas were permanently erased from their historic alcoves in Afghanistan, and terrorism was credited for destroying both. The Buddhas of Bamiyan and The World Trade Center were both imbued with meanings that rubbed certain terrorist groups the wrong way. The World Trade Center represented the excess of everything, whereas the Buddhas of Bamiyan represented absolutely nothing, but to the Taliban and Al-Qaeda, both all and nothing were equally ripe for elimination.

I can almost wrap my head around why Al-Qaeda felt a need to attack a symbol of capitalism, but I will forever find it difficult to understand why the Taliban felt threatened by the concept of nothing. Through the Taliban's eyes, those Buddhas were idols, but to those who knew what they were looking at, all they saw was nothing. Buddhism isn't so much a religion as it is a concept, and the notion of nothing and emptiness are central to Buddhist thought. The largest Buddha of Bamiyan represented the Vairocana Buddha. It was created very large to show man how small he genuinely was. Its imposing size encouraged humans to let go of their egos. Once humans let go of their egos, humans become free. Once humans become free, they become one with the void. It was truly the world's greatest irony that the Taliban removed the most prominent symbol of nothingness from this planet because they, in a sense, removed something that wasn't even there.

Once I understood who America's enemies were, I feared that the United States would enter a war that it couldn't possibly win. The Taliban and Al-Qaeda were a new breed of zealots that we had little experience fighting, so I wasn't excited about the prospect of the US starting a war with a group of people whose mindsets were essentially rooted in the Middle Ages. The whole idea of war generally sickens me anyway, but I knew it would be impossible for the US to allow the World Trade Center to smolder without retaliation. I knew that a war was coming; I just didn't know when.

I tentatively rescheduled my trip to Paris to depart on October 9th, not knowing that the United States would start its airstrike on Afghanistan just two days before. I decided not to cancel my trip as a consequence, and everyone thought I was nuts for still wanting to travel internationally and travel by myself, at that. Personally, I was ready to get out of this country and experience what the rest of the world was going through because I wanted to gain an international perspective on things. So long as the plane was going, I was going to go with it. So, hell ya, I was going to France because it seemed like there was no better time to get away.

When I went to the airport, I unceremoniously handed over my original paper ticket with the travel date of September 11th printed on it. The lady behind the Lufthansa counter reacted like I just handed her a hot potato once she took a look at the date, and it made me feel bad that I didn't think ahead of time to warn her that I was a rebook. I did, however, ask her if I could keep the ticket as a souvenir after she checked me in, and she handed the ticket back to me as if she was more than glad to get rid of it. Unfortunately, I have nothing to show for it today because the ink didn't stick to the thermal paper very well and has since Vairocana'd (faded into nothing) on me.

Paris

Paris was not having good weather when I arrived. A depressing downpour covered the city with a layer of gray that was disturbingly reminiscent of the gray that had coated

Dachau with so much sadness. War was in the air, and I could feel it even though the war itself wasn't happening anywhere near me. War was happening in my bones as it was happening inside the bones of everyone that I saw reading newspapers on the metro. I didn't have to know how to read French to understand what the articles that accompanied the photographs of missiles and men in fatigues said because the pictures told me everything. We were at war, and if I had any doubt about that, then all I had to do was open my eyes and see. Those were Americans in those photographs, and they didn't look like they were standing in familiar territory. The war was happening somewhere in Afghanistan, and I was glad that no one on the metro asked me to point to where Afghanistan was on a map because I wouldn't have been able to do so. I had no idea where the war was happening, and I almost didn't care that I didn't know where Afghanistan was. To be honest, I don't think that I wanted to know, not because I didn't care, but more because I did, if that makes any sense. I didn't need to know where Afghanistan was because I didn't think we needed to be there. My vote was for diplomacy, not that anyone asked.

By all appearances, the cloud that was parked over Paris harbored no intentions of leaving, and I knew that I was going to regret that I only brought along one pair of wildly impractical shoes. In a sense, they weren't really shoes at all but more like glorified socks made out of some meshy material, and they proved to be super ineffective at keeping out the rain. I grew slightly concerned about the prospect of developing trench foot after I walked for an hour on wet Parisian streets, but I was also well aware that I was too cheap to do anything about it. I basically channeled my inner World War I soldier and carried on. I figured that since war was going to be the theme of the trip that it behooved me to emulate it to a certain degree.

I initially planned on using Paris as a base for a few days before heading off on some day trips, but an inevitable train strike threatened to keep me hemmed in Paris for the duration of my stay. I wasn't too concerned about being stuck in Paris because I had a long list of museums that I wanted to see, but I started to panic when I walked over to the Louvre and discovered that it was on strike as well. I gradually learned the hard way that more than half of the city's museums opted to go on strike after I walked over to several of them in the rain, only to be confronted with one fermé (closed) because of la grève (strike) sign after another. I was seriously tempted to walk back to the Louvre at one point when I found a sizable rock lying on the ground because the idea came to me to throw it at the glass pyramid. I ultimately decided against doing so and instead rode the metro to Montmartre cemetery because I figured that if I was going to be wet and glum, there was no better place to be wet and glum than in a graveyard.

I naturally walked in the wrong direction when I exited the metro, so it took me an extra long time to find where the cemetery was. When I finally did stumble upon it, I came up against its massive wall and had to walk around the whole darn thing in the pouring rain just to find its one single entrance. By the time I was in, I was soaking wet from the knees down and was utterly convinced that I had just traipsed through an upside-down rainstorm. My overall impression of Paris at that moment was that the city was not being kind to me, and it made me want to tuck myself inside one of the cemetery's miniature gothic house-slash-tombs and bury myself. Montmartre cemetery had plenty of tomb residences to choose from, but I couldn't find a way to circumnavigate the need of being dead to get inside any of them. I had no choice but to stay outside, so I found the largest overhang that I could and tucked myself under it, and patiently waited for the rain to stop. Of course, the rain never did stop but only slowed to a trickle, and it seemed to take forever to do so once my nose noticed that I was standing in the center of stray cat territory. The smell of wet cat piss was a smell that I thought that I could handle until I realized that I couldn't, so I gave up my relatively dry patch sooner than I wanted to and ventured back into the drizzle. I soon joined the population of stray cats in their game of "try not to get wet" that was already in full swing, and tomb hopped behind them because they evidently knew how to stay dry way better than I did.

Overall, Montmartre cemetery was where I wanted to be because I honestly enjoyed how the cemetery mucked with my brain. I'm usually drawn to cemeteries in a way that I can't quite explain, and I think that my attraction to them has everything to do with the way that they feel. Cemeteries are strangely beautiful to me because they often look like artistic refuges in places where they seemingly wouldn't belong. My mind can easily tune out the fact that the ground is filled with dead people, but oftentimes I truly don't want to tune out a cemetery's most defining feature. I sometimes prefer to remind myself that I, too, will someday be gone. Life is incredibly short, and I hate that. I want to live forever, but I know that I won't because I physically can't. No one can. I don't even know if eternity is possible. Forever. Forever just seems so long. Too long, in fact. Forever. What does that even mean? To be never-ending? What right does anyone have to exist that long? Maybe we are all just a pile of atoms that never die. Maybe when our bodies die, our atoms' energy lives on, and they bond to create something new. Perhaps it's our atoms that are eternal, and we are what the Earth is made of. I may never be born a human ever again, but I might return as a blade of grass, a tree, a bird, a whale, a mountain. Sure, I'd like to think that heaven exists, but why would it be wrong to want to stay here? I enjoy planet Earth and wouldn't mind being a part of it, always. Everyone is entitled to their own beliefs, and this is what I want to believe in. It doesn't necessarily make it true, but it doesn't necessarily make it false either. I'm not rushing to die to find out, though, as I know that the answer will be waiting for me when I get there, at least that is what I hope. Death could possibly be a big nothing, and that would disappoint me, but I'd be dead, so thankfully, I wouldn't know. Dead will be dead when the time comes, and that time will eventually befall us all.

I regard death as being the greatest unknown. I know that death will happen, but a part of me thinks that it won't. When I am alive, I am dead to death, but I will be alive to death when I die. Only then will death become real, but then I won't be able to feel it. Death will happen, but I wonder if I'll know it when it does. Maybe some people don't even know that they ever died. The people in those tombs...did they even know that they were there? My hunch was that they did not. The tombs were built to house the dead, but the cemetery itself was built to host the living. Actually, I don't even know why I thought about such things because although I appreciate cemeteries, I personally don't desire to be buried in one. I much prefer to be cremated and have my ashes dispersed in the breeze, and I don't know how long I should allow myself to go on with this topic because it's going in a direction that I wasn't necessarily anticipating. I guess that what I'm saying is that cemeteries don't really make me sad, but rather, they make me think. It is my opinion that too many people are afraid to allow themselves to think about death, which also explains why I usually have entire cemeteries all to myself. The good thing with that is that I always have plenty of space to think in, so I never have a shortage of thoughts.

The rain eventually got to me, so I decided to head back to the hotel where I could change out of my wet clothes and ask the hotel staff if they knew what the heck was going on with all the stupid strikes. Luckily, they were well versed with Parisian strikes and gave me a list of all the privately-owned museums that were currently open. They also told me that the trains would be running again "soon," whenever that supposedly was. I thanked them for their information and climbed the twisty set of stairs to my hotel room, where I instantly ripped off the wet clothes that I couldn't stand another second to be in. I plopped on the bed and turned on the TV for background noise as I perused the list of open museums. Unfortunately, I immediately lost my concentration because the news was too quick to remind me that there was a war going on. Granted, I intentionally turned on CNN because that was the only English-speaking channel that I could find. I didn't bother to change it to some French channel instead because experience had taught me that listening to a language that I couldn't understand tended to get on my nerves after a while. So, CNN it was, and soon the words, "Anthrax! Afghanistan! Bombings! Al-Qaeda! Osama bin Laden! War on Terror!" filled the room on constant repeat. "Did we talk about the anthrax mailings yet? What about Afghanistan? How about those bombings? There's nothing that we don't know about Osama bin Laden except for where he is! The War of Terror has only just begun!"

The news said nothing at all about Saudi Arabia, which I thought was a curious omission considering that nearly all the men involved in the 9/11 hijackings supposedly came from there. However, I was well aware that Saudi Arabia was the United States' bedfellow, so there was no way the US would drag its mistress to the scaffold. The same 15 minutes snippets only revealed so much, though, and I didn't think that any of it was too important. The media decided to keep the public in the dark about anything that mattered and only succeeded in making everyone afraid to open their mailboxes.

President Bush's soundbite, "this is a new kind of evil," played so often that I didn't want to keep hearing it anymore. Unfortunately, I knew that this was only the beginning and that the sound of his voice was going to be inescapable for the next several years. It's always hard for anyone to live in a country when the party that one voted for doesn't win a place in office, and living in that country is even harder when one has to trust in a leader that one didn't vote for to take one's country to a war that one doesn't believe in. At least, that was how I saw it, and I was seeing it from a foreign country, which at least provided me a level of separation. It almost made me feel like I wasn't an American anymore, and it was the first time in my life that I considered not being one. The expat life suddenly appealed to me, and I wanted right then and there to stay in

Paris forever, even if the clouds rained every single day. I didn't care anymore. I didn't care if the rain never stopped, and I didn't care if I never went back home. Where was home anyway? It felt like my country was changing. Yet, who we were changing into was something that we, along with the rest of the world, were yet to find out.

I left the hotel room and went to some small art museum where I allowed myself to forget all about the news. After that, I capped off the day with a glass of abominable vinegar-flavored wine at the Chinese restaurant that I loved to hate and watched the colors of a wet sunset fade across Notre Dame's facade. The day felt like it was long, but also not really. It seemed like it was almost too soon that I was staring at my favorite Parisian view. It also seemed like I was just there not that long ago. When was I here last? About two years ago. Fooled me. Seemed like I was there just yesterday.

I woke up the next morning and reluctantly turned on the TV. I flipped through the stations and found a music channel to put on before I stepped away to take a much needed shower. I was disappointed when I came back into the room and saw that some French morning program was on instead of the music videos, so I once again had to decide between CNN or anything in French. So, CNN it was, and the cycle started anew.

"Good morning, Anthrax!" the TV blared at me.

Agh, fuck this new normal.

Reims

The hotel staff told me that the trains were supposedly running, so I took them for their word and headed to the station, where I pleasantly saw trains moving. I showed the attendant my Eurail pass and boarded a TGV train to Reims, and arrived there in what seemed to be an instant. I immediately made a beeline for Reim's famous cathedral because the quicker I got there, the sooner I would get out of the rain. I didn't necessarily think that the rain followed me from Paris, but I was slightly under the impression that it believed it was my chaperon and made the decision for me to accompany me to Reims. I wanted to tell the rain that I didn't need its company, but I refrained from doing so because I was worried about hurting its feelings and causing it to storm even more.

The rain started to come down in buckets by the time I got up to the cathedral. I was tempted to look up to see if a Quasimodo-type figure was giddily throwing them down on me because I was whole-hardheartedly convinced that every cathedral had some gothic-like creature living among its gargoyles. However, I decided against looking up because I didn't particularly want to take five gallons worth of water straight into my eyes. Instead, I tucked myself under a generously sized portal and safely admired the motley array of highly animated statues that populated every inch of space around the door jambs. I wasn't about to count how many statues decorated the cathedral's exterior, but it was undoubtedly a veritable museum's worth. I was moreover impressed that no two figures looked remotely alike and decided that it was worth the train journey alone just to look at them. Yet, I knew that this cathedral was more than just a facade, for this was the very place where men were crowned into kings.

The idea of kingship seems a foreign concept to me, but

that doesn't mean that I'm not attracted to the allure of it because I totally am. There is something romantic about kingship that I find hard to resist, and I never mind it when I fall into a historical rabbit hole filled with stories about royalty. It's super easy to understand how hereditary monarchy became an entrenched institution, yet I am somewhat under the impression that modern democracy hasn't officially shaken off its yoke. Kingship still exists, but we just call it something else, and that something else is called money. We are not ruled by someone; we are ruled by something. We are not in charge of our lives because something else is. Our actions are dictated by the dollar, and every decision we make comes at a cost. Life isn't lived freely but instead needs to be paid for at every moment. We may not think that we live under a ruler, but we most certainly do despite our inability to see it. Some people might talk of revolution, but revolution is impossible when there is nothing to physically overthrow. It's not just the top 1% that rules over America, but it is money that rules over us all. It used to be that each country had its own monarch, but now the entire world bows to the same single master.

When I went inside Reims Cathedral, I thought about how not much had changed in the intervening 800 years since that cathedral was built. The cathedral could still easily host coronation ceremonies in there today, and I imagined the president of Wall Street crowning the almighty dollar as the world's official leader. Of course, I believed that the dollar was already wearing that crown, so I felt disappointed when I realized that the world was deprived of the spectacle. I believed that the world needed a visual, an extravagant coronation ritual, something that we could throw loads of confetti at it!

But, alas, capitalism is not known for its parties, so such an event will never occur.

I must have spent way more time inside Reims cathedral than I thought I did because I walked back out into what looked like an entirely different day. The sun had finally decided to bestow its presence upon the land, and it shone like it hadn't shone for at least a million days. Of course, I didn't have any sunglasses on me, but I didn't allow myself to complain about it. I much preferred to be blinded by the light than soaked by the rain, so I took my lumps of sunshine and rolled with it. I was simply delighted by the prospect of not seeing Reims through giant slants of water, yet I grew slightly concerned about not seeing Reims at all when I couldn't seem to find it.

I believe that I was looking for a medieval city core that I didn't know wasn't there. I gradually caught on that all of Reims' medieval buildings got bombed off the map, not during World War II but during World War I. As I walked around Reims, I constantly encountered plaques planted in front of modern buildings or next to empty spaces that referred to "the bombardment of 1914." I admittedly knew very little about World War I, and I most certainly didn't know who it was that bombed Reims into smithereens. I narrowed down the culprits to having either been German, American, or Russian, as I figured those were the usual suspects. I kept hoping that one of the plaques would explain to me who it was that caused all that damage, but the plaques assumed that everyone already knew. Unfortunately, I knew absolutely nothing about Reims' history. For starters, I found it hard to correlate bombings with World War I. I had to dig through my brain to recall that the first major war to drop bombs from airplanes was indeed World War I. According to the plaques, Reims Cathedral took a direct hit and lost its wooden roof and most of its medieval stained glass. The cathedral, though, had since been so lovingly restored that its injuries were hardly noticeable to me.

I was blissfully unaware of the World War I era photographs of the cathedral looking like a shell of itself when it stood its ground after the bombings, but those pictures were apparently very well known to the general public during the immediate post-war years. Everyone who survived that war must have related to those images in their own personal way. People must have felt exactly like how those ruins physically looked, as it would have been almost impossible not to. It was unfortunate that the cathedral had to take on so many heavy blows, and it was an absolute miracle that it somehow managed to remain standing. That cathedral became a symbol of endurance to those who survived the war, and they did everything in their power to keep the cathedral from falling. It was almost as though if that building fell, something inside everyone would fall along with it. That cathedral stood above a gaping abyss, and it was the only thing that kept humankind from falling into a bottomless hole.

War is never pretty, and World War I was a particularly ugly one. The combination of trench warfare and the use of chemical weapons created a hideous battleground the likes of which the world had never seen before and will hopefully never see again. World War I made a scarscape out of the land and left an emptiness inside the soul. The air that those men fought in was not filled with oxygen but was filled with phosgene and mustard gas. The poisoned air would wrap itself around a soldier's body and engulf him in a suffocating squeeze. They fought a war in a world where trees had no branches, buildings had no walls, and windows were just empty holes where light used to be. It was impossible to fight that war and not be somehow affected by it, but the effects were usually so significant that they defied accurate description. Many men who survived that war never mentally stopped being choked by the gas they encountered on the battlefields and spent the remaining years of their lives in quiet suffocating silence.

Rouen

My plan that next day was to redeem myself of my past mistakes. The last time I tried going to Rouen, I ended up on the wrong train and found myself in a city that put cows on their cathedral (Laon). Not that I had anything against cows, but I didn't want to accidentally see them again, so I double and triple-checked that I was indeed getting on the correct train before I physically boarded it. Even though I was fairly confident that I boarded the correct train, I still had my suspicions that I couldn't do anything right, so I tentatively braced for a million-hour train ride to Siberia just in case. Naturally, I was pleasantly surprised when the train came to a stop less than two hours later and dropped me off in the correct city that I only half expected it would.

The city of Rouen boasted a magnificent cathedral that I was interested in seeing in person. The artist Monet did an atmospheric series of paintings that captured what that cathedral looked like when sunlight fell upon its facade at different hours of the day, and I was curious to find out if my eyes could see that building the same way his did. When Monet looked at Rouen Cathedral, he didn't see the tallest church spire in all of France but saw instead how the light and air played with the building's complicated features. What Monet saw was not a Rouen Cathedral that could be touched but rather a Rouen Cathedral that could be sensed, and that was the Rouen Cathedral that he painted over and over again. Monet's Rouen was a feeling, an idea, an emotion. Monet didn't so much as paint a building as he painted what the air and light around a building looked like. He gave color to the atmosphere and made the ethereal visible.

It took some doing to find a spot where I could plop myself down and try my hand at drawing the cathedral. I came to Rouen armed with a sketchbook and colored pencils, but the rain tried its best to deter me from sketching it because it apparently knew my artistic limitations way better than I did. Once I got started, I immediately stopped because I knew from the first line that I put down that my drawing wasn't going to come out right. That cathedral was way too intricate for me to capture, and I couldn't convince my eyes to look past the thousands of intimidating details. I had no idea how Monet managed to ignore most of the particulars of the cathedral's facade, and it was only right then that I fully understood what impressionism was. Impressionism was the ability to look at something and not see it, but possessing the skill to capture that something exactly as it appeared. My respect for Monet increased immensely after my pathetic attempt at trying to do what he did because I, for one, couldn't see the essence of the very thing that was before me.

I gave up pretty quickly, but I didn't allow myself to feel too terrible about not being able to pull it off. Monet was definitely in a league of his own, and I wasn't foolish enough to think that I had the talent to get anywhere near him. Besides, drawing in the rain was not my idea of fun, and the shelter that I was under wasn't much of a shelter at all. I figured that I had plenty of excuses to drop what I was doing, so I packed up and headed inside the impressive cathedral.

I adore visiting cathedrals because there is something about their human quality that draws me in. These buildings never fail to display man at his finest, and there is always a passion imbued in the stones. There is a certain feeling that is strictly reserved for cathedrals, and it is a feeling that Monet would have been able to give a color to had he painted the inside of such buildings. As it was, Monet was an outside man and a translator of plein air. He listened to the sounds that landscapes and buildings made and immortalized their voices on canvases that still speak to us today. Indeed, Rouen Cathedral's interior was all mine to figure out, and the first thing that I wanted to know was why it was so crooked. Many of the pillars that held up the ceiling appeared to be misaligned, and their general unevenness caused the vaulted ceiling to look wobbly. My stomach felt fine when I looked at the floor, but it started to turn when I looked up at the ceiling. I couldn't figure out if I just wasn't seeing the building right, so I asked whoever was standing next to me if he thought that the building was crooked too.

"Oh, the whole thing is totally crooked," the man kindly assured me. "It got bombed pretty badly in the war."

Given what I learned at Reims the other day, I just assumed that he meant World War I. I didn't ask him to elaborate on the subject because I thought that I knew what war he was referring to, so I thanked him for his information and went back to straining my neck. It wasn't until later that day that I found out that Rouen Cathedral, and indeed much of the city, was bombed by the "Allies" during World War II, and by "Allies" they meant the British and the Americans. I have since read quite a bit about both World Wars because this trip inspired me to go to the library and learn more; however, I was getting a first-hand glimpse of what those wars looked like in reverse whenever I encountered a restored building.

Monet's paintings of Rouen Cathedral during World War II would have been amazing pictures to see if only he had been alive to paint them. "The Disappearing Rouen Series" could have been the series' title. I imagined that his first painting would have shown Rouen Cathedral in full bloom. Then, a different piece of the building would go missing with each successive picture until finally, the whole cathedral would be gone by the final installment. There was no doubt in my mind that he would have painted what that war looked like as it reflected itself upon that cathedral's facade as the city itself gradually got bombed away.

Joan of Arc was also in Rouen, but she wasn't there anymore, for there was nothing left of her to bury after she was burned at the stake. Ironically, nothing much was left of the medieval castle where she was held captive either. All that remained of the once imposing structure reputed to be inescapable was a squat circular tower that went by the name of "The Tower of Joan of Arc." However, the brochure that I picked up kindly told me that her prison cell was not specifically located in there. It hardly mattered, though, because I highly doubted that she harbored any intentions to haunt her former prison anyway, for she was much too exceptional a person to bother with doing such a thing. Humanity let her down while she was alive, so I couldn't imagine that she'd want anything to do with humankind after her death. However, she was made into a saint, so people seemed to have convinced themselves that she somehow still cared about us. Then again, maybe I was wrong to think that she didn't care about us because I wasn't the one to say. All I know is that if I were her, I'd be pretty pissed at us forever, but I guess there is a reason why I wasn't the one born to lead an army and place the crown on Charles VII's head when no one else in the world had the talent to do so.

I didn't go to Rouen expecting to encounter Joan of Arc's spirit, but deep down, I was secretly hoping that I would. I have nothing but respect for her indomitable spirit, but I was seriously hoping that her spirit wasn't still hanging around the place where she was murdered. A small memorial marked the exact spot where the fateful pillar once stood, and a small patch of wildflowers was all that was there. Little snippets of purple and white blossoms snuggled the ground, and I found the simplicity of the memorial to be overwhelming to the point that I almost cried. Okay, I did cry a little bit. I couldn't help it. The flowers were too touching that I couldn't help but to be moved by them. I was expecting something huge to mark the site where Joan of Arc was killed, but instead, what I encountered was something unexpectedly small. The moment I raised my head, all I saw was air, and it was in the atmosphere where I sensed her spirit. The idea of Joan of Arc surrounded me, and I encountered her spirit to be a state of mind. Her spirit was a strength that I had to find inside myself, and musing about Joan of Arc felt empowering. She was someone who wasn't afraid, and her total lack of fear inspired me to confront my own hesitations. Emotionally, I was feeling weak because I lost all the confidence that I used to have in the world. 9/11 was still on my brain, and I still wasn't sure what I thought about the war that was currently raging.

War was something that Joan of Arc was good at, and how she discovered her talent for it was a mystery to me as it was a mystery to everyone else who encountered her. I suspected that her medieval mindset had everything to do with her ability to think beyond her id. Religion had probably told her that her own thoughts were distinctly separate from divine inspiration. I don't think that she believed that she was technically listening to herself when she followed through with what her visual and auditory hallucinations instructed her to do. All her actions were the result of what she thought was divine inspiration. That being said, I am utterly convinced that she would not have become the same person that she was had she been born in the modern era. For one, we would have loaded her up on high doses of medication, and for two, we would have totally ignored her. Joan of Arc was a one-shot deal, and shoot from cannons she most certainly did until she met her military end at the Siege of Compiégne. Curiously, history somewhat repeated itself when World War I officially came to an end in Compiégne and it repeated itself again when France signed an armistice with Nazi Germany there in the early years of World War II. If Joan of Arc's spirit was anywhere, she was over the commune of Compiégne. If anyone needed to keep a watchful eye over any sort of military truces, it was her, and any revenge that would result from broken promises would be hers to dole out.

Joan of Arc's memorial was located in Rouen's charming historic district, which was a section of town that would have been larger had not the Americans heavily bombed it during World War II. The historic district was a massive half-timbered fantasy of timeworn buildings that conspired to make me feel like I time-warped into the 16th century. The plethora of people in modern-day clothing was the only giveaway that the 16th century didn't lock up and freeze all around. However, I did keep my eyes peeled for any medieval holdouts because I desperately wanted to see what outfits they'd be wearing. Buildings typically reflect what the people who built them looked like, and medieval buildings exhibit loads of character. No doubt, half-timbered constructions were built out of economy because they used the least amount of expensive material (wood) and heaping amounts of cheap material (plaster). Those who built in half-timber presumably didn't look at their constructions as being "charming" or "adorable" but looked at them as being utilitarian. Even so, medieval cities, despite their unsanitary conditions, despite their lack of running water, and despite their suffocatingly close quarters, were definitely not ugly.

Paris, The Journey's End

I woke up the next morning to the familiar sound of rain. I decided to sleep in a little bit, thinking that if I buried my head under the covers that the rain would come to a stop. However, not even a buried head prevented the rain from coming down.

"Another day of this crap," I thought to myself. "More wandering around in the rain in my meshy shoes searching for the few museums that were magically open."

I made a concerted effort not to turn on the TV because I didn't see the point in making the morning any more of a groundhog day than it was already being. Besides, the news had been repeating itself for the last several days and was starting to bore me. It felt slightly wrong to admit that I was bored with hearing about a war that was happening not too far away. Distance didn't seem to matter too much when I stopped to think about it, though, because Afghanistan was just someplace that I couldn't relate to. My mind essentially placed the war as occurring somewhere on the moon.

I learned from the hotel staff that the Louvre was still closed, but they directed me to the Museé Marmottan (The Monet Museum) as a worthy alternative. That museum ended up being the most perfect suggestion for me as my mind was still very much on Monet. The museum was chocked full of his paintings, and most of them were of his water lilies. I don't explicitly remember counting how many of those paintings were of his water lilies, but if the museum claimed to own 100 Monet paintings, then I'd venture to guess that about 90 of them were of his water lilies. That man Monet sure never did tire of that subject. I had read that his sight started to go in his old age, but I left that museum fairly convinced that he could have painted the majority of those pictures with his eyes closed, for images of water lilies must have been permanently imprinted on the inside of his eyelids.

When I left the museum, I noticed that the line to get in had wrapped around the block, so I took that as a bad sign that not a whole lot of other museums were going to be open. It was evident that I would have to pick from the dredges, which explains why I ended up at the Army Museum next. However,

I did take advantage of the rare bit of sunshine that decided to come out and made a slight detour through the Bois de Boulogne along the way. The large public park contained a sizable forest that beckoned me to explore it, but the ground was so soaking wet that I didn't end up walking in very far. I merely got deep enough in the forest to appreciate how glorious the sun looked as it filtered beams of light through the wet foliage and how beautiful the droplets of water looked when they fell in the wind. My imagination soon got the better of me, and my eyes were convinced that they saw a knight on a horse with Robin Hood and his Merry Men following behind. I knew that Robin Hood was English, but my imagination didn't bother with such trivial details. The woodland was truly magical, and all my medieval fantasies were lurking behind the many beautiful trees.

I definitely would have never ended up at the Army Museum had other museums been open, but I ended up spending several hours in there, which really surprised me. The objects on display proved to be very interesting. The place was a tried and true time capsule of everything related to war, and I lingered especially long over Napoleon's objects. Napoleon's army bed was the one item that really got me thinking about how he wasn't just a historical figure but was once an actual living person. The bed itself was just a simple army cot dressed up under a velvety green drape, and that extra accouterment gave it a regal air. In a way, the whole contraption looked rather silly because it was just a cheap mobile army cot decked out to look luxurious, but I supposed that this one object likely summed up the whole of Napoleon in one visual nutshell. Outwardly, he lived in a palace, but inwardly, he resided on a cot, and I suspected that his body was laid to rest on one before he got buried inside six layers of coffins.

The day was nearing an end, so I wandered over to the Notre Dame Cathedral. I hoped to catch a scheduled organ concert, but I got there too early and accidentally caught the beginning of a sermon. I ended up staying through it purely out of curiosity because the whole thing was very elaborate and legitimately looked like performance art. The priest kept swinging an oversized incense burner over his head, but I suspected that his senility must have kicked in because he seemed to forget that he was doing it. The amount of incense that it generated got so intense that it almost choked out the entire congregation. Maybe it was because it sounded like we were dying that he eventually remembered to put the incense burner down. He then picked up an oversized golden candelabra and proceeded to walk around with that thing over his head for no apparent reason. I was pretty sure that the priest was a profoundly religious man and all, but I was much too concerned for his safety to focus on the spiritual aspect of the sermon when he looked to be much too old to be carrying such heavy things over his head. I was watching his feet more than I was watching his hands because I was waiting for the moment when he was going to trip on his robe and accidentally throw the candelabra at us like a javelin. Much to my relief, he put the candelabra down, but then he immediately grabbed an oversized communion holder, and I just braced for the whole production to end with the priest doing a faceplant.

The sermon went on for about an hour, and a woman was singing a rather pretty song throughout it all, but it sounded like she was repeating the same four lines over and over again.

That, and we (the congregation) had to stand up for like, forever. It sounded to my ears that the priest was speaking in Latin, so it made me wonder if anyone understood anything that he was saying. I wondered how many of us were tourists versus how many of us were regulars. I took a look around and noticed that it didn't seem that anyone was intentionally there for the sermon because it looked more like we were all there for the organ concert that was due to follow. That we were all there presumably by mistake seemed evident to me when I noticed that we all had the same befuddled look plastered across our faces.

The organ concert started immediately after the sermon, but ten minutes into it got me wishing for that singer to come back out because the organ music sounded so atrocious. The organist chose to play a piece composed in the 1980s, but five minutes into it got me wondering if the organist suffered from dyslexia. My hunch was that he was shooting for something composed in the 1890s and only realized his error when it was already too late. That diabolical music sounded sacrilegious to my ears and caused me to wonder why contemporary organ music needed to sound so darn experimental. I mean, organ music usually sounds weird enough the way it usually is, and I would have preferred to hear the soundtrack to Dracula than whatever it was he was pounding out on those poor innocent keyboards. I somehow managed to suffer through an hour-long Catholic sermon in a language that I couldn't understand, but I couldn't find it in myself to endure more than 20 minutes of torturous organ music, so I left along with over half of what was once the congregation.

I didn't feel the need to look back at Notre Dame

Cathedral once I exited the building, but I'm looking at pictures of it now, nearly 20 years later, and the building doesn't look the same. Fire destroyed its roof and took down its spire, and the cathedral now stands as a shell of itself. Work has recently begun on dismantling the 8,000 pipes and five keyboards that made up France's largest organ after heat, dust, and water damaged the instrument and rendered it unplayable. The organ will be cleaned, and a new roof and spire will rise again, but such things cost time, skill, and money which are all things in short supply during a pandemic. I'm not going to say that COVID-19 appeared on the planet at the worst possible time because the only better time for a worldwide health pandemic is never, but I am saying that it's a really bad time for COVID-19 to be here right now. The world was already in a whole lot of pain, and it didn't need a raging respiratory virus to make it feel worse.

I remember when I sat in my hotel room on my last day in Paris with a cheap bottle of wine and thinking that the world as I knew it was in the process of changing. I could feel a change coming on, but I couldn't sense what that change was going to be. I felt a negative emotion deep in my marrow because I questioned what good could possibly come out of starting a war with The Middle East. I had just spent the last several days tripping over the remnants of previous wars, and there was a feeling about those battered places that soaked my bones just as much as the rain did. There was a dampness about war that drenched my soul and made my insides feel dull. The feeling of war was innate, even primal, for I sensed it imprinted on my DNA. War is something that we always live with, for it is an element that courses through our veins. It took sitting in a dinky Parisian hotel room with the sound of rain pattering against the window to make me recognize that the same sound pulsated inside of me.

I went to Paris to escape war but instead learned that war was inescapable. Such is the beauty of travel when it teaches me something pivotal. It's those sorts of epiphanies that spur me to leave my surroundings and explore various corners of the globe. I never know what I am going to learn when I take myself out of my comfort zone, but I do always know that I am not going to return as the same person that I was. I travel because I want to *know*. I want to know what makes the world tick, what makes me tick, and what makes the world such an insanely special place. I feel very much a small part of a much greater whole, and I seek that greater whole to make myself complete. I know that I'm a very curious person, and I hope that I never stop wondering. The world is too big, and the questions are too many to make me want to stay home. I travel not only because I want to but more because I *need* to.

I positively despise the COVID-19 pandemic because it has kept me hemmed in for too long. That respiratory virus has not only been a thorn in my side, but it has been a ruthless stab in my back. COVID-19 paralyzed most of my travel plans for the immediate future and put my life on indefinite hold. Sure, I am aware that there are safe ways to travel, but I've been working at a hospital since the pandemic began, so I've gotten used to laying low. Travel is just not on my radar for the moment simply because I'm focused on surviving this thing. For now, I can survive on all my memories of my previous journeys and spend some quality time writing out my thoughts. I thoroughly enjoyed exploring the trips that made up this volume and am already looking forward to writing out the next decade's worth of experiences. I may not be physically going anywhere in my current situation, but there are more than enough places for me to go in my head.

I will never think that it was fair that Paul's life got cut short. I still think of him occasionally and wonder if he was better off missing out on all the crap that happened to the world. However, I will never say that he was better off dead because he deserved to be here with the rest of us. We may only get one chance to live on this amazing planet, so it's important to value that one chance and live the best life possible. Of course, everyone is born under different circumstances and faces unique obstacles, but we all have our shared humanity in common.

We are all on this planet together, whether we like it or not. One thing this pandemic has shown us is that we need to work together. If one country suffers, the entire world suffers with it. Isolationism doesn't work anymore, and no man is an island. If travel taught me one thing, it's that we need to open our eyes. We need to stop looking at our immediate surroundings and take a look at the entire world around us.

We need the Earth more than it needs us. If we overstay our welcome long enough, the Earth will have no problem shaking us off her back. When that happens, we will not land on Mars because that planet exists too far away, so odds are better that we'd land on the moon. From there, we could stare back at Earth and muse about everything that we did wrong and make promises to ourselves that we know we'd never keep. My faith in the human race is currently at an all-time low, but I hope that we as a species somehow redeem ourselves and work together to heal our wonderful planet.

I love this floating blue ball and yearn for the day when everyone else loves it as much as I do.

APPENDIX

Kat on the crappy motorcycle

Kat and the only photo the author has of Paul

Monument Valley at Sunrise

White House Ruins

Ruins at Hovenweep

Ruins at Mesa Verde

The author drinking a beer somewhere in Paris circa 1998

The author's husband, Ryan. California circa 2007

Front Page of 1999 Journal

"Notre Dame" Drawing

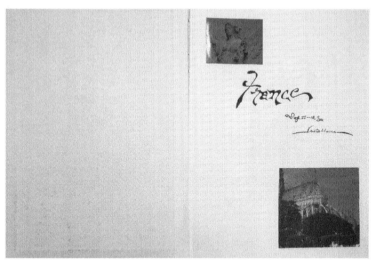

Front Page of 2001 Journal

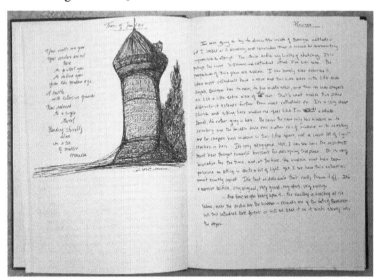

Joan of Arc Tower Drawing

"Grandma's house" postcard

Two photos taken by the author of her "grandma's" house

Link to the German propaganda poster:
http://photos.app.goo.gl/i5a7ecig8dqTKojt6

SELECT BIBLIOGRAPHY

The following is a list of sources used to substantiate certain thoughts and ideas.

INTRODUCTION

What You Should Know About Landmines in Cambodia. World Nomads website. https://www.worldnomads.com/travel-safety/southeast-asia/cambodia/watch-your-step-cambodian-landmines. Accessed August 1, 2018.

Bastard Costa Rican Wildlife: The Botfly. Leaving the Nest: An Expat Survival Guide website. cultureshock-survival.blogspot.com/2011/03/bastard-costa-rican-wildlife-botfly.html. Accessed August 1, 2018.

CHAPTER ONE

Musée Mécanique website. https://museemecanique.com/#. Accessed April 26, 2018.

Ruskin Z. Musée Mécanique owner working to keep the fun alive despite pandemic, fire. *Datebook*. September 2, 2020. datebook.sfchronicle.com/entertainment/musee-mecanique-owner-working-to-keep-the-fun-alive-despite-pandemic-fire. Accessed April 6, 2021.

The Dancing Ganesha, photo. File:Dancing Ganesha - Joy of Museums - Asian Art Museum - San Francisco.jpg. (2021, February 15). *Wikimedia Commons, the free media repository*. https://commons.wikimedia.org/wiki/File:Dancing_Ganesha_-_Joy_of_Museums_-_Asian_Art_Museum_-_San_Francisco.jpg.

Heaphy L. The Hindu God Ganesh – Who Is This Elephant Headed Fellow Anyway? *Kashgar*. May 2, 2017. https://kashgar.com.au/blogs/gods-goddesses/the-hindu-god-ganesh-who-is-this-elephant-headed-deity-anyway. Accessed May 11, 2018.

CHAPTER TWO

Valley of Fire State Park. NV State Parks. Department of Conservation and Natural Resources website. http://parks.nv.gov/parks/valley-of-fire. Accessed September 2, 2018.

John G Clark. Find A Grave website. https://www.findagrave.com/memorial/17080428/john-g-clark. Accessed September 10, 2018.

CHAPTER THREE

When Is a Desert Not a Desert? The Varying Landscapes of Arizona. ASU geoalliance website. https://geoalliance.asu.edu/sites/default/files/LessonFiles/Davis/DESERT/ DavisDesertT.pdf . Accessed September 28, 2018.

CHAPTER FOUR

Benjamin R Sjoberg. Missing Veterans website. http://www.missingveterans.com /1996/benjamin-r-sjoberg/. Accessed October 15, 2018.

CHAPTER FIVE

Rauschenberg C. *Paris Changing: Revisiting Eugene Atget's Paris.* New York, NY: Princeton Architectural Press; 2007. Lost Secrets of Chartres Blue? History of color, and why astrology in a church. Art history, symbolism and legends blog. artelisaart.blogspot.com/2012/03/secrets-of-chartres-bluehistory-of.html. Accessed November 1, 2018.

Caspar David Friedrich as quoted in *German Romantic Painting* (1994) by William Vaughan, p. 68. Wikiquote website. https://en.wikiquote.org/wiki/Caspar_David_ Friedrich, Accessed April 26, 2021.

Alfred, Lord Tennyson as quoted in his poem titled *In Memoriam A.H.H.*, Canto 27. 1850. Wikipedia contributors. (2021, February 16). In Memoriam A.H.H.. In *Wikipedia, The Free Encyclopedia.* Retrieved 21:59, April 26, 2021, from en.wikipedia.org/w/index.php?title=In_Memoriam_A.H.H.&oldid=1007194407.

Fitzpatrick A. Google Used to Be the Company That Did 'Nothing But Search'. *Time Magazine.* September 4, 2014. time.com/3250807/google-anniversary/. Accessed November 22, 2018.

CHAPTER SIX

Raga S. Gaudí's Accidental Death: Why The Great Architect Was Mistaken For A Beggar. *Mental Floss.* February 11, 2016. https://www.mentalfloss.com/article/72482/gaudis-accidental-death-why-great-architect-was-mistaken-beggar .Accessed July 1, 2019.

History of Carcassonne. Mescladís website. mescladis.free.fr/ANGLAIS/

pages%2ohtml/history.htm. Accessed July 13, 2019.

CHAPTER SEVEN

Lydon T. Alaska's Melting Glaciers Tell the Story of Climate Change. *Yes Magazine.* December 5, 2019. https://www.yesmagazine.org/environment/2019/12/05/alaska-climate-change-glacier. Accessed December 7, 2021.

Sutter P. How Venus Turned Into Hell, and How the Earth Is Next. *Space.com.* August 7, 2019. www.space.com/venus-runaway-greenhouse-effect-earth-next.html. Accessed December 15, 2021.

Lewis & Clark among the Indians. The Clatsop Winter. Journals of the Lewis and Clark Expedition Online website. lewisandclarkjournals.unl.edu/item/lc.sup.ronda.01.08#ln0802. Accessed January 10, 2019.

Clark's Journal Entry, December 21, 1805. Journals of the Lewis and Clark Expedition Online website. lewisandclarkjournals.unl.edu/item/lc.jrn.1805-12-21. Accessed January 10, 2019.

Duncan D and Burns K. Ken Burns and Dayton Duncan warn: Beautiful, unspoiled landscapes are disappearing. *USA Today.* May 25, 2018. www.usatoday.com/story/travel/nation-now/2018/05/25/wild-rivers-scenes-visionary-enchantment/593020002/. Accessed January 10, 2019.

First Emigrants on the Oregon Trail. Beginning the great migration to Oregon. Oregon-California Trails Association website. octa-trails.org/articles/first-emigrants-on-the-oregon-trail/. Accessed January 15, 2019.

Oregon Trail—Facts, information and articles about the Westward Expansion. History.net. www.historynet.com/oregon-trail. Accessed January 15, 2019.

Ravitz J. The sacred land at the center of the Dakota pipeline dispute. *CNN News.* November 1, 2016. www.cnn.com/2016/11/01/us/standing-rock-sioux-sacred-land-dakota-pipeline/index.html. Accessed January 25, 2019.

Nemec B. End of the Oregon Trail Historic Oregon City. Land Claims. *historicoregoncity.org.* April 3, 2019. https://historicoregoncity.org/2019/04/03/land-claims/. Accessed February 3, 2021.

Krock L. Case Closed. *NOVA*. February, 2005.
https://www.pbs.org/wgbh/nova/charters/case.html. Accessed February 11, 2019.

Lynch J. How to Protect the Constitution (Literally). *Popular Mechanics*. February
13, 2018. www.popularmechanics.com/technology/security/
a15895554/how-to-protect-the-declaration-of-independence/. Accessed February 11,
2019.

CHAPTER EIGHT

Geronimo (Goyaałé), a Bedonkohe Apache, kneeling with rifle, 1887 photo. Google
Arts and Culture website. artsandculture.google.com/asset/
geronimo-a-frank-randall/aQEWLlXAm2xrlA?hl=en. Accessed March 4, 2019.

Crazy Horse. Biography.com website. www.biography.com/military-figure/crazy-
horse. Accessed March 4, 2019.

Wounded Knee. History.com website. www.history.com/topics/native-american-
history/wounded-knee. Accessed March 4, 2019.

Sacagawea. Biography.com website.
https://www.biography.com/explorer/sacagawea. Accessed March 5, 2019.

Cochise. History.com website.
www.history.com/topics/native-american-history/cochise. Accessed March 5, 2019.

Red Cloud. The Famous People website. www.thefamouspeople.com/
profiles/red-cloud-5085.php. Accessed March 5, 2019.

Chief Joseph. Biography.com website. www.biography.com/news/chief-joseph-
quotes-surrender-speech. Accessed March 5, 2019.

Explore Mounds. Cahokia Mounds.org website. cahokiamounds.org/
explore/. Accessed March 10, 2019.

Birdman Tablet. Google Arts and Culture website. artsandculture.google.
com/asset/birdman-tablet-cahokia-mounds-state-historic-site/pAH45K-yp7vm3A?
hl=en. Accessed March 10, 2019.

Berg AS. The Spirit of St. Louis' Amazing Journey. *Smithsonian Magazine*.
November 2013. www.smithsonianmag.com/history/the-spirit-of-st-louis-amazing-
journey-4175294/. Accessed March 15, 2019.

White House Ruin Trail, Canyon de Chelly National Monument. The American Southwest website. www.americansouthwest.net/arizona/ canyon_de_chelly/white-house-ruin-trail.html. Accessed March 20, 2019.

Blau M. Jason Molina's long dark blues. *Chicago Reader.* October 1, 2014. https://chicagoreader.com/music/jason-molinas-long-dark-blues/. Accessed March 20, 2019.

Spider Grandmother. Myths and Folklore Wiki website. https://mythus.fandom.com/wiki/Spider_Grandmother. Accessed March 25, 2019.

Mesa Verde National Park History and Culture. US National Park Service website. www.nps.gov/meve/learn/historyculture/index.htm. Accessed April 1, 2019.

Hovenweep National Monument History and Culture. US National Park Service website. www.nps.gov/hove/learn/historyculture/index.htm. Accessed April 10, 2019.

Chaco Canyon National Historic Park History and Culture. US National Park Service website. https://www.nps.gov/chcu/index.htm. Accessed April 20, 2019.

Bandelier National Monument Tsankawi. US National Park Service website. www.nps.gov/band/planyourvisit/tsankawi.htm. Accessed May 1, 2019.

CHAPTER NINE

Temple Ehécatl. Atlas Obscura website. https://www.atlasobscura.com/places/temple-ehecatl. Accessed May 10, 2019.

Leffel T. Unbalanced in the Sinking City. *Perceptive Travel.* April 2009. www.perceptivetravel.com/issues/0409/mexico_city.html. Accessed May 15, 2019.

Travel Narratives, Selections from the True History of the Conquest of New Spain by Bernal Díaz del Castillo (1492-1580). Roy Rosenzweig Center for History and New Media. chnm.gmu.edu/worldhistorysources/unpacking/travelanalysis.html. Accessed May 20, 2019.

Letter to King Charles I of Spain dated October 30, 1520. HistoryWiz website. www.historywiz.com/primarysources/cortesletter.html. Accessed May 20, 2019.

Kennedy M. Murder most foul: British Museum unmasks who really killed Aztec leader. *The Guardian.* https://www.theguardian.com/artanddesign/2009/apr/08/

aztec-emperor-moctezuma-british-museum-exhibition . Accessed May 20, 2019.

The fall of Tenochtitlan. The History Press website. www.thehistorypress.co.uk/articles/the-fall-of-tenochtitlan/. Accessed May 20, 2019.

Hassig R. *Mexico and the Spanish Conquest*. Norman, OK: University of Oklahoma Press; August 4, 2014.

Minster C. Massacre at the Festival of Toxcatl. *ThoughtCo*. February 26, 2018. www.thoughtco.com/massacre-at-the-festival-of-toxcatl-2136526. Accessed May 20, 2019.

Kilroy-Ewbank L.Templo Mayor at Tenochtitlan, the Coyolxauhqui Stone, and an Olmec Mask. *Khan Academy*. www.khanacademy.org/humanities/ap-art-history/indigenous-americas-apah/north-america-apah/a/templo-mayor-at-tenochtitlan-the-coyolxauhqui-stone-and-an-olmec-mask. Accessed May 20, 2019.

Associated Press. Aztec skull trophy rack discovered at Mexico City's Templo Mayor ruin site. *The Guardian*. August 20, 2015. www.theguardian.com/science/2015/aug/21/aztec-skull-trophy-rack-discovered-mexico-citys-templo-mayor-ruin-site. Accessed May 20, 2019.

Wade L. Feeding the gods: Hundreds of skulls reveal massive scale of human sacrifice in Aztec capital. *Science*. June 21, 2018. https://www.science.org/news/2018/06/feeding-gods-hundreds-skulls-reveal-massive-scale-human-sacrifice-aztec-capital. Accessed May 20, 2019.

Minster C. Armor and Weapons of the Spanish Conquistadors. *ThoughtCo*. April 4, 2020. www.thoughtco.com/armor-and-weapons-of-spanish-conquistadors-2136508. Accessed September 15, 2020.

224th anniversary of Aztec Sun Stone's rediscovery. The History Blog. www.thehistoryblog.com/archives/34073. Accessed September 15, 2020.

President Abraham Lincoln's Cooper Union Speech. sonofthesouth.net. http://www.sonofthesouth.net/slavery/abraham-lincoln/abraham-lincoln-cooper-union-speech.htm. Accessed September 21, 2020.

Our Lady of Guadalupe. Britannica.com. https://www.britannica.com/topic/Our-Lady-of-Guadalupe-patron-saint-of-Mexico. Accessed September 21, 2020.

Teotihuacan. History.com website.
www.history.com/topics/ancient-americas/teotihuacan. Accessed May 30, 2019.

Olmec Civilization. World History Encyclopedia website.
www.worldhistory.org/Olmec_Civilization/. Accessed June 4, 2019.

Minster C. The Olmec Royal Compound at La Venta. *Thought Co.* August 27,
2020. www.thoughtco.com/the-olmec-royal-compound-at-la-venta-2136303.
Accessed September 15, 2020.

Stephens-Catherwood Connection. NephiCode website. nephicode.blogspot.com/
2016/06/stephens-catherwood-connection.html. Accessed June 4, 2019.

Pre-Hispanic City and National Park of Palenque. UNESCO World Heritage
website. whc.unesco.org/en/list/411/. Accessed June 12, 2019.

The sarcophagus lid of Pakal the great in Palenque. PeleoSeti.com.
www.paleoseti.com/grabplattepalenque.htm. Accessed June 12, 2019.

Palenque Mapping Project. Mesoweb website. www.mesoweb.com/
palenque/dig/report/mapping/mapping.html.

Zapatista National Liberation Army. Britannica.com.
https://www.britannica.com/topic/Zapatista-National-Liberation-Army .Accessed
June 22, 2019.

CHAPTER TEN

Outbound tourism statistics. Where do brits go on holiday? Finder.com.
www.finder.com/uk/outbound-tourism-statistics. Accessed July 23, 2019.

Albrecht Dürer's Self-Portrait with Fur-Trimmed Robe, 1500. Die Pinakotheken
website. www.pinakothek.de/en/modules/module-image-text-marginal/1052.
Accessed July 25, 2019.

J.W.M. Turner's Ostend (East End), 1844. Die Pinakotheken website.
www.pinakothek.de/kunst/meisterwerk/joseph-mallord-william-turner/ostende#.
Accessed July 25, 2019.

Thomas Gainsborough's Mrs. Thomas Hibbert, 1786. Die Pinakotheken website.
www.pinakothek.de/en/node/2736. Accessed July 25, 2019.

Caspar David Friedrich's, Giant Mountain Landscape with Rising Fog, 1819. Die Pinakotheken website. www.pinakothek.de/kunst/caspar-david-friedrich/gartenlaube. Accessed July 25, 2019.

Wirtshaus Maxvorstadt German Restaurant. Restaurant Guru website. restaurantguru.com/Maxvorstadt-Wirtshaus-Munich. Accessed July 30, 2019.

Ulm Minster. Atlas Obscura website. www.atlasobscura.com/places/ulm-mintser-ulmer-muenster. Accessed August 3, 2019.

Cook J. The Lion Man: an Ice Age masterpiece. *The British Museum Blog*. October 10, 2017. blog.britishmuseum.org/the-lion-man-an-ice-age-masterpiece/. Accessed August 3, 2019.

Nazi Camps. Holocaust Encyclopedia. encyclopedia.ushmm.org/content/en/article/nazi-camps#:~:text=Between%201933%20and%201945%2C%20Nazi,state%2C%20and%20for%20mass%20murder. Accessed August 19, 2019.

Dachau Concentration Camp. History.com website. https://www.history.com/topics/world-war-ii/. Accessed August 19, 2019.

CHAPTER ELEVEN

Vairocana. New World Encyclopedia. www.newworldencyclopedia.org/entry/Vairocana. Accessed August 22, 2019.

Sunyata. New World Encyclopedia. www.newworldencyclopedia.org/entry/Sunyata. Accessed August 22, 2019.

Perez-Rivas M. Bush vows to rid the world of 'evil-doers'. *CNN News*. September 16, 2001. https://edition.cnn.com/2001/US/09/16/gen.bush.terrorism/. Accessed August 25, 2019.

Boissoneault L. The Debate Over Rebuilding That Ensued When a Beloved French Cathedral Was Shelled During WWI. *Smithsonian Magazine*. April 19, 2019. www.smithsonianmag.com/history/debate-over-rebuilding-ensued-when-beloved-french-cathedral-was-shelled-during-wwi-180971999/. Accessed August 30, 2019.

Keller T. Destruction of the Ecosystem. *1914-1918 Online*. October 8, 2014. encyclopedia.1914-1918-online.net/article/destruction_of_the_ecosystem. Accessed August 30, 2019.

Stamberg S. Monet's Canvas Cathedrals: A Life Study Of Light. *NPR*. July 2, 2010. https://www.npr.org/templates/story/story.php?storyId=128221023. Accessed September 10, 2019.

Explore Rouen Cathedral, France's tallest church! French Moments website. frenchmoments.eu/rouen-cathedral/. Accessed September 12, 2019.

Whitlock F. Why America Participated in the Allied Bombing of France in WWII. *WWII History Magazine.* https://warfarehistorynetwork.com/2019/01/20/why-america-participated-inthe-allied-bombing-of-france-in-wwii/. Accessed September 12, 2019.

Tower of Joan of Arc, Rouen. French Moments website. frenchmoments.eu/tower-of-joan-of-arc-rouen/. Accessed September 12, 2019.

La Tour de la Pucelle - Jeanne's prison. Jeanne d'Arc website. www.stejeannedarc.net/dossiers/plan_prison_jeanne.php. Accessed September 12, 2019.

Manning S. Joan of Arc's Military Successes and Failures. *Historian on the Warpath*. January 6, 2010. scottmanning.com/content/joan-of-arc-military-successes-and-failures/. Accessed September 2, 2019.

Armistice - The End of World War I, 1918. Eyewitness to History website. www.eyewitnesstohistory.com/armistice.htm. Accessed September 5, 2019.

Franco-German Armistice 1940. Britannica website. https://www.britannica.com/topic/Franco-German-Armistice. Accessed September 9, 2019.

Miller S. What Really Caused the Voices in Joan of Arc's Head? *Live Science.* www.livescience.com/55597-joan-of-arc-voices-epilepsy.html. Accessed September 7, 2019.

Garcia-Navarro L. After The Flames, Notre Dame's Centuries-Old Organ May Never Be The Same Again. *NPR*. April 21, 2019.

https://www.npr.org/sections/deceptivecadence/2019/04/21/715271953/after-the-flames-notre-dames-centuries-old-organ-may-never-be-the-same-again. Accessed September 10, 2021.

Thank you for reading MEMORY ROAD TRIP: A Retrospective Travel Journey

Please consider posting a rating or review to your favorite book site. Reviews are the lifeblood of authors and help more readers like you find their new favorite books!

Krista Marson has a blog!
Please visit: https://kmarson.com/blog/ for weekly musings.

Be the first to know when Krista Marson's next book is available! Follow her on her website: https://kmarson.com/ to get alerts whenever she has a new release, pre-order, or discounts!

Feel free to contact her at: memoryroadtrips@gmail.com

Made in the USA
Middletown, DE
23 November 2021

53295075R00187